GOODBYE IS NOT FOREVER

AMY GEORGE
WITH AL JANSSEN

HARVEST HOUSE PUBLISHERS
Eugene, Oregon 97402

Cover art by Thomas Kinkade

Thomas Kinkade, an enormously popular and internationally published artist, is most famous for his light-filled landscape paintings. A devout Christian, he readily acknowledges God's hand in his life and career. Limited-edition prints of the painting portrayed on the cover of *Goodbye Is Not Forever* are available; readers can request details by checking the appropriate box on the Amy George free tape form at the end of the book.

The song "Two Different Worlds" is used by permission of HollyHill Music Company and Myra Music.

GOODBYE IS NOT FOREVER

Copyright © 1994 by Amy George with Al Janssen
Published by Harvest House Publishers
Eugene, Oregon 97402

Library of Congress Cataloging-in-Publication Data

George, Amy.
   Goodbye is not forever / Amy George with Al Janssen.
      p.   cm.
   ISBN 1-56507-123-9
   1. George, Amy.   2. Ukrainian Americans—Biography.   3. World War, 1939-1945—Personal narratives, Ukrainian.   4. World War, 1939-1945—Conscript labor—Germany.   5. Political prisoners—Soviet Union.
   I. Janssen, Al.   II. Title.
   E184.U5G46   1994
   973'.0491791'0092—dc20   93-23528
   [B]   CIP

Printed in the United States of America.

94   95   96   97   98   99   00   —   10   9   8   7   6   5   4   3   2   1

This book is dedicated to my Mom, the most wonderful Mom in the world. She gave up her life for us and totally loved and accepted each of us children just as we were. With her, we felt safe. Kindness was heard whenever she spoke, and from her heart she showed mercy toward all people. Ann (Hanusia), Thomas (Tarasik), and I stand in unison and praise God for our Mom. Together, we rise up and call her blessed.

> *Strength and honor are her clothing; she shall rejoice in time to come. She opens her mouth with wisdom, and on her tongue is the law of kindness. She watches over the ways of her household, and does not eat the bread of idleness. Her children rise up and call her blessed; her husband also, and he praises her: "Many daughters have done well, but you excel them all." Charm is deceitful and beauty is vain, but a woman who fears the LORD, she shall be praised. Give her the fruit of her hands, and let her own works praise her in the gates.*
>
> —Proverbs 31:25-31 NKJV

I wish to offer special thanks to my brother, Thomas, and my sister, Ann, for helping me reconstruct some of the events in this story. And a special thanks to my husband, Bob, for his invaluable insight and encouragement.

Contents

Before You Begin

Mine is not an unusual story. Millions of people suffered heart-wrenching separation in the 1930s and during World War II. Many died violent deaths, or suffered in cruel labor camps. The traumas shaped a generation. But as the years go on, the memories of those events fade. It is imperative that we learn the lessons from that era. As we hear about the tragedies of the 1990s and observe the turbulence in republics that were once part of the Soviet Union, we wonder how much more suffering people must endure. Haven't we learned the lessons of Stalin and Hitler? Those despots set the course for my life—ripping my father away from me as a little child and forcing me to leave my home to live in a concentration camp where I watched my mother work as a slave for the Third Reich. Then in the rubble of war, they used me and my mother as pawns and abandoned us as people without a country. We fled for our lives, hid from Russian agents, and fought daily for survival. Though mine is just the story of one family, it represents millions who were uprooted by the momentous events of this century.

Many of the events I share in the following pages occurred before my teenage years, and more than four decades have since intervened. While I have done everything in my power to ensure the historical accuracy of the story, these are my own recollections, and as such, may err in certain small details. It is my desire that the reader will catch the heart of the story, which is absolutely true. While there is much here that grieves the heart, there is much greater reason to rejoice as I see the hand of God on my life and the lives of my family. I pray that this personal account will bring added insight to a very important era in history and also give you encouragement in your own personal journey.

Perhaps it may seem I've waited a long time to write of my family's experiences. But it is only now, with the perspective of time and maturity, that this story can be told. Only now do I understand what was happening as my life intersected with the momentous events of World War II. Only now can I see that God was in control before and after the Iron Curtain fell. This is really His story.

1

Soviet Justice

SPRING 1936
DRUSHKOVKA, a village in Ukraine
FYODOR (Amy's father)

The crow of the neighbor's rooster awakened the man. It was about 4:30 in the morning, with another hour until sunrise. Yet Fyodor Philipovich Wasylenko eagerly slipped out of bed and put on his pants and shirt. His wife stirred but didn't awaken as he kissed her on the cheek. Next to her slept a baby, barely three months old. Across the room, he heard the rhythmic breathing of his ten-year-old son and fourteen-year-old daughter. He smiled at the sight—for what more could a man want in life than a beautiful, healthy family! Then he tiptoed through the living room and kitchen to the door where his fishing pole was leaning against the wall. He slipped on his boots, grabbed the pole, and quietly left the house.

This was his favorite time of the day. There was a hush over the village. The sky was beginning to glow in the east. It was a mile-long walk through a meadow to the small river where he loved to fish. One spot in particular, where the stream expanded into a pool, almost never disappointed him. There, young fish would be jumping. He would have no problem catching his limit.

Fyodor chuckled as he walked briskly, slowed only slightly by a stiff leg—the result of a childhood accident. He was a cheerful man, his smile amplified by a chiseled face and a bald head he shaved every other day. He savored life, relishing theater and music and nature. Educated at the university, he read voraciously, eager to expand the horizons of his knowledge. He might have looked like a simple Russian peasant, but he refused to live a complacent life. His desire to help his people obtain a better life was never dampened by the oppression of communism.

As he walked, he thought of his wife, who sometimes tired of all the fish he brought home. She fixed it every way imaginable. Pan-fried, baked, in soup, and stuffed—she had learned that last recipe from a Jewish friend in the village. Some of the fish went to another friend who smoked it and divided it with him. Fyodor liked smoked fish best and often took it with him for a lunch or snack as he went about his work. Sometimes his wife got so sick of fish that she would secretly dig a hole in the yard and bury the extra. That was all right; he would just go fishing again the next day! How could one complain of too much fish? Not after the years when they had endured empty stomachs, especially during the famine of 1933. That was still fresh in his mind. Then, they would have given anything for a piece of bone-filled fish.

It still made him mad. The foolishness of Stalin and his henchmen had produced that famine. Of course, he could never express that opinion publicly. But it was so obvious: Stalin had worried about Ukrainian nationalism and was determined to crush it. In the late 1920s, in an effort to eliminate the *kulaks* (wealthy and educated "peasants") he ruthlessly collectivized the rich farmland and arrested any who might be considered part of the resistance. This fisherman had been one of those arrested in 1928, and he had spent three years in exile at the very end of the national railway system in Shadrynsk, Siberia. Then in the early 1930s much of the grain harvest in Ukraine was appropriated and sent to feed other parts of the Soviet Union. In many homes, every last scrap of grain was confiscated. By the winter of 1932-33, millions were dying of starvation. During the spring of 1933, he could remember walking down the streets of Kursk and stepping over the bodies of the dead and dying. The star soprano of the local opera company lay with her hand outstretched on the sidewalk begging for a piece of bread—crying with a voice that had once lifted people to their feet in applause, but now was raspy and faint. He had also heard about people going mad. In one village, a man had killed and eaten his child. Yet there was no offer of relief from the Communist authorities. He knew the government had hoarded grain. In fact, they exported grain, or allowed it to rot in storage bins while armed guards kept hungry masses away. But publicly, they never admitted there was a problem.

Such thoughts made his blood boil, only to be cooled by the memory of a story he had heard during the famine. It was about two men who met at a road crossing and chatted for a moment about where to find a piece of bread. "Do you know of any place?" asked one. "No," answered the friend, "I don't even know where to find an old, shriveled potato skin! In fact, I haven't eaten in three days. But three nights ago, I had this vivid dream. There I was in this kitchen, and on the stove was a huge pot of delicious soup. My heart raced with joy. But there was a problem—where was the spoon? I looked desperately for a spoon, but there was none in sight. I woke up in frustration, with a growling stomach.

"The next night, I had the same dream. Same wonderful soup, delicious to look at. But again I woke up in frustration, looking for a spoon. So last night, before going to bed, I got smart. I took a spoon and tucked it under my pillow before turning out the lights. Just in case I would dream about that soup again!"

"So what happened?" asked the friend.

"The dream didn't come back!" was the reply.

Fyodor chuckled at the story. How typical of Russians—they had not lost their sense of humor. It was often the only way to ease the stress of daily life. No, he would never apologize for providing too much food for his family! He would never depend on a hostile and incompetent government to feed his children. Now he was no longer in exile. He had work, and there was money to buy bread. And every morning, he could fish. In the winter, that meant cutting open a hole in the ice and bracing himself against bone-chilling winds. But during the spring and summer there was no need to hurry. He could enjoy nature, soak up the sun, and think. Fishing gave him perspective on life. It was an escape from the daily oppression of communism, where every action and word had to be carefully weighed. One never knew for sure who were his friends and who were his enemies. But the fish—they didn't care. Give them worms, and they would attach themselves very nicely to his hook!

Ah, here was his stream. Fyodor's shaved head gleamed in the early morning light as he prepared his fishing gear. He was an expert. The line on his pole danced as he wound up and cast out to where he knew the more mature fish were congregating. Then he sat on the slightly muddy shore, stretching out his free hand to brace himself as he first stretched out the stiff leg in order to sit. Soon he was on his feet again, scooping up his first catch. Occasionally he would catch a young one, four or five inches long. When that happened, he would gently remove the hook and toss the fish back into the water. Let them grow; he would catch them later!

Fyodor was startled when a group of men suddenly appeared behind him. Usually the only other fishermen at this hour were a couple of older villagers who staked out spots further upstream. He looked over his shoulder and saw a carriage parked on the road just fifty yards behind him. He recognized the three men as workers from a brick and coal factory where he was used as a legal consultant. There was an air of importance from the fourth man; he swaggered as the men made their way down to the pond. He was clearly a party leader—you could tell one every time. He was probably the new factory boss; Fyodor had heard that one had just arrived a few days ago. One of the workers helped the boss unfold a large net and the others carried it into the water.

Fyodor was alarmed. "You can't do that!" he shouted to the group.

The men with the net looked up, surprised that anyone would challenge their actions.

"You're obviously new here," Fyodor said to the leader. "This is not a commercial fishing area. Only amateur pole fishing is permitted. No nets."

The culprit's face turned red. "Who are you to tell me where I can fish and where I can't fish?" he growled.

"I'm a citizen who knows the laws. Nets are not allowed here. This is a breeding pond. Only poles are allowed." Apparently the boss didn't know the local ordinances, or he didn't care. Fyodor knew that type—one who was on the side of those who made the laws and therefore felt no need to obey them. Under communism, laws were for everyone but party members.

The man with the net wasn't used to being challenged. He stared at his accuser and demanded, "What is your name?"

This was dangerous. "Tell me yours," Fyodor replied.

"You impudent swine. Tell me where you work!"

"I serve various enterprises. I give legal counsel."

"A *lawyer!*" he spat the word out with an oath. "So you think you know everything."

"I know the ordinances here."

"Do you know who I am?" the boss shouted.

"Does it matter?" Fyodor gestured toward the water, as though performing lines on a stage. "The law doesn't say certain people may fish here with nets, and others must only use poles. It says no nets allowed. That's true for all citizens of our great Soviet Union."

"You know nothing about law. I am Mikhail Tschikalin, and I am the new general director of the Drushkovka Brick Factory. You are just a stupid peasant!" He moved closer to the fisherman, as though considering an attack.

But the fisherman was not alarmed. He made no move to retreat. The party boss reconsidered: "Do you think our great leaders in Moscow care about your stupid local ordinances? Do you think they are worried about your petty little fish when they are trying to defend our great motherland? You insignificant little worm!"

If the fisherman was afraid, there was no evidence of it in his face or posture. He had confronted petty bureaucrats before. He knew they could imprison him, but they could never break his spirit. He had spent time in jail before, and had acquired a firm confidence that revealed no fear.

Maybe the factory boss sensed that and, being a coward at heart, didn't want to chance a physical confrontation. They glared at each other for a moment. Then he smiled and tried a new approach.

"I see you care a great deal about our nation," he said in a conciliatory politician's voice. "So why are you worried about these fish? They are here for all of us comrades."

"But if we take them with nets, there will be none left. This is a stocking pond. We must let the small fish grow and produce more fish for our great country."

"This is only one pond. There are so many other fish in our great rivers. Why shouldn't the people of my factory enjoy the fish we have here?"

"Then why do we have laws? Why did our wise leaders say no nets here? It was so all the people in our village could enjoy the fish, not just a privileged few who would scoop them all up and leave none for the rest of us."

"You stupid idiot!" Again the tone changed, and the party leader's face turned red with anger. "You will pay for this." He nodded to his helpers, who folded up the net as they started back toward the village. "Throw him into the water," he ordered the men.

They hesitated, then headed toward the fisherman. Fyodor snapped open his pocketknife, which he used to clean fish, and held it in front of him. He shouted, "If you dare to attack me, I will slice your bellies open as I do those of the fish!" The anger and disdain in his voice made the factory workers think he might even welcome the fray. But the boss called it off. "Forget it! There are better ways to deal with this kulak. Let's go!" The men angrily retreated to their carriage and left.

The fisherman sighed with relief, but he knew instinctively that he would pay a price for this confrontation. Party leaders were not to be trifled with. He knew that, yet he couldn't help himself. What good was law if it was ignored? And what good was a man if he didn't stand for truth? He knew what was right. No one—not even a party leader—was above the law.

Was that belief worth another prison term? Probably not, but for some reason Fyodor could never back down from what he knew was right. He put a fresh worm on the line, reached back, and cast out into the middle of the pool. No party hack was going to ruin his fishing.

OCTOBER 1937

A fist hammered on the door. The sound split the silence of the autumn night. Fyodor and Maria awakened with a start.

"What was that?" an alarmed Maria Wasylenko asked her husband. She sat up, shaking in fear.

Fyodor knew who the intruders were. He remembered the warning from a neighbor that morning: "They are coming for you tonight. You must run!" Sometimes, if you ran, they would leave and not come back. But he was not one to run away. He had nothing to hide. He was not ashamed of his life. And if he did run, where would he go? Sooner or later, they would find him anyway.

Fyodor stumbled to the kitchen, flipped on the light, and asked, "Who is it?"

"Open up immediately!" a voice demanded.

"I will not open the door unless you identify yourselves."

There was a loud bang, then suddenly the door flew open as three men forced themselves into the house. They headed for the bookshelves and started ransacking Fyodor's belongings.

"What do you want?" Fyodor demanded.

No answer.

"What are you looking for?"

Still no answer.

His face and bald head became flush with anger. "Tell me what you want and I will give it to you! You don't need to tear up my house!"

But the intruders ignored him and kept tossing books and periodicals and papers onto the floor.

"I am a Soviet citizen!" he shouted. "You can't come in here without a warrant. I know the laws. I demand you identify yourselves!"

"Fedija, please!" cried Maria, her long black hair flowing down over her nightshirt. She knew how the men could hurt him if he resisted.

One of the men skimmed through a journal that contained information about the condition of European countries. Such publications were forbidden to most citizens. "What is this?" the man demanded.

"I read them for my work! I must keep up with what is going on in other places, in factories like ours." The intruder set the journal on the kitchen table and continued his search.

Again, Fyodor asked, "Why are you doing this? What do you want? Tell me, and I will give you what you are looking for."

His pleas were ignored. Two sleepy-eyed children emerged from the bedroom. They huddled together with their mother, shaking with fear. Drawers and boxes were now turned upside down. A pile of clothing, papers, books, and journals grew on the floor.

One of the men bent down and picked up a notebook. It was a diary that belonged to Fyodor's older daughter—written in German. "Give me that!" Fyodor shouted as he lunged for the book.

The man shoved him out of the way and set it on the table. Fyodor's heart skipped a beat. He had made it a rule that whenever he and his wife needed a sitter for the children, they would hire one of the women from the German settlement nearby. He insisted they speak only German so his children could learn the language. For the past year, he had encouraged his daughter to write her diary entries in German for practice. He knew there was tension between Germany and the Soviet Union, but surely there was nothing wrong with teaching his children a foreign language. He was certain, however, the men would use this against him.

"Where is your search warrant?" Fyodor asked. "You can't come in here without a warrant. I'm a Soviet citizen. I know my rights."

No answer. A drawer splintered as it was turned upside down and thrown aside.

Fyodor began yelling. He pushed one of the men. "Show me your identification!"

"Fedija!" his wife pleaded.

A baby began to cry. Maria retreated to the bedroom to pick up the baby, trying to comfort her.

As she returned to the front room, an eleven-year-old boy asked, "Mommy, what are the men doing? Why are they—"

"Shhh! Quiet!"

Fyodor went after another of the intruders. "Do you have a badge? Show me your badge!"

No answer.

He turned to the third man out of frustration. "What are you looking for? Tell me! I will give it to you, I assure you!"

One of the searchers pulled out a gun and pointed it at Fyodor's face. The fifteen-year-old daughter lunged to her father's side to protect him. The gunman shoved the girl back against the wall. "Shut up and stay there!" he ordered. Then he stood facing Fyodor with the gun while the other two men finished the search.

They set aside several law books and works of literature. There was a collection of newspaper clippings, and also some photographs. These they put in Fyodor's crocodile-leather portfolio.

Finally the leader spoke. "Put on your coat!" he ordered. "You're going with us." At that point, he flashed his badge.

NKVD!*

Fyodor didn't move. "Fedija, please do what they say!" Maria pleaded. The two older children were now crying and trembling in fear.

This was it! Fyodor and Maria looked at each other. They knew. Sooner or later, they had to come. The NKVD always came. He had been arrested before. He had lived in exile for three years. And even after he was released, he was never really

---

* The Soviet secret police from 1934-43, which later became the KGB.

free. They watched him. They warned him. They applied pressure. And the pressure built, until now . . .

There was no sense in arguing. So the men had not properly identified themselves. What could he do? You couldn't fight the NKVD. He removed his nightshirt and put on his pants, a shirt, and a coat. Over his shaved head he placed a fur hat.

He kissed his son and older daughter. Without a word, he kissed his wife. He then bent over, gently took his baby daughter's hand, and kissed it. *"Auf, nedovho, Emotshka,"* he whispered. "Goodbye. I'll see you soon, my little daughter."

Shaken, but with proud determination, he allowed the men to escort him out the front door into the pitch-black night. After a few steps down the narrow path, he turned for one last look. His wife was standing in the doorway, the baby cradled at her breast.

The men led Fyodor down the path, over a narrow stream, and back up an embankment to a waiting truck hiding on the outskirts of the village. Then he heard a familiar sound—a two-tone whistle from his wife. She wanted to know where he was. He whistled back the same two tones.

Then it was silent.

2

I'm Yours Forever

NOVEMBER 1937
ARTOMOWSK, Ukraine
MARIA (Amy's mother)

M aria wore a red scarf and a tattered wool coat. She hesitated for a moment before stepping off the train onto the crowded platform. Jostled by the mob, she nearly dropped her meager package of food and clothing. The jail was only a few blocks away. She quickly made her way to the entrance and found a huge waiting room packed with women, most of them like her, looking for their husbands or sons.

Where she got the energy to make this long journey, she didn't know. That morning she had walked a mile to her mother's house to leave her baby, walked five more miles to the train station, then changed trains again before arriving in Artomowsk. But she took a deep breath and elbowed and shoved her way toward a small window. An hour passed before she got close enough to learn that there were forms to fill out. Papers—there were always papers. She did her best to complete them without surrendering her place near the window.

Reaching over the heads of two *babushkas* (older women clad in the traditional Russian scarves) she shoved the papers toward the official inside the window.

"Outside! Wait outside!" she was ordered.

"Can I see my husband?" Maria shouted over the crowd.

"Outside! You will be called when it's your turn."

19

Maria felt as if she was going to faint as she shuffled through the crowd to the door. But once outside, the cold air braced her and she recovered some strength. A round-faced woman stood next to her. She was clutching a bundle wrapped in newspaper. She smiled at Maria. "You might as well relax. I've been waiting for three hours."

They talked briefly, comparing notes about their families. Neither said a word about their husbands.

A loud voice called from inside the waiting room. "Kordova!" Others in the room repeated the name. A tiny woman on the outskirts of the crowd moved and the women parted to let her into the building.

"Semchenko!"

"Semchenko!" went the message through the group. The round-faced woman brightened, then instantly revealed a worried look. Maria watched her as she pushed her way through the crowd toward the official with a list in his hand. Maria couldn't hear what he told her, but she suddenly screamed, dropped her parcel, and fainted. Rumbles went through the crowd as two officials carried her outdoors. What happened? everyone was asking. The word was passed from inside. Maria's heart froze as she heard: "They told her that her husband was executed." No one knew why or when; one didn't ask such questions.

Maria wondered about her Fyodor's fate. It was clear on the faces around her that all the women shared similar fears. But each of them suffered alone. Maria wanted to escape from the crowd and cry. But her body wouldn't move. She would stand and wait and silently worry.

A few minutes later, another name rang out. Then another. "Sokolov!" "Petrovich!" "Burkovsky!" "Fyodorov!"

She began to despair of ever hearing her own name. She waited two hours. Three hours. Maybe longer.

"Wasylenko!" For a moment she stopped breathing. "Wasylenko! Are you Wasylenko?" asked a woman near her. Maria headed back into the building. The crowd parted slightly; the fight to the window wasn't quite so difficult this time. She made her way to the official with the list.

"Are you Maria Denisowna Wasylenko?"

"*Da!*" she answered.

"Husband's name?"

"Fyodor Philipovich." The official, she noticed, was in an NKVD uniform. That should have been no surprise, yet it upset her. "May I see him?" she asked.

The man ignored her as he marked his list.

"May I see my husband?" she asked again.

"It is not possible," he said.

"When can I see him? I brought him some things. Can I leave them?" She tried not to sound desperate.

"Come back when it's your day. Butkovski!" Maria heard "Butkovski" shouted back, through the door, into the crowd outside.

"When is it my day?" But she was already being elbowed away from the window.

"You're W," said one woman. "Each letter of the alphabet has a different day."

"What day is for W?"

"Anyone know what day is W?" someone shouted.

The question was passed back. Finally, someone answered, "Third Thursday of each month."

"Can I leave a package for my husband?" asked Maria.

"Come back on your day. Third Thursday of next month."

She felt weak-kneed again. How would she find the energy to walk back to the train station and endure the long trip back? And the long hike from the station back to her home? She was only 34, but she felt old—and very tired.

SUMMER 1938

Maria Wasylenko came faithfully every month to try and see her husband. She left her baby daughter with her mother, and many times when she returned, she collapsed at her mother's, too tired to carry her daughter the final mile to her own home and bed. But she exerted that effort for the possibility of a moment with her husband. He had to know she cared. Maybe it would enable him to survive the horrors of prison life.

But she was not allowed so much as a glimpse of Fyodor. She was only permitted to hand over her package consisting of a change of clothes and a little food—mostly some dried fruit and maybe a potato or two from her garden. In exchange she received a package of dirty clothes—her husband's laundry—soiled almost beyond recognition. Stained with sweat and blood . . . and perhaps his tears. There was no assurance that her husband was well, that he was not seriously injured by the beatings she knew occurred, that he was not psychologically crushed by the sleepless nights and incessant interrogations. Most of all she ached for the chance to touch him, to embrace, to feel his arms around her and know that he was well, and that somehow he would survive this ordeal.

Maria knew her husband. He had been through this before. He would never let them break his spirit. Yet who could withstand the constant pressure? Eventually they all broke. They would make him sign a confession. Violation of article 58 of the criminal code of 1926. Crimes against the state. Anything could be considered a crime against the state. A neutral statement about Stalin. Perceived lack of support for party policy. Interest in another nation's affairs. Or an offense against a party official. Fyodor, of course, would never admit to any crime. In his heart he knew he was innocent of all charges. But it didn't matter.

After one of Maria's monthly visits, as she trudged back to the train station, a man motioned to her. Glancing around before he spoke, he said, "You must not tell anyone that you saw me."

She stared at him but said nothing.

"If anyone learns I told you, it could cost me my life."

The man nervously looked around again, then said, "I saw them beat your husband. They beat him so bad that he lay there as if dead. They stopped until he regained consciousness, then they beat him again."

As soon as he finished speaking, the man was gone. Who was he? A troubled guard? A former inmate? Her cynical self considered that he was a plant by the NKVD. His job: to terrorize her. Or to motivate her to plead with her husband to sign a confession of some kind. She was sure if she wrote a letter with that message, it would be delivered.

* * *

It was hot this day. Maria sat in the waiting room, sweat pouring from under her red scarf. Outside, in the courtyard, groups of prisoners were being marched out of the compound. New prisoners were coming in; old ones were being transferred. The transfer of each group was preceded by a security shutdown. No one could come or go from the waiting room until a transfer was completed.

Maria waited for the usual exchange. Besides her usual package, she carried a pair of black boots. They had been handed to her during the last visit, and she had them repaired. When her name was called, she would hand over her package. Then she would wait a while longer. Finally, she was given a package in return. But the thing she desired most—the chance to talk to her Fyodor—to touch him, to hold him, just to see him—was always denied.

Today, the wait was longer than usual. More prisoners were herded out of the compound. There was agitation among the women in the room. Someone shouted, "They're taking them away!" Many of the women got up and hurried outside. At that same moment, Maria heard her name called. "Wasylenko!"

Maria went to the door where the guard stood empty-handed. "Your husband is no longer here."

"Where is he?"

"I cannot tell you."

"I have this package for him. How can I get it to him?"

The guard shrugged. What did he care? He turned and walked away. She fought to quell the panic she felt rising within. Then she noticed that the room seemed deserted. She remembered that they were transporting the prisoners, but where to?

Maria dashed out the door and saw the crowd moving down the hill toward the freight yard. She hurried, pushing her way past babushkas who couldn't move so quickly. At the yard was a swarm of people. The commotion, yelling, and screaming disoriented her. A long train of cattle cars was parked on a siding. Prisoners were being marched onto one of the cars, and many of the other cars were already full. Arms hung out through the narrow slats, waving, searching for loved ones. A line of guards patrolled the railroad siding, and no one was allowed near the train.

"Misha!" screamed a woman nearby. The shriek startled Maria. A woman pushed through the guards and clasped a teenage boy around the neck. Piercing sobs tore the air as two soldiers grabbed the woman's arms and threw her back into the crowd. "Why?" she screamed at the uniforms. "You already have my other two sons. Why Misha? Why do you take all my sons away? Tell me, why!"

Maria felt pity for the woman and her son, but there wasn't time to dwell on that. Where was her Fedija? She looked up and down the length of the train. It would be impossible to find him. But she had to try. She pushed through the crowd, searching each train car for some sign of her love. Fyodor knew that today was her day to come, so surely he was looking, too. Maybe he would recognize her red scarf and try to send her a signal.

Maria pushed her way up to the front of the train. Steam hissed from the engine, but the engineer was leaning against the coal car, puffing a cigarette and showing no signs of moving yet. She looked back down the line of cars. She could see arms waving through the slats and strained to see if a shirtsleeve matched her husband's. It was impossible; they all looked alike! Around her, other women shoved and shouted and strained to find their loved ones. But the intimidating line of guards kept the crowd from getting near the train.

Undaunted, she began to work her way back toward the end of the train. The oppressive heat and surging crowd drained her energy. At one point she had to stop to try and regain some strength. But her eyes never left the train, never stopped looking.

Maria looked up at the small windows near the top of the cars. Men were lifting each other up on one another's shoulders so they could search the crowd for loved ones. Desperately she scanned each window . . . there he was! He was waving frantically at her.

She waved back. Her instinct was to push forward, to rush toward him. But the guards . . . she had to think this over. Looking around, she saw a pile of building materials. She clambered up the pile for a better look. Now she could see his face. They waved at each other. Maria held up the package and the boots. Fyodor grinned and pointed down. What? The door? What was he thinking? She couldn't just hand them over. And they couldn't expect the car doors to be opened. Yet she did not want to just stand there, either. She had to try something; her husband needed the boots and the clothes.

Maria looked at the engine and counted back. Her husband was in car six. She then scanned the length of the train. It appeared that every wagon was loaded to capacity, which meant that soon the train would start moving. Would one of the guards have mercy on her? She had to try. Adrenaline propelled her into the crowd and she pushed her way to the front. Which guard should she approach? She was afraid; a guard would probably just push her away. Was it worth the risk?

Yes, she had to take a chance! She stepped out. "I beg your pardon," she said to a soldier. "Could you find it in your heart to open the wagon door, even just a crack, for a moment, so I could see my husband's face for the last time and hand him these things that he needs so badly? This is my day to visit, and I have come such a long way. . . ."

The young man appeared to be a teenager, not much older than her son. He grinned at her, making her more uncomfortable as she pleaded with him.

"I have his clothes and boots." She held out the parcels. "Could you at least hand these to him?"

"Which one is your husband?" asked the young guard. "Is he young or old?" He was smiling, trying to ease her fear. "Do you know which wagon he is in?"

"The sixth wagon from the engine."

The man took her parcels, then went to get a ladder. When Maria tried to follow, he held up a hand to indicate she was to remain in the crowd. He placed the ladder against her husband's wagon, climbed up, and unlocked the sliding door. He shoved it open a few feet. There, beaming, stood Fyodor!

They stared at each other, unable to speak, as the guard handed Maria's package to her husband. How long had it been? Nearly a year since the arrest. How long until they would see each other again? She knew he would probably receive a ten-year sentence. That's what everyone got now—ten years. He was going to Siberia, and she couldn't follow him . . . she couldn't leave the children. This moment had to be savored.

"How are you? And how are the children?" Fyodor asked, the loud voice from his barrel chest projecting through the bedlam.

"Fine, fine. We're all just fine," she answered as loud as she could. But he couldn't hear her over the noise of the crowd.

Fyodor grinned and shrugged his shoulders. There were other ways to communicate. He cupped his hands in front of his chest, as if reading a book, then acted out a writing motion, and finally held one hand about shoulder-high.

Maria understood. Her husband was a born actor. His signs were asking her how their oldest daughter, Hanusia, was doing in school. The education of his children was the most important priority to him, and what few notes he had managed to send always urged his wife to provide for that education, no matter what the price.

She smiled, nodded her head, and cupped her hands to her face, as though burying her nose in a book. Fyodor understood and was obviously pleased. He held his hand chest-high. How was their son Tarasik doing in school? She signaled again that he was studying, and added a hoeing motion with her arms to indicate he was also helping her tend their garden.

Fyodor beamed his pleasure. He cradled his arms now; he wanted to know about his little daughter.

Maria, too, cradled her arms, then smiled as she pretended to hold her baby to her breast. Their special little girl was healthy. She held her hands apart and then slightly expanded the space to demonstrate she was growing.

All during this exchange, Maria watched to see if her husband was in pain. She couldn't tell if he was hurting; he looked reasonably healthy, though he had clearly lost weight. There was no evidence of serious injury from beatings.

Fyodor now called to the guard, who was obviously pleased to watch this reunion. Maybe it reminded him of the family he missed in some distant part of the Soviet Union. Maria strained to hear her husband's voice. "Could you do me a favor? Could you let my wife come close for a moment so I can put my arms around her? Would you allow that?"

The guard shook his head.

"Please!" Fyodor pleaded. "Just a moment? A hug and a kiss?"

"I can do everything else for you, but this is impossible. It is against regulations and strictly forbidden. Anything else you ask is fine. But this is impossible."

"But you don't understand. She's not going to be mine after I'm taken away."

Maria heard that. "I'm yours no matter what!" she shouted.

Did he hear her? He blew her a kiss and soberly hugged himself to convey the deep affection he felt for her. She felt a chill, despite the muggy heat. Clouds were darkening the sky. A late thunderstorm would arrive soon.

"I'm yours forever!" she shouted, and blew back a kiss. At that statement, the prisoners around Fyodor applauded and cheered. That's what all of them wanted to hear—that their wives and loved ones would wait for them.

Fyodor looked up at the sky, then lifted his hands above his head to indicate that his wife should consider taking cover.

She shook her head. "I'm okay!" she shouted. She would not surrender this moment.

They gazed at each other as darkness began to descend on the crowd. Were others making connections with their loved ones? She neither knew nor cared. For now, time had stopped. Who could know when, or if, she would see her husband again? She couldn't bear to think the unthinkable. Yet she knew that many never returned from the gulags. A few drops of rain, the prelude to a downpour, splattered on and around her, but she didn't care.

The bang of wagon doors being shut broke the trance. Some women began weeping and wailing. Maria's tears would come later. She continued to stare at her Fyodor as the door was slowly pushed shut. She heard a loud clank as the lock was put into place. The rain was heavier now, and the crowd was quieter. There were no more conversations. Yet no one left. The women waited.

The engine released a burst of steam. Then slowly it gave its initial tug, jerking the cars in a chain reaction. It began inching ahead. Fyodor's wagon moved past Maria and picked up speed, heading into the darkness. With it went her dreams. A chill descended on her spirit. Would she ever see him again? Could he survive the harsh conditions? Could she survive without him?

Wagon after wagon passed—hundreds of prisoners. Thousands more would join them by the time they made all the other stops along the way to their frozen destination. The last car slid past, moving quickly now. She heard the engine whistle blow as the train turned a corner and disappeared. She heard the whistle shriek one more time. And then it was silent.

In her heart, she sensed this goodbye was forever.

SPRING 1939

After a long day of shoveling coal, Maria had dragged her exhausted, rain-soaked body back home. With bitterness she remembered the humiliation just a few days after she had seen her Fyodor taken by train to Siberia. She had gone with a friend to Konstantinovka to the NKVD headquarters to try and retrieve her husband's portfolio and the contents that had been confiscated the night of the arrest. Particularly, she had wanted her daughter's diary and the photographs returned. She asked to see Colonel Woronov, the local head of the NKVD, but his secretary would not let her in the door. As she was leaving the building, the colonel had leaned out of his third-story office and fired the portfolio at her feet. It was empty.

It was obvious to everyone that Maria was a marked person. How much could she take without breaking? The authorities had tried every way possible to demoralize her. She would stand in line to apply for a job. Everyone in front of her got a job. Everyone after her got a job. But she was denied a job.

She would stand in long lines to buy bread. She would finally get to the front only to be told they had just run out. She would then point to a couple of loaves on the shelf. They were always "reserved." She would gladly have baked her own bread, but there was no flour or any other ingredients available anywhere.

The electricity to their home had been cut off, so she could no longer listen to the radio. Instead of electric lights, she had to use two oil lamps—when she could get oil. And it was her husband who had worked so hard to bring electricity to Drushkovka!

When Maria ran out of money and items to trade for food, she traded her wedding ring for a loaf of bread. It was no use asking her family for help because they were suffering, too. She did not want to add to their burdens.

Maria knew what the NKVD wanted. They wanted her and her children to starve to death. They viewed her as a worthless drain on society because she was married to a man they considered a counterrevolutionary. And everyone around her knew that whoever tried to help her would endanger his or her own life.

But that winter, Maria had secured a job. The state desperately needed every available body, and this was work no one else wanted to do. With the wives of other political prisoners, she shoveled coal onto trains in a cold, drafty tunnel. It was filthy work, and she couldn't even take a few lumps of coal back to her freezing house. Her work meant she had to leave her three-year-old daughter at home for twelve or thirteen hours at a time, all by herself with no toys in an unheated house.

One evening she had run into her brother on her way home from work. Upon arriving at her house they tried to open the door, but for some reason it was blocked. Together they had gently shoved until the door inched open. Inside, they found her little girl asleep on the floor, lying against the door, her dirty face streaked with tears and marked by impressions from the floorboards. They had wept at the pitiful sight. How long had she lain at the door, crying in despair for her mother?

How could a mother bear such scenes of suffering? How long could she survive without food for herself and her children? How long did she have to endure the pressure, the humiliation? It never ended. She was tired. Utterly, totally, bone-weary tired and discouraged. Totally drained in body and mind. She felt she had no more reserve. No more strength. No more will.

It seemed that there was only one answer: She had to have an escape. The means lay on a shelf in the pantry—an old frazzled rope. It had once been used to tie up a cow in the small stable. Now it sat alone in the pantry. The rough wood shelves were empty. Where once there was flour and grain and various food items from the garden, now there was nothing.

Maria looked up at the trapdoor in the ceiling. Above it was the attic. It would be fairly simple to climb up there and tie the rope to a beam, loop the other end around her neck, then jump through the door. She would have her rest.

She tiptoed back to the bedroom and peered in for a moment. There was the baby, now three years old, sleeping soundly. It was her afternoon nap. For a moment Maria hesitated. Tears formed in her eyes. What kind of world would this child know? If there was a God, and if He was merciful, she would be spared from having to suffer in this sick world—a world that took her father without cause and put him in a brutal labor camp and that ostracized her mother and her sister and brother and herself just because they had a father who lived by his convictions instead of by the frivolous dictates of a ruthless state. No, this wasn't a world fit for an innocent child.

But what about her son? He was ten years older. What would happen to him? She couldn't bear to think about that. Fortunately, he was in the village with some friends. He would manage . . . somehow.

One thought continued to dominate her, gnawing away at her heart: *I cannot go on.*

She would give the NKVD what they wanted, and in the process relieve her own misery. She went back to the pantry, pushed a wooden ladder in place, and opened the trapdoor. It was a simple matter to tie the rope to a beam on the roof. She tied a loop at the other end of the rope, and opened it wide. She pulled again on the rope. Despite the frayed parts, it was strong. It would hold. She then stepped to the edge of the trapdoor opening and held the noose in front of her, ready to slip it over her head. Once it was in place, she would jump. At last, the misery would be over.

She hesitated, staring at the noose.

"No! Mamo, no! Don't do it!"

The shout startled her.

"Mamo! What are you doing?"

The rope dropped from her hands. She stumbled and almost fell through the trapdoor. She stared down at the pantry entrance. It was her son.

The boy burst into tears. "Mamo, how could you? We need you!" He scrambled up the ladder and into his mother's arms. "Please, don't do it, Mamo. Don't leave us!" He hugged her and clutched her, as if by sheer willpower he could save his mother.

Tarasik's actions were like a pail of cold water shocking her. "My God, what am I thinking?" Maria began to sob uncontrollably and clutched her son. "I'm sorry. I'm so sorry. I don't know what I was thinking. How could I. . . . I love you, little son."

The spell was broken. Darkness had overtaken her; she had felt as if she was in a long, black tunnel with no exit. Now, she saw a light at the end of the tunnel. It was faint, but sure. She knew the answer. She had misplaced her focus on her pain. She had looked only for an escape from her agony. But at what cost? What about her children? How could she have allowed herself to lose all hope?

There *were* reasons for living; one was clutching her now. Another was asleep in the house. An elder daughter was away at school in Stalino. They all needed her. There were others—her mother, brothers, and sister. They were hurting, too. How could she even think of adding to their pain?

No, she must find a way to survive. She could not afford to worry about the future. Maybe her husband would come home someday. Maybe they would be a family again. But if not, she would at least live for their three children, who looked to her for strength. They needed her. If she could just hold on, then maybe, just maybe, something better would come along for them. She could not look too far ahead. She had to cope with problems as they came along—one day at a time.

In that moment, a tiny flame of hope ignited. It wasn't much, but it was enough to keep her alive. She determined then that never again would that flame go out. She would finish her job.

She would survive.

And if fate was merciful, then let fate determine her future.

3

A Picture for Daddy

SPRING 1940
DRUSHKOVKA, Ukraine
AMY

There was barely enough light for me to make out the form of my mother, still sleeping next to me, and my brother across the room. I quietly slipped out of bed, tiptoed through the living room and kitchen, opened the door, and welcomed the new day.

There was a crisp freshness in the air. Compelled by the sights and sounds of nature, I sat down on the stone stoop, pulled my nightshirt down over my knees until it touched my toes, and watched the sun begin to rise. Soon its rays would begin to warm my shivering body and somehow remind me that I was loved. Sjun, our wolf dog, saw me from her bed of straw by the shed. She stood, stretched, then shuffled over and settled at my feet. Her presence helped cut the chill as I stroked her thick brown and black fur.

The yard in front of me was slightly muddy. A few weeks earlier, the mud caused by melting snow made it almost impossible to walk in front of the house. Now just a trickle of water flowed past, the last remains of snow on the hills behind. Pebbles in the water glistened in the morning light and I followed their path as they escorted the water down to a larger creek, which separated our house from our neighbors. A few carefully placed stones allowed us to cross the stream and enter the village.

That creek served as a barrier for anyone attempting to invade what I considered our property. When neighboring children played in the stream, I would stand on the bank like a little general with my hands behind my back and my stomach sticking out and in my deepest voice instruct them to get out of my river. Mother would laugh at my spirit, put her arms around me, and gently say, "You be kind, little daughter!"

My attention was drawn back to the wonders in front of me. I looked up and gazed at our orchard of fruit trees, bathed in dew. Years before, the trees were planted all around the house by my grandmother and father. We had twenty-five kinds of apple trees, plus pears, plums, apricots, and cherries. They formed a wall around me, protecting me from the great big world beyond. And in those trees right now I could hear a chirping symphony of birds contributing their celebration for the new day.

Besides the house, the only part of our property without trees was the garden. Standing between the orchard and a line of weeping willows along the stream, the plot of land was full of cabbages, tomatoes, giant sunflowers, and grapes, under whose vines our chickens found cool, shallow nests in the sandy dirt during the hot summer days. Many times I joined them, helping them find raisins among the grapes that had fallen. The garden and orchard provided most of the food we lived on.

We had flowers, too. White and purple irises lined a path down to the stream. Large lilac bushes hugged the house and filled my nose with their rich fragrance. A yellow rosebush was at a far corner of the vegetable garden, and I was well acquainted with its tender aroma.

A chicken emerged from the shed and started to forage for food. Every day, when a chicken indicated by walking to her nest that she was ready to produce an egg, I would sit on a small wooden stool at the door of the shed adjacent to our house and wait as long as it took the chicken to do her job. As soon as she stirred and carefully stepped down, I would pick up the still-warm egg and bring it to my mother with pride—as if I had laid it myself. My mother would compliment me on the beautiful egg, and I thrived on her praise. But recently I was told to not disturb the eggs. One of the hens was sitting on the eggs and soon we would have some chicks. I could hardly wait! I thought fluffy yellow newborn chicks were the most lovable beings. My mother would gently pick one up and place it in my palms, which I cupped around the peeping noisemaker. I would hold it to my face to feel the soft fluff and then kiss the chick on its tiny beak.

The sun rose above the horizon and I soaked up its warming rays. With the warmth, I felt loved and secure. Was it really the sun, or was it the love of my mother? A little girl of four years doesn't try to answer such questions. She simply accepts the love and thrives on it, as if it is life itself. For me, I believe it was.

I was named Emma Fedorowna Wasylenko. My sister nick-named me "the twig." I think she gave me the name because I was so small and skinny. I was born prematurely, on February 25, 1936. In the deep of winter my mother had to make her way through the snow several times to a nearby well to fill two buckets with water which was used for cooking, washing, and drinking. Carrying that heavy weight caused her to go into premature labor. My family was always anxious about my health because they believed that a child born prematurely wouldn't live past the age of thirteen. Such myths permeated the thinking of the peasants in our village.

My little world was quite simple. Our home was on the out-skirts of Drushkovka, which was located in southwest Ukraine, somewhere between the cities of Dnepropetrovsk and Doneck. The great cities to the north—Kiev and Moscow—were totally beyond my world. I knew very little about them, or of the political leaders there who shaped our lives.

My heroine was my sister Hanusia, fourteen years my senior. She was studying medicine at the institute in Stalino, a large town about thirty miles away. I couldn't wait to see her in a few weeks when school ended for the summer. My brother Tarasik, ten years older than me, still lived at home, but his world of friends was different from mine. Apart from my cousins, with whom I played occasionally, most of my time was filled with exploring nature. My friends were our dog, the chickens, and the bugs. Without doubt, my total security was my mother.

"Little one, it's time to come inside." I hadn't heard my mother stirring in the house. I went inside and mother had a *blintzick* (pancake) waiting for me on my favorite plate, which was hand-painted with pretty little flowers and plums. "Eat quickly. I need to get you ready."

Most of my days were spent in this tiny, simple world of nature. But today there was something special to occupy my atten-tions. My mother had told me the day before that we were going to Konstantinovka, a small town about five miles from our little village. "We're going to get your picture taken for the first time," she explained. "It's for your father. He is asking about you in his letters. He hasn't seen you for two-and-a-half years." But when I pestered her with further questions, she only smiled and said, "You will see tomorrow, Dotshitshka!"*

I was too excited to eat more than a few bites. I went into the bedroom and there, laying on our bed, was my special dress—a simple little frock my mother had made from an old skirt that she had worn to the point of threadbareness. Though she had never had sewing lessons, she made a pattern for me and placed it over the areas of her skirt that were the least worn. This became the dress that I wore only on special occasions. I jumped up and down as I pulled off my nightshirt, pulled on my wool leggings, and slipped into the dress. But mother had an even bigger surprise. She held up a vest made of gray wool and embroidered with colorful silk flowers.

"Mamo! It's beautiful!" I exclaimed.

My mother slipped the vest on over the dress and I turned around, trying to admire every inch of it. "Mamo, did you make this for me?"

"No, Dotshitshka. I found it at the bazaar in Konstantinovka. Do you like it?"

I ran into my mother's arms and hugged her. "I love it, Mamo. It's beautiful!"

She wasn't finished. Next she combed my hair and pulled back the curls from my face and tied them together with a white satin bow. Then she produced another surprise. "Here, let me put this little bag over your shoulder." How much excitement could a little girl stand! The strap of the shoulder bag was made of black satin ribbon. The pouch itself was also black satin, with a contrast border across the top which matched the bow in my hair.

Before we left, mother had some instructions for my brother. "Senok [little son], after school, I want you to hoe the cabbage patch and around the fruit trees. I expect you to hurry home; no playing with your friends. If you don't hurry home, you won't have enough daylight to finish your work."

We didn't have a horse and cart, so the only way to reach Konstantinovka was to walk. It would take us nearly two hours. My mother took me by the hand and we went down the path into our village. It didn't take us long to walk through Drushkovka. It

—————————————————

* Little daughter—a term of endearment.

consisted mainly of a few mud and straw houses—in contrast to our home, which had brick walls and a tile roof.

Then the dirt road wound through a large *kolchoz*, or collective farm. There was little evidence of any activity. Periodically, we saw small homes, and surrounding them small private plots where the occupants had planted cabbages, potatoes, sunflowers, and other vegetables. Several women were working hard in their gardens. There were also a few pigs and cows that wandered freely, looking for food.

"Mamo, I'm getting tired," I complained.

"All right, let me carry you." She reached down and picked me up. I clung to her neck and wrapped my legs around her waist. I felt myself begin to doze off as my mother trudged on. I was small for my age, and my mother didn't find me much of a burden as long as she didn't have other packages to carry. All she needed to do was sidestep the frequent mud puddles that dotted the road. Thus carrying me also served to keep my nice clothes from getting dirty.

As we approached Konstantinovka, my mother stopped and put me down. I clutched her hand. This small town was slightly larger than our own Drushkovka. It had a train station which was actually little more than a rickety wooden platform and a shack for the ticket seller. There was also a village square where the bazaar was held. People came from all around to sell or trade food and clothing. My mother often came to sell or trade some of her garden vegetables and the fruits she dried—that's how she had obtained my new vest.

We passed the station and square and at the edge of town stopped at a simple thatched house with whitewashed walls. A small man with a bushy gray beard came to the door. "Come in, come in!" he said to mother. "This must be your little daughter. I have a surprise for you, little girl!" My ears perked up with anticipation.

Inside was a dark room that contained only a single chair in the middle and, a small distance away, a strange-looking thing on three legs and covered by a black cloth. As he fussed with it, he asked me, "What is your name?"

"Emma," I whispered.

"Emma. What a nice name. Do you know what we're going to do today?"

"You're going to take my picture."

"That's right!" He pulled the chair over to a specific spot on the floor.

"Maria Denisowna, would you please put your daughter on the chair?"

My mother picked me up and stood me on the chair. I stared at the man who was doing something underneath the cloth that sat on top of the three legs. As he worked, he talked. "Now Emma, you need to be a good girl and watch very carefully because under this cloth there lives a bird, and it is ready to come out and see you."

My mother wrapped her arms around my waist and whispered, "Look at the camera, Dotshitshka. Look closely so you will see the bird."

Nothing was going to take my eyes away from that cloth! The man had disappeared under it, but I could hear him saying, "Watch carefully; the birdie is going to appear any moment." I saw something that looked like a glass eye come out. And then there was a flash and I saw stars in my eyes. But no birdie! I kept staring, looking for the bird.

"We're all done!" said the old man. "Now that wasn't too hard, was it?"

But I was still looking for the bird! I stared more, but all I saw was the black cloth.

"Come on, Dotshitshka. We're finished." My mother took me by the hand.

"But Mamo, where's the bird?" I started to cry.

The photographer knelt down before me. "That bird is tricky. Sometimes he comes out only for a second. Maybe next time you'll see him."

I stopped crying and tried to hide my deep disappointment. I had never seen a camera before, and I had not known what to expect. Maybe the bird had come out while my eyes were blinded by the flash.

At the door, the photographer told my mother that she could pick up the picture the next time she was in town. We walked away hand in hand, my eyes blinking and adjusting to the bright sunlight after being in the dark room.

We stopped at the market, but this day there wasn't much activity. My mother didn't buy anything and we started our long walk back to Drushkovka. We walked for some time in silence; my mother was not one to talk much. And I was content just to be near her. But my curiosity finally prompted me to ask a question that was arising inside. The photo was for my father, whom I could not remember because he had been arrested when I was an infant. I wanted to know more about him.

"Mamo, where is my daddy?"

"He is far away, in the northernmost part of Siberia," she answered quietly. But she gave no extra details. That was her way.

"Why is he in Siberia? Why isn't he with us?"

My mother shook her head. "It's hard to explain, little daughter. He is in a labor camp."

"When is he coming home?"

"Not for a long time. We don't know how long."

"Why? Why is he there, Mamo? Why did they take daddy away from us?"

"They accuse him of many things, and they say he is a counterrevolutionary."

"What's a counter . . . re, revolu . . . ary?"

My mother let out a deep sigh before she answered. "They say he is an enemy of the people."

Such concepts were too complicated for my young mind. "My daddy isn't an enemy. He wouldn't hurt anyone."

"You're right, little daughter. He is a great man. People listened to him and looked up to him. But there were a few people who were afraid of him—who didn't like him because he was educated." Mother paused, then continued, "It isn't safe to speak what you believe. It is better to be quiet than to talk."

This was the most important lesson of life—as my mother often reminded me. Every person had to learn it. Survival depended on it. Those who had opinions and talked too much were sent away. Only the opinion of the government was right.

"Remember, Dotshitshka, there's an old saying that goes, 'Never spit into the well. You may have to drink out of it later.'" Mother often used pithy little proverbs to help me remember her lessons.

I thought about that for a while. Then I asked, "What is my daddy like?"

My mother didn't answer for a moment, and as I looked up at her face, I saw a mixture of emotions. What was she feeling? Sadness, joy, anger, and resignation. "He's a wonderful man," she answered. "He is full of life. He loves to sing. He loves to dance. He likes to help people. He talked to all the villagers about getting electricity in our village, then made sure we got it. He is a lawyer, and he also taught school. He is very creative. He has written songs and plays. Children and adults in the village participated in his productions."

She paused. These things helped to describe my father, but they couldn't replace his presence. Her eyes moist, mother added, "Dotshitshka, your Tato loves you very much."

"When will I see him, Mamo?"

"I don't know." She shook her head. "I don't know."

We walked along in silence, until I started lagging. My mother picked me up and carried me the rest of the way while I dozed off on her breast.

SUMMER 1940

The next few weeks were busy. Mother worked in our garden. Tarasik was now out of school, but was less than enthusiastic about helping with the work. Mother frequently had to prod him, especially when it came to hoeing the weeds around all of our fruit trees and in the vegetable garden—a job he detested and often neglected. Each morning my mother let Zorka (which means "sunrise"), our calf, out of the shed. In the evening, the cow would return to the shed where mother would milk her. I would sit on the milk stool by the stall entry, tired from a day spent running and exploring. Zorka always walked slowly by me and carefully lifted her legs so as not to kick or hurt me. Mother often marveled at the sensitivity of the animal.

Zorka provided a critical part of our diet. Mother had obtained the cow the previous spring, when it was still a calf, in exchange for dried fruit. The weather was so cold that the calf had spent the first few weeks in our living room until it was warm enough for her to survive outside. Because mother was so concerned about my petite size, she made sure I had fresh milk daily. That and the daily exercise from running all over our property and climbing the hill behind our house all worked together to make me stronger.

The day my sister was due to arrive home, I got up early and sat at the door in my nightshirt, as usual. It was warmer now and mother was no longer worried about me getting cold. Still, when she rose soon after I did, she gently urged me to get dressed. "Hanusia won't be here for a while."

I dressed immediately and ran back outside to wait. My sister had once told me that she was embarrassed when she learned mother was going to have another baby. But when I was born, love took over and she became a second mother to me. She taught me my first words, and much of what I learned was through music—she had a beautiful singing voice. The previous summer, she had helped me learn how to walk barefoot outdoors. Since I had only one pair of shoes and they could never stand the rigors of a summer's play, Hanusia carefully walked me shoeless outside the house. At first, the rough ground pinched my tender feet. But over time, the bottom of my feet toughened and now I ran all over the place without pain.

Hanusia was also a marvelous nurse. She had been home for a week the previous winter when I was extremely sick. She nursed me through that time, pressing cold cloths on my face to bring down the fever, preparing and feeding me hot soups, and rubbing my back and legs to relieve my aches. Hers were healing hands.

It was late afternoon when I finally saw my sister coming up the path, carrying a small suitcase in one hand and a bag of laundry over her other shoulder.

"Hanusia!" I yelled as I ran down the path and across the stream, almost slipping on one of the rocks. My sister dropped her bags and opened her arms. I eagerly jumped into her embrace and hugged her around the neck. "Sistlitski!" I greeted her. "We're sisters!"

"Sistlitski!" she repeated, happiness radiating in her eyes as she swung me around. When she set me down, I looked into her face and saw a golden-brown tan. Her hair was curly and its black sheen glowed in the sun. To me, she was the most beautiful girl in the world. She held my hand and together we crossed the stream to where my mother waited to greet her oldest daughter.

That night after supper I sat on Hanusia's lap and she rocked me, as she had so often over the four years since my birth. "Little sister, do you remember the songs I taught you?" she asked.

"Let's do the song about the little bird!" I said.

Hanusia started the song and I sang with her: "Little bird stay with us, and please don't try to flee. We give you many things like candies, cookies, and tea."

We giggled as we finished. "You sing pretty," I said.

My mother overheard me and said, "Her friends call her a nightingale!"

"Aw, Mamo," Hanusia blushed, but she was obviously pleased by the compliment.

"Let's sing another song!" I pleaded. "Please!"

"Do you remember this one? 'The winter wind is bitter cold...'"

It was a song my father had composed. I joined in: "And everyone has taken cover. Except for the little sparrow, sitting sadly in the tree."

This was a Ukrainian rhyme, and it tugged at my heart as we sang the words and melody:

> You don't need to be so sad,
> I will be your mother.
> Come inside and eat some food,
> And drink a cup of tea.
>
> My hunger and my thirst, my friend,
> Are not my great concern.
> For I have lost my lifelong love,
> Never to return.
>
> The villain buzzard saw his chance
> To feed his greedy pride.
> And now my life is at its end
> From the loneliness inside.

I looked at mother and saw tears in her eyes. All of us were sad and thinking of my father. What caused him to write such a sad, yet beautiful song? I wanted to know, but Hanusia diverted my attention by telling me a story before putting me to bed.

The next afternoon, members of my mother's family arrived. Grandma (my mother's mom), walking slowly as she hung on the arm of my Uncle Alyosha, carefully made her way up the path. Alyosha had five daughters and after the death of his wife, they all moved in with grandma. The youngest girl, my cousin Tosia—she was my favorite because she was nearly my age—ran ahead of the rest. Grandma was carrying some special treats, including a loaf of white bread and a bottle of soda pop. It was a celebration whenever we had food and drink different from what we ate every day.

I played outside with my cousins while the adults sat and talked and ate sunflower seeds, spitting the peels out into the yard. As it got dark, we moved inside the house and the food was set on the table. Mother put on pickled apples and cucumbers—the remainder of last year's batch, plus some fruit compote. There was an early cabbage, cut up and fried with onions, then mixed with sour cream. Finally, she brought out some salted pork. This was truly a feast, for we almost never had meat. Occasionally we would slaughter a chicken, but even that was put in a soup and made to last many days. When we ate bread, it was almost always a heavy black bread—not the light, white kind.

My sister took a slice of bread and put some pork on it and gave it to me. Everyone seemed to be talking at once as they helped themselves to the food at the center of the table. There were no separate place settings; everyone took what they wanted from communal plates. I ate slowly, savoring the white bread and pork. Hanusia poured a couple of ounces of soda pop for me. It was a pink liquid, and I took just a sip and let the bubbly sweet taste sit on my tongue for a long time.

"Look what I have!" my mother announced. She was holding the picture of me taken a few weeks before. She had picked it up on a recent trip to Konstantinovka, where she had traded some dried fruits and fresh garden produce for the pork. The picture was passed around. "Look at those eyes!" said my uncle. "What was little Emma looking at?"

I was silent, but my mother explained: "She was waiting for the bird to come out. You know how photographers always say, 'Look at the birdie.'"

"I bet she would still be looking today if you hadn't pulled her away!" he laughed and passed the photo to grandma.

"It's a good picture of Emma," grandma told my mother. "Fyodor should be pleased."

Mother blushed, but with the mention of my father's name, a chill settled over the house. "Have you heard anything from him lately?" Alyosha asked.

Mother shook her head. "I write to him once a month; that's all I'm allowed to send. I don't know how many of the letters he gets. I sent him a copy of this picture last week. We'll see...," she shrugged her shoulders, as if to say she was powerless to do anything.

Hanusia picked up a guitar and started playing. My brother began strumming a mandolin, a small stringed instrument. Others began to hum, trying to remember the words to some of the traditional Ukrainian tunes. After a couple of songs, someone asked my sister to sing a solo. With accompaniment from the guitar and mandolin, she sang a coy song:

Mother waited and waited for me,
Looking out for me to the late hours.
But I was kissing my love,
Kissing my love in the orchard.

My mother had a faraway look in her eyes as my sister sang. When she finished, my uncle asked his sister, "Maria, are you all right?"

"I was just thinking about how much Fedija loved music. I miss hearing the radio. You know, one night he was up late listening to the radio, and he came and woke me up." She laughed lightly at the memory. "He pulled me out of bed and we danced around the room to this very song."

I tried to picture the scene, my mother in her nightshirt and her long black hair, which was usually braided or pulled back tight, loosened and flying freely as father swung her around the room. Our house once had other evidences of his love for music. A *kobza* (a Ukrainian harp-like instrument) had once stood in a corner—father had played it and mother had sung with him in harmony. That instrument was now gone, for in times like these, food was more valuable than an instrument.

Those must have been happy times, when music filled the air in our cozy home. But now, I think my mother wondered if they could ever be captured again.

The sun eventually disappeared behind the trees. Uncle Alyosha lit a lantern. The music started up again and cousin Tosia grabbed my hand and pulled me out into the middle of the living room. We bowed melodramatically, then like dancers in a chorus line, we began stepping to the music. Everyone clapped in rhythm. The faster the music got, the more we bent from hip to hip, kicking out our legs as they do in the distinctly Russian gopak dance. The adults began tittering at our efforts, which only made us try harder. As the music got faster we followed along until we were whirling and kicking out of control. I finally collapsed on the floor as the adults howled with glee. My mother and grandmother had tears in their eyes from the laughter.

"It feels good to laugh," said my mother. "It's like medicine."

Grandma praised us: "Emma and Tosia, I believe that is the finest dancing I have ever seen!" We glowed in her approval and the love of our family.

Later I sat in a corner of the room, fighting against tiredness after the excitement of the day. I didn't want to fall asleep; such happy moments were rare. Hanusia must have carried me to bed, for I don't remember seeing everyone leave. The next day when I woke up, my relatives were gone. I played, but mother, sister, and brother worked. They had to, for the fruit of the soil was all we could depend on when the harsh winter came.

As soon as the harvest was completed, Hanusia went back to school in Stalino. I keenly felt her absence. She was my best friend, but I wouldn't see her again for months. Apart from my cousin Tosia, whom I saw rarely, I had no real friends my age. Occasionally I saw kids from the village, but we were separated from them by the stream, and I wasn't old enough that my mother would let me go into the village alone.

Most of the time, nature was my only friend. Spring and summer were my favorite times of the year, when I was free to wander all over our "property." During spring I would walk through the orchard and pick off the hard sap from the cherry trees and suck on that sweet, gooey juice. Or I would explore the well where we drew water for the garden. Or, I would dip a pail into the stream and fill it with pollywogs. I would give each one a name and make up stories about them. By fall, the pollywogs had grown into frogs and they weren't so thrilled about a little girl playing with them. That's when I would adopt some wiggly bugs and make up stories about their lives. But that was only a diversion. The changing leaves on the trees told me the hard truth. Winter would soon be on its way, and for me that was the worst time of the year. Once the first snow arrived, my life would face the worst possible confinement.

4

The Battle for Survival

We rode with a neighbor on a horse-drawn cart to Konstan-tinovka to sell some of our fruits and vegetables. There, besides the fresh produce, people sold homemade sour cream, butter, eggs, jam, and various handcrafted items. I stayed close to my mother as she conducted business and continually examined the people around me and the products they were selling. Suddenly my eyes caught sight of a little white dress. It was mounted on a makeshift stand, and it was exactly my size. Now how could I, a four-year-old, possibly know my dress size? I can't explain it; I just knew it would fit me, and I longed for it. I had never had a new dress; in fact, no one in our family had enjoyed new clothes in years.

I pulled on my mother's hand, and pointed. "Mamo, may I have it?"

My mother looked at the dress and then squatted down so her eyes were even with mine. "My sweet Dotshitshka, it is not possible. We can't afford it." Her voice was soft and gentle, and in her eyes I could see that if there had been any way possible, she would have bought the dress. But no disappointment on my part could change the situation. Mother's answers were always final, and the sorrow in her face let me know the sad condition we were in.

That moment gave me my first real glimpse of the stress my father's situation placed on mother. We were desperately poor. I

45

had no warm clothing, nor boots, nor a heavy coat. What little clothing we had was old and worn and patched—that is, when mother was fortunate enough to find a piece of cloth. If there were no patches available, the garment was mended in a rough way, for what thread we obtained didn't match our clothing. After that day at the market, whenever I saw something I wanted, I didn't bother to ask for it because deep down I knew the answer: We didn't have any money. I learned to look at pretty things, admire them, and then go away and forget them.

Our situation became even more difficult after the sale of our cow Zorka. I cried as Mother led the gentle cow off to town. Later, she tried to explain that we had no choice. There were taxes to pay, and the cow was the only possession we had that was worth enough to cover the taxes.

I didn't understand. "What are taxes?" I asked.

"Taxes are what we owe the government. We have to pay money, or some of our fruits and vegetables, or whatever they ask."

"Why do they need it?"

"Everyone has to pay their share."

"But we have only one cow. Why do they have to take it?" I protested.

Mom hugged me tight. "I know it's not fair," she whispered. "But we don't fight it. We can't fight it. Your daddy spoke up for what was right, and they crushed him."

*   *   *

Cold weather was approaching—I could feel it in the air as I rose later each morning to see the sun rise. Now I couldn't sit in my nightgown on the stoop; I had to dress and my light jacket wasn't enough to cut the chill. While it was still very early, mother would leave to go and stand in long lines, hoping to find work. Sometimes I went with her; sometimes I had to stay home.

One day I went with mother as she applied for a job at the government office in Drushkovka. She looked unusually tense and weary as I stood next to her outside the two-story building. I danced lightly on my feet, trying to chase away the cold. But I refused to complain, afraid that mother would send me home. I didn't want to go home; even standing in line was better than staying at home alone.

Since the time my father was taken away nearly three years before, my mother had found work only twice. For each job, there had been dozens of rejections. Her first job was to deliver mail and newspapers throughout the region surrounding our village. That was grueling work, requiring her to hoist a heavy bag and hike several miles each day. Sometimes she had to fight off stray dogs that were trying to attack her. Later, in the winter, she found work shoveling coal onto train wagons. That, too, was heavy work meant for men. The boss could not stand to see her resting between trainloads, and transferred her to another job where she had to pitch heavy chunks of brick mix high into a firing oven. This job exhausted her to the point where she thought she would die. The only people who worked these jobs were women like mother—women who were outcasts because their husbands and sons were rounded up in the same group as my father. They were labeled as families of the repressed.

We slowly made our way into the building. Mother clutched the small leather portfolio that had belonged to my father. It contained her birth certificate and a booklet that recorded her work history. Every Soviet citizen had similar documents. Without them, one could not travel or gain employment. The line continued up the stairs. Every little while, a woman came back down the stairs, squeezing past the line. Usually they looked happy—they had gotten jobs.

We eventually reached the top of the stairs and turned into the tiny room where one man was interviewing candidates and a woman was assisting him with the paperwork. Mother recognized the man—Woronov, the local head of the NKVD. This was not a good sign. He had humiliated her on more than one occasion, particularly when she tried to retrieve the portfolio and papers from him after my father's arrest.

Finally it was our turn. My mother set her portfolio on the desk, but Woronov didn't bother to look up. "Name?" he demanded.

"Maria Denisowna Wasylenko." My mother articulated each syllable slowly.

"Job experience?"

"Clerk and bank teller. Also sales. I managed a small grocery store..."

The man interrupted her. "Your last job. When?"

"Last winter, shoveling..."

"As a clerk or bank teller!"

"In Kursk. 1933."

"Why were you dismissed?"

"I wasn't dismissed. My husband and I moved back to Drush-kovka. This is our home."

"Your husband. What is his occupation?"

Mother hesitated before answering. "He's a lawyer."

"And what is your husband's name?"

She could not refuse to answer. "Fyodor Philipovich Wasy-lenko."

The man looked up for the first time, and his scowl made me cringe and lean closer to my mother. "Fyodor Philipovich Wasy-lenko. I don't believe I've seen him about lately, have I? He used to come by the factories around here. But not lately."

"No, not lately."

"So what do you wish with me?"

"You have posted several jobs," my mother answered, trying to gain her composure. "You have openings for bookkeepers. I am a good bookkeeper..."

"Are you?" he sneered. "Then why have you not worked a job since 1933? Perhaps you're not as good as you think?" He opened the portfolio and pulled out mother's documents. He skimmed over the pages and stopped at the last stamped page, which showed her work shoveling brick mix. "What's the matter? This last job wasn't good enough for you?"

My mother was shaking in anger. "I had no one to take care of my children..."

"Hard work keeps you warm. During the winter, you should be glad for a job that keeps you warm. Besides, why should I give you a job as a bookkeeper? Anyone in this line could do that job better than you. If you want work, go back to shoveling brick mix. Maybe they will let you work there again. And then, maybe not!" With a wave of his hand, he dismissed her.

Mother started to protest, but a voice behind her snarled, "Come on, come on! Let's move along!" We turned and walked out the door. We could hear the man ask, "Name?" Mother stopped and looked back. "You want the bookkeeper job?" the man asked. "Report for work tomorrow morning, 7:00 sharp!"

I looked up at my mother's eyes. They were full of hurt and frustration. But she held up her head and walked down the steps. If my mother cried that night, it was after I was asleep. In front of me and Tarasik, she kept her composure. This had happened many times before. She could have quit and given up the idea of working, but she needed money for food to supplement our diet and to support my sister in school. Mother was determined not to quit. She showed up every time there was a job posting. Sometimes she was just dismissed. Other times, like this day, she was humiliated. In either case, there was no work for the wife of a "traitor" to the Soviet Union.

* * *

There was always plenty of work to do around our house. Each morning, mother and Tarasik began the day by searching for kindling or chopping wood to stoke a fire in the kitchen stove. Fuel was a daily worry—where would we get a little firewood, some coal, a little kindling, some paper? Sometimes we waited until late in the day to start the fire in order to cut the bitter cold in the house. The heat from the stove was so valuable that we often slept on a shelf above the oven. The lingering warmth, the proximity of my mother and brother, and the *kozhuch*, a large goatskin, usually provided adequate warmth on cold winter nights.

There was no indoor plumbing. All food had to be prepared from scratch, but we rarely had all the necessary ingredients. One common dish was called *potapzi*. It was made from stale bread mother was usually able to obtain. It was cut in cubes, put in a bowl, sprinkled with water, a bit of oil, and a little sugar, then tossed. Mom also cooked *kesil*, a delicious jello-type fruit dish made with our dried fruit. On the rare occasions when we had flour, milk, eggs, *and* sugar, mother would bake all day—and what a happy day that was!

Laundry was a major ordeal. Mother washed at the river in the summer, but during the winter she had to carry water in from the well and heat it over the stove. Soap was a rarity, and no one had even thought of dryers. Mother had to scrub the clothes, using water as hot as her hands could stand, then wring them and hang them as best she could in the living room.

One welcome relief from this arduous life was a visit to grandma's house. We often went on Sunday afternoons. When winter came, mother had to carry me because I lacked warm clothes; she would bundle me in a blanket and hold me underneath her coat. This trip was treacherous when there was a lot of snow. One misstep off the packed path and a person could sink to the hips. Mother had carefully memorized the road and landmarks so she could find her way when the area was heavily blanketed with snow.

I loved grandma's house because my cousin Tosia also lived there. Grandma was a mother figure for the whole family, and her constant encouragement to all of us was to "love one another." She often reminded us that not to share was a sin.

Sharing was not the norm in our Communist state. But grandma lived it daily in front of us. One summer day, I was playing with Tosia in front of grandma's house. A man walked by, obviously hot and tired. Tosia and I stood and stared at the man, who was a stranger to the area. He had just about passed the house when we heard grandma behind us. "Stranger, could you use a little rest?" she shouted. She ran past us to the picket fence. "Please, come in and have a glass of fresh water and a piece of bread. It will give you strength to go on."

A smile came over the man's face. "*Spaciba*. Thank you. I could use a little rest."

"Of course!" said grandma. "Just come over here and sit down."

I watched this exchange with amazement. Later, as I was leaving for my own home, grandma reminded me that we were responsible to help one another, including strangers. "Remember that. Maybe someday you will be a stranger on the road. Then you will be pleased if someone offers you some rest and a drink of water and a little bread." It was this caring heart that caused all of us and all of her neighbors to love her.

*   *   *

Books were an important part of our home. We didn't have many, but they were valuable to us. Even though as a young child I could not yet read, it was not unusual for me to flip through the pages of a book—especially if it had pictures.

Like most children, I also liked to draw. Whenever I had a pencil in my hand, I would put my creative talents to work on whatever paper was near me. In our poverty a new, clean sheet of paper was precious and hard to find, so mother couldn't offer me anything to draw on.

Tarasik came home from school one day with a book he had borrowed from a friend so he could study for school. He left it on the table and went about his chores. I began to look through it, and noticed a picture. A pencil was also handy. Without thinking, I scribbled over the one picture in the book.

The next morning, Tarasik returned the book to his friend, unaware of my artistic labors. Later that day, a woman appeared at our house, waving the book and shouting, "You enemies of Stalin!" It was Borsha, the wife of a party member, whose son was in the same class with my brother. "Look at what you did!"

Mother was shocked, but tried to calm Borsha as she brought her in the house. "Please, now, show me the problem," she said gently. "I don't know what you are talking about."

"Right here!" She opened the book and set it on the table. My mother gasped. I came up behind her and peered at it. There was a portrait of Stalin, and in my absentminded scribbling, I had drawn over his face. I looked up at my mother. She looked at me and understood immediately that I had done it. Her face turned white.

"God have mercy! How could you let this happen?" Borsha demanded.

"She's just a little girl," my mother protested. "She didn't know what she was doing. I must have been outdoors for a few minutes, bringing in some water to cook with . . ."

"But Comrade Stalin! . . ."

"Borsha, I beg of you, please understand the circumstance. A child has no prejudice against anyone."

"What if my son's teacher discovers this? They will ask why I didn't report it. I can't ignore it!"

"Borsha, she's just a little girl! She certainly didn't mean any harm. Please, we've suffered so much already. Please don't report this."

Borsha looked down at me for the first time but said nothing. Maybe it was the innocent eyes of a little girl that softened her. Maybe it was the fact she had suffered, too. She shook her head and closed the book. "I know, Maria. I know."

She turned and walked out of the house. My mother followed. "Borsha, thank you for your understanding. We are so sorry. Maybe when our apples and pears are ripe you can come and help yourself to as many as you want . . ."

In bed that night, mother held me for a long time. "I'm sorry, Mamo," was all I could say as tears streamed down my face.

"I know, Dotshitshka. You didn't mean harm. But there are people who don't understand. If Borsha reports this, we will be accused of a crime against the state."

"What crime?"

She sighed, then replied, "Of course you can't understand. I find it hard to understand myself. Whatever we do, we must never say or do anything that shows we don't like Stalin, the

Communist party, or any of its leaders. That is why it is better to say nothing. It is too dangerous to think out loud or to express any opinions."

As I rested within my mother's arms, I wondered about this man Stalin. Why was everyone so afraid of him? Of course, his picture was everywhere. It was prominent on the wall behind the officials who interviewed my mother for a job, and in every building and room where official business was conducted.

Stalin's name was rarely mentioned in conversation. But his presence pervaded daily life. I don't know how I learned about Stalin; but I must have absorbed a lot. I knew he was from Georgia and that his given name was Iosif Vissarionovich Dzhugashvili. I knew he controlled a powerful secret police under the direction of a man named Beria. I knew everyone feared him, but no one spoke a negative word about him. Even among family, people were careful what they said; a child could unknowingly say something to a neighbor or stranger that would get his parents labeled as "counterrevolutionaries."

Discussion about politics was carefully woven into everyday conversations. Rumors were exchanged frequently, but always with the utmost caution, for people were fearful of the repercussions should they get caught. Stalin was never blamed for any problems. Beria and Molotov were mentioned. People would say, "It's not really Stalin doing this; it's his secret police." It was as though we were grasping for some single person we could trust. We needed hope, and it wasn't to be found in any of the local party officials, the NKVD, or in the bureaucracy.

But unspoken, I sensed that Stalin was the cause of our problems. That confused me. I was also amazed that this ruler everyone was afraid of had a favorite song that was also one of my favorites—"Sulikor." It was a love song and its melody captivated me even though I did not understand the meaning of the words. Why was everyone afraid of a man who loved such music? Wasn't he someone who could sing and dance with us?

Apparently not. Life under Stalin was difficult. The stakes were high for anyone who was perceived to be against him and his political machinery. Danger was always imminent. That was made abundantly clear to us one summer day when the wife of a party official passed my mother in the village and whispered, "They're coming for you tonight." Mother didn't hesitate. She hurried home. "Emotshka! Tarasik! Come quickly! Tarasik, take this sack and fill it with bread and dried fruit. Emotshka, let me get a blanket for you. It will be cold. . . ." Within a few moments, we had gathered the necessary items.

"Mamo, what is the matter?" I asked as she hurried us out the door.

"We can't talk now," she said. "Quickly. We will go up into the hills and hide."

She took my hand and we walked as quickly as my little feet would move. Then she picked me up and carried me. In times of fear or concern, she seemed to have unusual strength. We walked through the brush and stopped only as it got dark. Mother set me down and looked for the right place. "Here, we will spend the night among these bushes."

There were three blankets with us. Mother placed one on the ground. Tarasik wrapped himself in another, and mother and I shared the third. "Why are we sleeping outside?" I said as we settled down for the night.

"Shhh! We must be very quiet," she answered. Then she whispered, "It is safer here tonight. Your father was warned, and he didn't listen to the warning. It is better that we hide . . ."

I was too young to fully understand what was happening. But I felt my mother tremble as she hugged me tight and wrapped me in the blanket. The next day, we stayed in our hiding place until late afternoon. When we returned to our house, there were strange footprints around the door. Mother stood for a long time, wondering what to do. Finally, she announced to us, "We will sleep in our beds tonight."

She slept fitfully the next few nights, but the NKVD didn't come back.

WINTER 1940-41

On the day of the first snow, mother began her work shoveling coal. A cold wind drove the temperature down inside our home. She scurried around the house, gave instructions to Tarasik, and ordered me back to bed fully dressed. Whenever she could, mother brought home a few lumps of coal or some pieces of kindling or wood, but we rarely had enough fuel to keep our mud stove warm all day. Tarasik, who was fourteen, would come home from school at noon. His job was to make me a pot of *manka*—a kind of boiled Cream of Wheat. It was quite bland, and we had no butter or milk to put on it. I would eat a few bites, and Tarasik would go back to school, having completed his responsibility. Then I had to go back to bed to keep warm.

There wasn't a single toy in the house except for a homemade doll made out of a handful of straw that was doubled up and tied with a string at the neck. The knot of straw at the top was the head, and the rest, which looked like a broom, was the body. I didn't like that toy very much, so it lay in a corner most of the time.

Cold was my worst enemy, worse even than hunger. The worst cold wasn't when it snowed, but during the dead of winter when the temperature plunged and the sun shone but brought no warmth. Many days, the temperature in the house plunged well below freezing. Without fuel for their stoves, many people, especially children and the elderly, were confined to bed in order to stay warm. Mother always warned me about the danger of straying outside the protection of my blankets and the *kozhuch*. But sometimes, out of boredom, I would briefly sit up and breathe on the window to melt a small patch of ice. Then I could look outside for a moment at the white landscape before cold drove me back under the covers.

Regardless of how hard she tries, a little girl won't be as careful as she should. One day my hands slipped out from under the covers and I accidentally fell asleep. No one knew how long I lay that way, but it was long enough to give my fingers frostbite. The result was that from then on, every winter when the weather got cold, my hands and fingers would swell up. The swelling was worst in the morning and I had a hard time bending my fingers until they warmed up. Then the swelling would subside and the tingling and itching would start. It became just another reason why I dreaded winter.

My deepest desire was to be free to spend time outdoors every day of the year, not just when it was warm. I yearned to explore the winter landscape and to play in the snow. One of the happiest days of my life was one winter afternoon when our neighbor Pashka walked up the shoveled path to our door, walls of snow nearly over her head on either side. She was carrying a pair of children's boots made out of gray felt. My excitement rose as Pashka talked with my mother, offering to trade the boots for some dried fruit.

I looked longingly at those boots, now sitting on the kitchen table. My mother seemed hesitant, perhaps calculating how much food she had left for the winter. Then Pashka noticed me. "Why don't you try them on?" she suggested.

I didn't wait for my mother's permission. I pushed a foot into one of the boots. It pinched my toes, and I had to curl them in order to make the boot fit. But I didn't know what boots were supposed to feel like. I quickly put on the other one.

"Do they fit?" Pashka asked.

I nodded my head to say yes. I know now they were a good two sizes too small. But they were my first chance to get winter shoes, and I wasn't about to say they pinched my feet and lose the opportunity to go outside. Who knew when such an opportunity might come again?

The next day I explored the snow for the first time ever. Since I didn't have a winter coat, my mother loaned me an adult jacket—perhaps my brother's. The sleeves had to be rolled up and the hem dragged in the snow. A pair of socks served as mittens. But I didn't care. For a few exciting moments, I could play outdoors, and that meant I was free!

Meanwhile, mother's coal-shoveling job taxed her limits. She reported to work in a tunnel where a freight train with empty wagons pulled up. As the women worked, the black dust lodged in their pores and stuck to the sweat on their faces. Sometimes the air was so thick with soot that the women would have coughing fits. The icy wind in the drafty tunnel penetrated their clothing and numbed their hands, making it difficult to grip their shovels. The motion of shoveling the heavy loads and tossing them above their heads into the wagons made their bodies scream with pain.

When the day was over, mother would stagger home, her legs barely able to hold her up. Though blackened with soot all over, she would collapse on the bed, not caring how filthy she was or if she would ever get back up again. It was at times like these when life seemed most hopeless.

While life was harsh, it was predictable. We didn't have much food, but we were loved, and we knew it. Mother ached because she missed daddy and was persecuted because of him. But she shielded us from the worst of the suffering and bravely pressed ahead.

Little did we know that all around us momentous events were occurring that would soon alter the course of our lives. The news arrived via Pashka, who lived with her husband across the stream at the edge of the village. There had been rumors of war in Europe. Hitler's Germany had invaded Czechoslovakia and

Poland. But that didn't affect us. Our leader, Stalin, had signed a treaty with Hitler. We were safe, we thought.

Pashka kept us posted. One warm June day, my mother was working in the garden when Pashka came running across the stream and up the path toward our house. "Maria Denisowna!" she yelled. "It's started, Maria Denisowna!"

Mother looked up in alarm.

"The Germans are coming," Pashka reported, huffing and puffing as she tried to catch her breath. "Yesterday. I just heard on the radio. The Germans have invaded. They have come across the border, pushing into Ukraine and Russia."

"Oh my God!" mother whispered.

"We're at war," announced Pashka.

A force was changing the world map, and would soon change my life forever.

5

War!

The village of Drushkovka was troubled. Times had always been hard, but something worse was on the way. I could tell by the way the adults talked in hushed tones and the concern on their faces as they discussed "the political situation." They questioned how they would survive a war. The war, whatever that was, was coming closer every day. They talked about Germany. *What is Germany?* I asked myself. They talked about the invasion and that the Germans were coming. I had climbed the hill above my home and looked beyond our village to the horizon. *Germany must be just beyond where I can see,* I thought. I couldn't discern anything unusual happening, and I couldn't picture this Germany. What was it? What was war? Why was it so terrible? Why was everyone so afraid? And why did I have such a persistent, uneasy feeling?

The adults talked about airplanes and bombs. They said that when an airplane came and dropped its bombs, we were supposed to run in the opposite direction. But I had never seen an airplane. I tried to imagine a huge bird, flapping its wings, making a terrible screeching sound. I had never seen bombs, either. But they had to be terrible things because the adults talked about bombs killing people and blowing up houses. I imagined giant birds spitting balls of fire out of their mouths and destroying everything. It sounded horrible, and deep inside, reflecting the fear in my mother and others, I felt alarmed.

The people in our village didn't seem too frightened about the possibility of living under German rule. Most of us were barely surviving. We were hungry. We had no money, no clothes, no heat. My mother had been cut off from any significant livelihood. The cow had been sold to pay taxes. We had no chickens left. Next winter we would eat only what we could grow during these few warm months. People didn't talk openly about it, but sometimes you heard whispers. "Life under Hitler couldn't be any worse," said Pashka.

"Pashka, be careful!" mother whispered to her friend. "Such statements could get all of us in trouble."

"No, I am serious. We starve under Stalin. We can starve just as easily under Hitler," Pashka protested. "What difference does it make whether we die under Soviet rule or German?"

What did my mother think? I couldn't tell. Her thoughts were hidden, but I saw her bowed back as she labored in the garden. Work was her answer. She couldn't change the world situation, but she could work hard and know she had done everything in her power to provide for her family.

I chattered away at my mother as she worked. "Mamo, where does a pollywog's tail go?"

"It doesn't go anywhere, Dotshitshka," my mother said while watering the cabbages in the garden. "It just gets shorter when the pollywog becomes a frog."

"Where does the frog live after it becomes a frog?" I asked.

"You know! It lives by the stream. You see frogs there every day."

"Do frogs sleep in the water like the pollywogs, Mamo?"

"Yes, but their heads stick out a little."

"Do they have pillows to sleep on?"

My mother laughed and continued her work. I wandered back to the well where my brother was filling another pail with water. I sat down and looked in my pail. There were half a dozen pollywogs. Some had short tails and little feet close to their bodies. Others looked like small black fish. They had become my friends and I named each one: Three were boys—Misha, Ivan, and Boris. And three were girls—Vera, Katya, and Natasha. My mother had told me how special each one was. "Every creature is special, Dotshitshka. And remember: You are very special, too!"

I looked up from my pollywog friends and stared at my mother. Her skirt had so many patches that I couldn't see the original pattern. I looked at my own dress. It wasn't patched, but it had been washed so many times in the river that the blue flowers had faded and the white background had turned a muddy gray.

I looked up into the clear sky and soaked up the hot sun. I set down my pail of pollywogs and listened. It was quieter than usual. I heard the buzz of a few flies and the babble of the little stream. The birds, however, were mute. Usually at this time of day they were singing noisily. Instead, from a distance, I heard an unfamiliar sound, a deep drone. My mother and brother stopped working and looked up to the sky. Their faces showed alarm. I looked up with them but saw nothing. Yet I could hear somewhere far above us a persistent hum that seemed to approach just beyond our orchard. I scanned the sky, looking for the source of the sound.

It was not until Tarasik pointed his hoe that I saw it through the trees. It was shaped like a bird, but the wings didn't move. It was so high in the sky that it looked like a tiny toy bird.

Suddenly it dove down toward the village with lightning-like speed.

"Put that hoe down!" my mother shouted at Tarasik. "They will think we're shooting at them!"

I heard a hissing noise, like the sound of a whistle. My mother grabbed me by the arm and pulled me toward the house. We ran as fast as we could. With my other hand I clung to my pail of pollywogs. Water splashed out onto the ground, and with it my pollywogs.

Before we could reach the house, mother pushed me to the ground. "Stay down!" she ordered. There was an explosion behind us—the loudest sound I had ever heard. The ground shook beneath me. The pail slipped from my hand and rolled away.

Within seconds the machine in the sky roared directly overhead. The sound overwhelmed me and then, just as quickly, it faded. I lifted my head to peek into the sky but the plane had already left. It was now silent.

I could feel my mother breathing heavily next to me. I was shaking, too weak to stand up.

"Don't move!" said my mother. "Let's make sure it doesn't come back."

We lay still for a long time. Then we rose slowly to our feet, trembling and brushing off the dirt and leaves. From the village we saw smoke. Flames danced and crackled from a thatch roof. There was no other sound, though we strained to hear those awful engine noises. My brother looked pale.

Our neighbor from the house next door hurried across the stream. "It's started!" shouted Pashka.

"Are you OK?" asked mother.

"Yes, yes, we're OK!" said the older lady. "And your children? I see they are OK, but frightened. The Germans are coming our way. It won't be long now."

"Do you think our soldiers can hold them back?"

"I don't know. I'm sure the Germans are pushing as hard as they can for Moscow. That's the goal."

"But the news of our victories? How can the Germans advance so quickly if we are winning?"

"Ah, you should be glad, Maria Denisowna, that the officials cut your electricity. It keeps you from listening to your radio and hearing the lies of the announcers."

My mother nodded with a knowing look on her face. I stood by her side, still shaking and clutching her dress. I had never felt this way before. For the first time in my life I was really afraid. My secure world, pitifully poor as it was, had been shattered.

"Maria, remember, I have a cellar," said Pashka. "When the Germans come, bring Emotshka and Tarasik. We'll hide below. It's safer there."

*   *   *

I couldn't sleep that night. Images of what I had experienced that day played tag with questions in my mind. *Would they come back again? Would they bomb our house? Were we going to die?*

I knew very little about death. I recalled an aunt's funeral. I brought up my last memory of her, dressed in black clothes and lying perfectly still on a kitchen table. The shutters on the windows were closed. The house was dark and though filled with people, everyone was quiet. I had stared at my aunt, but she didn't move. I reached out and touched her foot, on which had been placed a black stocking. She didn't respond to my touch; the foot was stiff. My mother saw and gently removed my hand. "Dotshitshka, don't touch!" she whispered.

Then I remembered the wailing. In my mind I could hear the women, their cries increasing in pitch. "Why? Why did you go?

Why did you leave us?" they howled. It became a chant, a song of lament. *Where* did *my aunt go?* I wondered. Her body was there, yet she wasn't. Would women weep and wail for me when I died?

What if my mother died? My body shuddered and I felt tears well up in my eyes. That was the worst thought of all. How could I survive without my mother? Life couldn't exist without her—of that I was sure. The tears flowed as I failed to chase the awful possibility from my mind.

There were no planes the next day. But now that they had come, we knew they could come again at any time. A blanket of fear settled over the village. Everyone seemed agitated. We worked all the harder in our garden, as though our efforts could make the fruits and vegetables grow any faster. We had to store up food for the winter. But what would happen with war around us? Would our crops be destroyed? Would the Germans or Soviets confiscate them? We were isolated. We could depend on nothing except what we could produce with our own hands.

Planes came again several more times that summer. I learned to identify them by sound. If there was a low drone, the planes were loaded with bombs and we immediately took cover. But if they had a high-pitched sound, that meant they were empty and we didn't need to run; they had already dropped their bombs somewhere else.

Yet even the loaded bombers didn't seem interested in us. They were focused elsewhere on the Russian army. "It's a pushing match," said one adult. I pictured in my mind two giants in a shoving match. But the German giant was pushing harder.

Through our daily routines, mother tried to reclaim the order in our lives that had been so rudely interrupted by war. I, too, tried to live as if there was no danger. Grandmother had assured us that "no one is interested in simple people like us." She refused to take cover when she saw airplanes. "No one is interested in an old woman," was her answer, and she would continue working in her garden.

I climbed the hills behind our house with our dog Sjun and played in the stream with the pollywogs. But I never strayed too far from the house or mother. When I could, I helped mother by picking cucumbers or beating the seeds out of the sunflowers with a stick. But the fun was gone. Just as pollywogs grew into frogs, I was forced to abandon my playful, carefree life. A German airplane had changed everything. The cares of adults had become my cares, too.

WINTER 1941-42

We waited for the war to reach us. But war didn't come; at least, not yet. The great armies weren't interested in fighting over an insignificant village. One night we heard rumbles in the distance—like thunder. The Germans were getting closer. "They're pushing for Moscow," said adults, soberly shaking their heads. But after a few days the sounds died away. Everyone breathed a sigh of relief.

In preparation for winter, potatoes were stored in a partial cellar that was being dug between the house and orchard. Mother put cabbage in a large barrel to make sauerkraut. Sunflower seeds were pressed for oil and stored in earthenware pots. Apricots, grapes, apples, prunes, and cherries were dried. This time, mother didn't trade any of it. No one knew how long this harvest would have to last. She particularly treasured the corn—she had grown extra this summer. A friend had a mill, and occasionally mother would go over and grind some of the corn so she could make bread or cornmeal.

The snow came early that year and then it turned bitter cold—colder than usual in this cold climate. Knowing people recalled how another overconfident army had bogged down in the unending Russian winter—they mentioned a man named Napoleon. That name meant nothing to me. Rather, winter meant that once again I was imprisoned in my own home. The snow level rose higher and higher, and drifted nearly to the roofline of our house. My mother and brother shoveled a path from our door and partly cleared the windows so we could see outside. They came back into the house drenched in snow and sweat, totally exhausted. It was at times like this that we keenly felt the lack of hearty food to replenish lost energy.

Mom didn't go to work this winter. There were no jobs available, so we waited. The distant rumbles started up again. We could hear them during the day, and sometimes at night. They were coming closer. I would spend my days trying to see out of the window, searching the skies for any sign of planes. We were trapped in this prison of snow and ice, waiting. There was no place to run, and no place to hide.

One morning the first week of February, we were jolted awake by an explosion. The big guns we had heard in the distance were now all around us. I ran quickly to a window to look out, scanning the sky for planes. There was one, and then another, over our village. Mother yanked me by the arm. "Stay away from the windows! If they shoot, the glass will cut. Or, the bullets may kill you." By that time the planes were roaring overhead, and came so low that I could see the pilots peering through their canopies. The sound shook the house.

Fear fought with curiosity. I knew in my mind the terrible damage these planes could inflict. But the little girl in me also wanted to see these fighters, who were now buzzing around above the house like angry wasps. I had no idea of tactics; I could make no sense out of what the pilots were trying to do.

Within moments, I saw one plane coming right toward our house. It was very low. It grew larger and larger, until it looked as though it might smash into us. I froze. I knew this plane could destroy me, yet I couldn't move. I couldn't even scream. It zoomed just a few feet over our roof and then I heard a rapid, popping sound.

"Grenades," said Tarasik.

"Come, Emotshka!" My mother grabbed me and thrust me in a corner next to the mud stove. "We must stay away from the windows," she said, wrapping me in her arms. My brother huddled next to us, and mother wrapped her other arm around him so that we formed a human ball.

After that, it was quiet for a moment. "I wish we could make it to Pashka's cellar," said mother. She pulled us up to our feet and hurried to the door. Then she stopped and ran back to get a blanket. She then ran to the door again and started to open it when a nearby explosion rocked our house. "Oh my God!" she cried. She grabbed our arms and pulled us back to the corner near the mud stove. Gunfire once again surrounded our house.

Now that I could no longer watch up close through the window, I was more afraid. With every explosion, my eyes squeezed shut and and I wondered if this was the moment when we were going to die. Cannon fire. Rifles. Airplanes. Machine guns. Grenades. Shaking like a tree in a strong and gusty wind, I wondered when we would all blow up. We were terrified and much too afraid to speak. "Oy Bozshe! Oh my God!" my mother wailed with each explosion. Those were the only words spoken.

Our dog Sjun added to the sense of terror. We had brought her inside, and with every explosion, she would tear from one room to the next, try to hide under furniture, and wail—thus sounding more like the part wolf she was. She would hide under a bed for a while and then scurry around some more. "Stop it!" my mother shouted, but Sjun was too frightened to obey. Finally mother got up, grabbed her by the neck, dragged her to the pantry, and locked her inside. But we could still hear her whining and scratching frantically on the door, trying to get out.

We huddled in that corner for hours. It seemed like we were plastered against that wall with the cement of terror. Any moment I expected a bomb to hit our house. Yet strangely, my fear wasn't as great as my mother's, for as I clung to her, I felt secure. With her I could face anything—even death.

Through all this, I could see a small area of sky out one window on the opposite wall. Planes flew in and out of my view, circling and shooting at each other. Explosions and machine-gun fire surrounded the house.

Finally there was a lull in the fighting, and the silence lingered and was absolute. It seemed unearthly quiet in contrast to the frenzied turmoil of howling airplanes and explosions.

We waited in fear, expecting the sound of guns to resume. But instead, we heard footsteps crunching on the snow outside our house. Now I was really frightened. The possibility of facing a human enemy was worse than any airplane or gun. Were the visitors Russian or German? What would they do to us? Would they throw grenades into the house and blow us up? Would they seize the house and chase us out into the snow, leaving us to freeze to death as the sun set and the temperature plunged?

Time seemed to stop. Fear froze our thoughts. Then someone pounded on the door!

My mother's body went rigid. She couldn't move. There was the sound again, a loud pounding that reverberated throughout the house. Sjun barked wildly. The door was locked. They couldn't get in unless they broke the door down.

They knocked again. "Open up, please!" we heard. The words were Russian.

Mother scrambled up to her feet and ran to the door. She hesitated, then turned the lock and opened the door a couple of inches. I crept up behind her and, peering out from behind her leg, I saw two soldiers. Their cheeks were bright purple from the cold. Their hats and coats were encrusted with ice. One was holding a bucket, which he held out to my mother.

"Mama, could you heat this up?" he begged. He looked back over his shoulder, frightened, wondering if anyone was following him. "We are starving. We must eat some food. We are frozen and weak."

My mother stiffened in fear, and I instinctively understood why. What if Germans saw them? They, and we, were targets. Yet what could mother do? She had to help her countrymen; she felt sympathy for their condition. In another couple of years, that might be her son standing there in front of another mother's house.

"Don't stand there. Come in!" she said as she grabbed the bucket and slammed the door behind the two men. They stamped the snow off their boots at the entryway as my mother rushed to the kitchen stove. Inside the pantry, Sjun growled. The two men looked at each other, but didn't move. After all, what danger could a dog pose compared to what faced them outside?

I stayed with my mother as she set the bucket down, grabbed a few sticks, and started a fire in the stove. I peered inside the pail and saw a frozen blob that looked like purple oatmeal. *Yuck*, I thought. *How could they eat that?* I stared at the soldiers. They rubbed themselves and stomped their feet, trying to drive the cold from their bodies. But their faces revealed no emotion.

Then the shooting started again, only now it sounded more distant. Mother jumped and dropped a couple of sticks of kindling she was about to put into the fire. She obviously wanted these men gone as soon as possible. She recovered and fed the fire, then put the bucket over the opening above it.

It seemed like forever as we waited for the fire to get warm enough to thaw the frozen blob. The soldiers watched, but said nothing. We said nothing. I quietly wondered what these men were feeling. Did they expect to live out this day? Were they thinking of their mothers and other loved ones? Or had they shut out all emotions, concentrating only on survival and killing Germans?

Finally, the purple oatmeal began to thaw. Mother took a spoon and tried to break it into pieces. Then she stirred rapidly for several minutes until it was a soft, sticky mush. Then one of the soldiers grabbed the bucket and together they rushed out the door. My mother was right behind them, shutting and locking the door as they ran off in the direction of the hill behind our house. I looked up at mother's face and saw that her eyes were moist. In the midst of fear, there was still room for compassion and pity.

Mother leaned against the door for a moment, then saw me staring at her. "What could I do?" she said, shaking her head. "They were so young. And hungry. They are just boys. I had to help them." For a moment I thought mother would cry, but then her face filled again with resolve.

I took her hand and followed her back to our corner by the stove. I tried to picture the soldiers fighting. It must have been hard for them to move around—if they stepped into unpacked snow, they could sink to their knees or higher. They had to be tired from the energy they exerted. What if they got too tired? Naturally, they would want to stop to rest. But that was suicide, my mother had said. I pictured men frozen solid in the brutal cold. How would it feel to be frozen like that? I flexed my fingers, which tingled from the cold—a reminder of the frostbite I had suffered the previous winter. *Is this how the whole body felt as it froze to death?* I shuddered at the thought.

The battle continued until late afternoon when the light began to fade. We still heard an occasional shot from tanks in the distance, but around our house it was quiet. The rumblings of the big guns were now coming from the opposite direction. Did that mean the Germans now controlled our land? We couldn't tell.

Fifteen minutes passed. Then half an hour. Hesitantly, mother got up to give us some food when again we heard footsteps crunching in the snow. We froze in fear, then relaxed when we heard, "Maria! Maria, are you all right?"

Mother rushed to the door. "Pashka, what are you doing here? It's not safe—"

"It's OK, it's OK," she said, coming in. "I was worried because you didn't come to the cellar this morning. It would be better for you and the children if you stayed there tonight."

"I wanted to come, but the shooting happened too fast. We were trapped."

"Come now! This is your chance. One never knows if they may come back after it turns dark."

My mother picked me up and ordered my brother, "Senok, let the dog out, and grab some fruit. Sjun, outside now!" said mother.

"Hurry!" Pashka said as she searched the landscape. "There's almost no light left."

Mother wrapped me in her coat and a blanket and stepped outside. Tarasik shut the door. Sjun cowered against the shed and whined as we started down the path to the frozen stream. She cautiously started to follow. "Stay!" mother ordered, and the dog slunk back to the shed. She was on her own.

It took only a few moments to go down our path, cross the frozen stream, and come to the neighbors' house. Their cellar was really a hole in front of their mud-walled home. A mound rose above it, and in the mound was a door. I had never been in this "cellar," but I knew that similar dirt-covered basements were used by others to store milk, cheese, sour cream, and other items that needed to stay cool.

"Careful now," warned Pashka as she opened the heavy wood door for us. Tarasik turned around and carefully went down the steep dirt steps. Mother set me down and followed. "You go now, Emma," said Pashka as she lifted me onto the first step. I sensed my mother's guiding hand as I carefully made my way down. There were six steps.

Once on the dirt floor, I quickly glanced around. There was only one dim candle, and the benches on either side were shrouded in darkness. Pashka's daughter Ljuba was also there with her two children. Pashka's husband was trying to stay warm in one corner. My mother and I sat together as Pashka closed the door above us and made her way down the steps. There were eight of us in the little dugout, but we didn't feel crowded as we huddled into groups. Mother was exhausted from fear and worry; all she could do was lean against the wall and close her eyes. Tarasik gave me a piece of dried apple and I chewed on it and nestled into my mother's side. No one talked. We could hear nothing outside. Gradually, I drifted off to sleep.

When I woke up later, it was pitch-black and for a moment I thought I had died. Then I felt the reassuring warmth and breathing of my mother next to me. I put my hand down and felt the dirt floor. The adults were talking softly. I caught bits and phrases: "Wonder what's going to happen now?" "German occupation . . . resistance efforts . . . survival. We'll need to help each other."

I closed my eyes again but couldn't tell if I was awake or asleep. My mind was filled with the image of an airplane. I could see inside the cockpit, and the pilot was laughing at me. Out of the plane came spits of fire as it roared just a few feet over the top of our house. Then there were soldiers running all around us. I could hear the crunching of their feet on the snow. One of them burst into the house and he was ten feet tall. He loomed over me, and lifted his gun as if to shoot me. I moaned. Mother stirred, and I felt her arms as she wrapped me in her coat and placed my head against her breast. Within that cocoon, the nightmare faded. I relaxed and drifted back to sleep. Early the next morning, I was only vaguely aware that Pashka's husband was slipping out the door of the cellar to check the situation.

After he left, a sudden crash woke me with a jolt. The cellar door had been forced open and a stream of light was shining in. No one spoke. I looked up and saw a black boot on the top step, then another as the soldier carefully climbed down. A flashlight was in his left hand, a rifle in his right. Above him was another soldier carrying a rifle pointed at us. They were Germans. I could feel the tension; we sat petrified, expecting to be shot.

"Nur frauen und kinder hier. Only women and children here." Ljuba stuttered. Apparently she knew a little German. The soldier didn't acknowledge her, but carefully shone his flashlight on each face, examining everyone carefully. "Only women and children," she repeated.

My eyes focused on the other man's rifle. Would he really shoot us? The flashlight landed on my mother's face, then mine, briefly blinding me. Then it moved on to the others.

"Keine soldaten oder partisanen," said the soldier as he turned and made his way back up the steps, slamming the door behind him. We were back in darkness.

"What did he say?" Pashka asked.

"They are looking for Russian soldiers or partisans," Ljuba explained. "He said there were none here."

No one dared to move. Although the sun was shining outside, we waited.

"So we really are occupied," someone ventured.

"I suppose we will have to learn German," said another.

"But is it really over? How do we know that the fighting won't come back? The Germans could be pushed back."

"We must wait."

My mother said nothing. I dozed some more, wondering if we would hear the sounds of fighting again. But there were no noises. No planes. No guns.

Sometime around midday, we heard footsteps. We recoiled as the cellar door opened. It was Pashka's husband. Pashka made her way up the steps and met him. Together they walked out and

I could hear their boots crunching in the snow. Then I heard nothing. We waited tensely. Finally we heard her walking back.

"It appears that all is clear for now," she said.

Ljuba and her children left first to go back inside their house. Then mother, Tarasik, and I went up the stairs. I blinked my eyes at the top. After all that fighting, it seemed that everything should be dark, but the sun shone on the snow and all was bright and quiet. It almost looked as if nothing had happened—as if a bad dream had come and gone. Mother picked me up to carry me back to the house. Tarasik ran ahead of us. As we got closer I saw that he was comforting Sjun, who was huddled against the door and happy to see us return.

Inside the house, Tarasik started a fire in the mud stove. Mother gave me a *sucharik*—a piece of dried bread. "I need to check on Babusia [grandma] and Uncle Alyosha," she said. "I must see how they are doing after all of this horrible fighting."

But the day was already half gone, and we weren't sure whether it was safe to go anywhere, so we stayed inside and as soon as the sun set, we huddled near the stove and tried to sleep.

We didn't go out the next day, either, as we heard more shooting in the distance. It was sporadic, but mother wasn't taking any chances. The following morning, mother bundled me up as best she could, wrapping me in a blanket for added warmth. Tarasik, who was to stay behind, was told to fetch a little sled she had somehow acquired. I was too heavy to carry the mile-long walk to grandma's place, and the sled was just large enough for me to sit on.

The trip to grandma's house took us north of the village. Along the path I noticed some unusual tracks. They were not normal tire or sleigh marks, but looked rather like two sets of railroad tracks pressed deep in the snow. My curious eyes looked all around for signs of the fight that had taken place two days before. They were few—bullet holes in houses, footprints where soldiers had trudged. One farmhouse had a huge hole in the wall, and the roof had collapsed. We also passed one small, blackened truck that had slid off the road into a tree. I expected to see dead bodies, but there weren't any.

We passed only a couple of people on the path; most of the villagers were staying inside. We were almost to grandma's when we approached a woman my mother knew—she was a neighbor to grandma.

"Maria Denisowna!" she shouted. "Maria, I am so sorry." She ran up to my surprised mother and threw her arms around her.

"Vera, what has gotten into you?" my mother asked, holding Vera by her arms. "What are you talking about?"

"You mean you haven't heard?"

"Heard what?"

"I'm sorry, Maria. I assumed you knew. Your mother was killed yesterday . . .

"It was so uncalled for. The fighting was over. Some idiot German tank just shot at random at the house. No reason for it . . ."

The woman seemed compelled to babble, but mother couldn't listen. In shock, she turned toward her mother's house, which we could now see up the road. The news was overwhelming; it numbed her. I desperately wanted to look up into my mother's face and to know how she felt. But she moved ahead quickly, pulling me on the sled behind her.

We reached the house a few minutes later. Uncle Alyosha met us at the door. I saw tears in his eyes, and he hugged my mother for a long time. Then he lifted me off the sled and set me inside the house. My eyes had to adjust for a few moments; it was so dark compared to the bright sun reflecting off the snow outside. I was aware of my older cousins in the room. Each of them came forward and hugged mother, then me. Last of all was my cousin Tosia. I felt comforted by her presence, though she, too, was very quiet and sad.

I then focused on the table. There lay my grandmother, dressed in a tattered, gray wool skirt, a gray wool sweater, and a little headscarf that she always wore. My mother could only stand and stare. I looked at my mother, not knowing what to think or how to react. Tears flowed down her cheeks. She walked over and stroked her mother's face, shaking her head.

"What happened?" she quietly asked her brother.

He pointed to the wall and I followed his finger. There, in a line, were dozens of holes. "All of us were in the back room. Grandma insisted on fixing us something to eat and so came into this room. The machine gunner—who knows what he was thinking? I hear they are trying to root out insurgents. Anyway, he shot bullets into the house. One hit her in the side."

My uncle shook his head and started to cry. "We tried to help her." He pointed to a spot on the floor and I saw for the first time a pool of dried blood. From there a trail of blood flowed toward another spot in the middle of the room. "She didn't die right away. And she wouldn't lie still; she dragged herself to that chair. The children were hysterical."

"Our dear Mama," my mother whispered. "May you rest in peace."

"So senseless. She was only seventy. She was healthy. She could have lived another ten or fifteen years."

"Yes, but what kind of life is this? Now she won't have to suffer anymore. She's happy now." Mother hugged her brother again, then asked, "What do we do now?"

My uncle's shoulders sagged as he thought of the implications. "What am I going to do with all my children? Who is going to be here with me?" He looked frazzled and completely hopeless. Grandma had been the cook, gardener, and mother to my uncle's five daughters.

The rest of the day was a blur of activity. Somehow, by the next day, everyone was notified. People began arriving from the village. There were Uncle Kolka and Uncle Pilka from my father's side of the family, as well as neighbors who loved and respected my grandma. Tarasik also arrived—someone had gone to tell him. I followed mother to grandma's bedroom, where there was an old wood trunk. Mother opened it and took out grandma's good outfit. Adults kept one set of clothes that was used only for special occasions, such as weddings, church (if there was one open), and most important, for their own funeral. Mother dressed grandma in these clothes.

I watched through a window as my uncle dug a hole in the snow in front of the house. The ground was frozen, and he would have to wait until spring to dig grandma's final grave. Then the women wrapped the body in a blanket and the men carried it outside and laid it gently in the hole. We watched solemnly while my uncle filled the hole with dirt and snow, then placed a crude cross on top of the grave. A couple of the older women bowed their heads and whispered some words no one could hear and motioned their hands in the shape of a cross—a custom I had seen before but didn't understand. Everyone was crying. As we went back inside, the adults hugged one another again.

According to tradition, a meal was always served after a burial. This wake consisted of a meager selection of kasha, fruit compote, and bread—all of which was contributed by the neighbors and family. I sat at a table with my cousins. Each of us had a wooden spoon and we took turns eating from a dish in the middle of the table. Somehow we did this without fighting over whose turn it was to dish out a bite. At a time like this, it felt good to be part of one big family.

We returned home late that day as the sun was setting. I observed my mother carefully. It was clear that she hurt deeply over the loss of her mother, but she kept it all inside. Other than shedding some tears, she said nothing and did nothing to show her grief. Maybe it was because there were two children to feed and care for. Or, perhaps she felt numb from all the recent tragedy. With the German occupation, we had no idea what to expect. Perhaps mother realized that survival depended on keeping a hold on her emotions.

Mother and the people of Drushkovka were simple, humble people sobered by the struggle to survive, taking one day at a time without grumbling. The war was just another invisible rock that fell on all. There was no time for self-pity . . . survival was all that mattered.

6

The German Occupation

One morning I heard an unusual rumbling sound. Cars and other machines were rare in our village, so I ran to a window to see what it was. Down our path, on the other side of the stream, was a strange-looking object—a motorcycle with a sidecar. Two soldiers parked the cycle at the edge of the frozen stream and started to walk toward our house.

"Mamo, soldiers are coming!" I yelled. My mother came and looked over my shoulder.

There was a strong knock at the door. Mother answered while I stood behind her, practically hanging onto her leg.

"*Dobraye utra, Mama.* Good morning, Mama," said one of the men, speaking slowly. He obviously didn't know much Russian and he carried a small phrase book with him. "We will, uh, inspect your house."

My mother stepped aside to let the men in. Their tall, shiny black boots made a loud thumping sound as they walked across the wood floors. The tops of the boots disappeared under long over-coats that were covered with a light frost. Each man had a heavy belt around his waist, and on one hip, a holstered gun. On their heads were boat-shaped hats, which looked funny compared to the Russian *mikhavoy shapka*—the traditional fur hats. Their ears were a bright red from the bitter cold.

The men quickly inspected our home. Tarasik sat on the edge of his bed and stared at them. He looked much younger than his sixteen years, and they ignored him. The soldier who didn't speak Russian nodded to his partner, who then said to my mother, "Later today, two officers will come. They will stay here."

That was all. It was an order, not a request, and we understood that we would have German soldiers billeted in our house. What did that mean? Did we have to feed the men? Did we have to surrender one of our rooms? There were no explanations. My mother raised no objection; any protest would have been futile anyway. This was just another consequence of war, another circumstance to endure. I watched the men carefully walk back down the path, trying to keep their balance on snow that had been packed to an icy sheen. They made it to their motorcycle without falling and drove off.

Two different officers arrived later that day and set up lodging in our living room. They took turns sleeping on the couch or on the floor. After about a week, they moved on to another assignment and were replaced by two new officers. This pattern continued for the next couple of months. We got used to the visitors and our daily life didn't change significantly, for generally the men kept to themselves. Their schedule was unpredictable; we never knew if they were leaving early in the morning or coming back at night. They were never rude or abusive; we stayed out of their way, and they did the same with us.

A sign was posted on our front door—"*Belegt*"—Occupied. Most of the houses in Drushkovka had similar signs, as they also sheltered German soldiers. Such were the orders of the victors.

We never saw the soldiers eat; apparently there was a mess kitchen set up somewhere in the village. The one exception was when a soldier named Willie Schatz took Sjun and went rabbit hunting. They returned with a plump rabbit and Willie asked mother to cook it. She was delighted, as we were all hungry for any kind of food. Mother skinned, cut, and boiled the rabbit. Tarasik fetched some potatoes. Then mother browned the meat with the potatoes, and everyone enjoyed this special feast.

Another soldier named Herbert took a particular interest in me. "*Ich habe ein kleines madchen daheim*," he said as he squatted down in front of me and pulled out a picture of a little girl.

"I think he is telling us he also has a daughter," mother said.

The man must have missed his daughter, for he was the one soldier who played with me. He would stick out his booted leg and invite me to hold on to it with both arms. As I clung to his leg, he would give me a ride, dancing and pulling me along around the floor. I laughed and giggled and enjoyed the attention.

As winter began to release its incredibly harsh grip, a package arrived at our house for one of the soldiers. By now I was bolder in my approach to the men. So far, none had been cruel. Since I had never seen a package before, I silently placed myself by the kitchen table and watched as the two men opened the box.

Once the brown paper was removed and the box opened, a strange and wonderful smell emerged. The recipient smiled and pulled out a green sprig of some kind of pine. It had a little red mushroom with white dots tied to it. He held it up for all to see, then set it on the table. *"Weihnachten!"* he exclaimed.

I had started to pick up some German words and phrases, but I didn't know that word and couldn't figure out its meaning from what he was doing. Next, he pulled out a piece of fruit—a round, orange-colored object. He broke open the thick skin and a wonderful aroma filled the house. This was my first introduction to oranges. It was too cold to grow oranges in Ukraine, and I doubt if anyone around our village had ever seen one.

Then he pulled out a small tin box. It was orange with white stars in a pattern. Reverently the man opened it and I was introduced to another new smell. The soldier held the tin down so I could look in at the brown—nearly black—squares nestled in foil. I couldn't imagine what it was.

"Schokolade!" he said. *"Das schmeckt sehr gut.* It tastes very good. Try it."

He broke off a small piece, about the size of one of my fingernails, and popped it in my mouth. I let it sit there to absorb the taste. It was unlike any flavor I had ever experienced—bitter *and* sweet. I made a face, swallowed, and shook my head.

"Das gefällt dir nicht? You don't like it?" Then he lifted his head back and gave a huge laugh, the first truly joyful sound I had heard in months. He picked up a large piece of chocolate and popped it in his mouth. His friend did the same. They savored the flavor. The soldier patted me on the head. "That's OK," he laughed again. "Someday you'll learn what a treat this is. Here! A piece for your mama. I'm sure she will enjoy it!"

"Danke," I answered timidly, not exactly sure what I was thanking the man for. It was only much later that I realized that the soldiers were celebrating Christmas. Their package had caught up

with them three months late. At our house, we had never celebrated any holiday that I could recall. Each day was the same as the
next.

While I didn't like the taste of chocolate, I did recognize the
opportunity it gave for me to make friends. The next day, while
mother bartered for some food with a neighbor, I took the chocolate
meant for my mother into the village. Immediately three or four
boys and girls surrounded me. Breaking off pieces, I handed each
one a bite of this unusual thing. They found it enjoyable and all of
them paid attention to me. I felt important! However, my mother
was quite upset when she discovered what I had done; a rare treat
for her had disappeared.

Soon the men with the chocolate were gone, too, and no
soldiers took their place. In fact, there was now little evidence of
German occupation in our area. Pashka whispered to mother, "All
the soldiers have been sent to Leningrad, and none of them are
coming back alive." This was the first we learned of the siege of
Leningrad, and how the Russians, despite starvation-sized rations,
were resisting heroically.

SPRING 1942

With the Germans gone, there was virtually no economy. We
were completely isolated from the Soviet government, and the
Germans ignored us. There was no paying job for my mother, or
for anyone else in Drushkovka. What we produced from our garden and orchard or obtained via barter was all we could expect in
the way of food or income.

My sister was fortunate to have work in Stalino, though her
only payment was in the form of food. After the invasion, her
school had shut down and all resources were thrown into the war.
When the Germans seized Stalino, they opened a bakery and
Hanusia was put to work there.

One early spring day, she came home to visit us. Mother and
Tarasik were cultivating the soil in the garden and preparing it for
planting. I was down at the spring, which was full and rushing
with water from the melted snow. While there I happened to look
up and saw Hanusia walking toward us from the village. I yelled
and skipped across the stream and ran into her open arms.

She wasn't her usual exuberant self. "Sistlitski," she whispered
in my ear as she held me close. This kind of emotional embrace was
most unusual. I sensed immediately that something very important was happening.

Mother greeted Hanusia on the other side of the stream and, with arms around each other, they walked up to the house. In the kitchen, mother fired up the stove and put on a kettle to heat some water. I pulled up my little wooden footstool and cuddled next to my sister as she sat at the table. Mother poured some tea leaves made of dried rose petals into two glasses. She then poured hot water over them, creating a beautiful aroma. It made for a cozy intimacy among us three girls.

According to Russian custom, Hanusia poured some of the hot tea into a saucer to cool it, then held the saucer in both hands. She sipped the hot mixture before stating her purpose for the visit.

"Mamo, this is the situation. People in Russia are being rounded up and taken to Germany to work on their farms and in their factories."

My mother looked puzzled. Hanusia backed up and explained. "It started last week. Young women like me are just picked up off the street or out of their homes and shipped to Germany. They are starting with the youngest, healthiest adults. It's slave labor, Mamo. That's one of the reasons they invaded us. The Germans want our fields and natural resources, but they also need workers. It's just a matter of time before you, me, and Tarasik are all expected to work for the Third Reich."

"What kind of work?" my mother asked, her calm voice not betraying the anxiety I sensed was underneath.

"They need laborers for the farms that help feed the army. They need workers in the ammunition factories. All of Germany's able-bodied men are involved in the war. Two days ago, a German officer, Major Euler, who runs the bakery, started talking to me. We were standing outside the bakery and a truck filled with teenage girls passed by. He told me that soon I would be on one of those trucks to be taken to Germany.

"He started telling me about his family. He has a photography shop that his wife is running for him, and she is raising two small boys. He would like to get her some help."

Hanusia paused, then continued, "He told me about the plans to round up workers. Major Euler says it will be hard to survive. Many die in the work camps. If I don't do something, I'll be at the mercy of the Nazis. I'll have to go wherever they want to send me, and do whatever they want me to do. Eventually, that will happen to all of us."

Hanusia stared into her tea, as if it held some answer to our dilemma. Some of the tea leaves floated along the edge of her saucer. I felt a little like one of those petals, at the mercy of a strong hand I could not see.

"Major Euler's home is in a city named Göppingen. It's a town near the city of Stuttgart, in the heart of Germany. Major Euler wants me to go be a maid and take care of the house and the boys so his wife can concentrate on running the business—that is, if it can be arranged. He says his wife's sister is married to an important Nazi official who may be able to arrange things for him. It will be hard work, but I know how to work hard. And besides, at least I'll know where I'm going. It's better than being forced by strange people to go into the unknown. If that happens, we may end up separated forever."

Mother seemed to comprehend the enormity of the situation. Our family was at the mercy of powerful forces. With a heavy heart, she said, "We don't have a choice."

"We are all at the mercy of the victors," said Hanusia.

"We're at the mercy of our own government when they rule," said mother. "We're at the mercy of the Germans when they rule. We are caught between two evils."

I was surprised; I had never heard my mother and sister talk openly and so matter-of-factly about the government powers that ruled us.

"That's why I need to accept Major Euler's suggestion. Maybe when I get to Germany, someone will be in a position to help the rest of you."

Mother's eyes welled up with tears. "You'll be so far away."

Hanusia took mother's hand. "Mamo, this might be for the best. Think of Tarasik and Emotshka. What will happen to them? Sooner or later the Germans will round us up. Anyone strong enough to do productive work will be taken back to Germany. Major Euler told me that if I cooperate, maybe he can do something to help you when the time comes. It's not a promise, but it's better than nothing."

"I don't want you to go," mother said quietly. "So far away ...a strange country... by yourself."

"Mother, I've been away from home for some time now. I'm scared, but maybe I should take his advice."

"Do you trust this man?"

"As much as you can trust any German. I've seen pictures of his family. The children look adorable. He has two boys—Uli, six years old, and Wolfgang, who is four. I believe Major Euler because I know he is trying to help his family. I would rather be with them than in a camp. We have no idea of the awful things happening in those places. I hear people are starving. They are dying from illness, homesickness, and exhausting work. They're in the middle of the war . . ."

Mother sighed. "I understand. You are probably right. How will all this be arranged?"

"Major Euler gave me a letter to mail to his wife once I get to Germany. He insisted I always carry it with me. I'm to sleep with it, keep it in my clothes, never be without it for a moment. Any day now, I will be rounded up and put on a train with other people to Germany. That's why I'm here. He suggested I come and tell you, because there is no way of contacting you once this happens. In fact, he says there is another train leaving this Friday, and he suggested I might as well get on it so that you will know when I am leaving. When I am put in a labor camp in Germany, I will try to mail the letter. It will be up to Mrs. Euler to make arrangements to get me out and take me to her home."

My sister paused, then admitted, "It's a risk. There are many things that could go wrong. But, we have no choice. . . ."

I looked at my mother, trying to sense what she was feeling. I suddenly realized what a strength her oldest child was to her. Would she fall apart after Hanusia's departure? She had no husband to consult with and encourage her. Tarasik and I were too young to help her emotionally or to offer encouragement. Tarasik was growing up, yet he still looked to mother for strength. And I absolutely depended on my mother. I needed her presence more than I needed food. But who did mother have? Her own mother and father were dead. Her brother Alyosha and sister Newnia had their own problems. Hanusia was not only her daughter, but also her friend. Though they were often separated because of Hanusia's schooling in Stalino, just the thought that they could be together at any given time, with just a few hours of travel, was encouraging. But Germany? It might be years before they saw each other again. And with the war so widespread, it was very dangerous to travel. This could mean separation forever.

Hanusia turned to me and said, "Sistlitski, let's practice the little song that I taught you about the snowflakes. Remember?" This was my sister's way of easing the pain of her news. She raised both of her arms and wiggled her fingers to simulate snowflakes falling from the sky. I loved that song because I could

sing and dance at the same time, demonstrating with my arms
and body how the snow came down and lay on the ground.

"Let's start and sing together," she said cheerfully.

> We are little white snowflakes,
> Falling gently from above.
> We are light and fluffy flakes,
> That cover you with love.

"Very good!" Hanusia hugged me. "You keep practicing.
When I come back from Germany we will sing it again. Maybe
you can teach mother so she can join in with us." Her enthusiastic outlook temporarily lifted the cloud that had gathered over
our lives.

Before Hanusia left home, she shared an interesting observation with mother about her meeting with Major Euler. "You
know, maybe there is a good reason why I learned German as a
girl."

SUMMER 1942

It was the middle of the summer before we received any word
from my sister. A short letter informed us that she had arrived
safely in Germany at a location that was clipped out of the letter
by a censor. "I'm working hard, but I'm all right." That was all
the news we could expect. We knew all mail was censored, so it
wasn't safe to say more. But that worried us. There was no news
about her going on to Major Euler's home. Had something gone
wrong?

The next letter arrived a few weeks later, at the height of
harvest season. Again, it gave few details except to say that
Hanusia had made it safely to the Euler family. A few days later
we received a package. We had never received a parcel of any
kind before, for my mother's family all lived locally. Thus there
was no need for any of us to ship packages. With me clinging to
her side, mother eagerly opened the package. She pulled out a
beautiful doll and held it up for all of us to see.

"Isn't she the most beautiful doll you have ever seen?"
mother exclaimed. "And she is so big!" I could tell that mother
was tempted to play with it. "Look at this lovely face!" she said.
Then she cradled the doll much like one would a baby, and the
doll's eyes closed.

The doll was made out of some kind of stiff plastic material, and it wore a pastel-colored dress covered with flowers. When we lifted the dress to inspect the doll, we found pants underneath. And molded on the back was a picture of a turtle.

"Does that mean the doll is made out of a turtle?" I asked.

"I don't know, Dotshitshka." Mother handed the doll to me. "Be very, very careful."

This was the first real toy I had ever had. Naturally I was excited to receive such a gift, but having to be so careful took some of the fun out of playing with it. Through the years, I had become used to playing outdoors and enjoying nature. The pollywogs, chickens, dog, cow, insects, and flowers that I called my friends weren't so fragile.

I noticed another feature of the doll: "Mamo, she doesn't have any hair! What happened to her hair?"

Mother looked at the doll's head, which was molded to make it look like it had hair. "Dotshitshka, that's just the way they made this doll in Germany."

I was disappointed. With hair, I could at least comb and braid it.

"Is there anything in the box for you, Mamo?"

"No, but there is a pair of shoes for Tarasik. They are about two sizes too big, but he will enjoy them. Hanusia wanted to make you happy, and she made me happy this way." Mother then gave me a big hug. I set the doll on our bed, and went outside to play.

FALL 1942

One day while we were outside, a German soldier came through our orchard and gazed at the cherries ripening on one of our trees. He went over to my mother, who was bent over working in the garden. *"Entschuldigen sie bitte. Kann ich kirschen haben?"*

Mother was flustered. *"Ya nye panimayu.* I don't understand."

I, however, had heard enough German during the weeks that officers had lived in our house to understand some words and phrases.

"Excuse me, please. May I have a few of the cherries from your tree?" the soldier said most politely.

But my mother couldn't understand German and just shook her head and shrugged her shoulders with an embarrassed smile. The man pointed again and I finally figured out what he wanted.

"*Tagody, Mamo!*" I yelled. "He wants some of our cherries!"

My mother smiled. "*Pozhalusta.* Please, help yourself."

"*Spaciba.* Thank you," said the soldier.

I laughed. "Thank you" was the one phrase most German soldiers had learned to speak in Russian.

Mother ran inside the house and brought the man a dish. He picked some cherries. Mother then folded a newspaper into a homemade paper sack and poured the cherries into it. Pleased with his accomplishment, the soldier continued on his way.

My mother shook her head. "Such discipline," she said to me in amazement. "I would expect them to just come and take what they want. I've heard reports that they can be barbarians. But those who have been with us have been most cordial. And so mechanical—almost like machines."

Apparently the German forces found little to worry them in this simple family—a woman with a teenage son and six-year-old daughter. Of course, there had to be another side. Some of our fellow Ukrainians, we knew, were resisting. Before Hanusia left, she told of partisans who were hung in the town square as a warning to all who might think of resisting the conquerors.

My father had a cousin who was a partisan. His name was Pawel; we called him Paulo. He was only nineteen years old and had just become a Communist party member not out of conviction but for personal gain—to have plenty of food and access to goods and places that only Communist leaders enjoyed. When the Germans occupied our area, someone informed on him, and he fled into the woods.

Late one night we were roused from bed by a loud knock. Mother cried out in surprise when she opened the door. Paulo put a finger to his mouth and slipped quickly inside.

"Please! You must be quiet!" he whispered as he shut the door. "I need your help."

"What are you doing?" mother asked. "You will get us killed!"

"It's OK, Tiotia Maria [Aunt Maria]. I'm sure I wasn't seen. Please, may I come in?"

Mother stood back and clutched her chest, as though trying to restart her heart. I stood at the door of the bedroom and watched. Paulo quickly looked around and was satisfied that all the windows were shuttered and no one could see in. Then he sat at the kitchen table. "Do you have anything to eat?"

Mother went to the pantry to get some food. She brought out some bread and cut up a fresh cucumber. "Would you like some tea?" she asked. Paulo nodded and she lit the stove to heat some water. She poured the tea, then sat down as father's cousin devoured the food.

"I'm tired," Paulo whispered. "I need to hide out for a day or two. I've got to get some sleep."

"Where have you been?" mother asked.

"Don't ask. It's better that you not know. I have been running and hiding since the Germans took over. Several of us have banded together and given the Germans some trouble. Two nights ago, we stumbled into a patrol. We didn't have any way of fighting them, so we didn't have a chance. They shot at me, but I managed to climb a fence and get away."

"Paulo, why? Why are you doing this?"

He finished his last bite before responding matter-of-factly: "If they find me, I'm a dead man. So I have to fight. There is no other choice."

"What if they catch you with us? . . ."

"Do you have any place to hide?"

Mother thought for a moment. "You could sleep in the shed."

"Too obvious. That's the first place they would look."

"There's the cellar."

"That won't work either. How about the attic?"

"There is not much room up there."

"I don't need much. Let's take a look."

Mother showed him how to get upstairs through the pantry. He found a tiny space between the ceiling boards and the roof. The only way he could fit in the space was to lie flat. "Perfect!" he whispered. Mother handed him a blanket and pillow, and he fell asleep immediately.

Paulo fled two nights later, and mother heaved a sigh of relief. No Germans had come near our house during that time. He told us nothing about where he was headed. But a few days later, Alyosha came by and gave us the gruesome report. "The Germans captured Paulo two nights ago," he said. "He was executed on the spot." One of Paulo's partisan friends had brought my uncle the sad news.

Most of us couldn't think of resistance. How could we possibly challenge the might of the German army? Pashka told us that all villages had been ordered by Communist authorities to burn their homes and crops before the Germans arrived. But in our area those instructions were never obeyed; to do so was tantamount to suicide. The Germans certainly weren't going to feed and shelter us. How could we have survived? Yet we also knew that if the Soviet army recaptured our villages, we would be considered traitors because we had not followed the official policy of "scorching the earth."

Despite the fact we were now under foreign occupation, we actually felt less fear than before. In many ways, the war had brought the most peaceful time of my young life. The hardest part was that mother missed Hanusia. So far, we had received only three letters from her, plus the package. But we no longer lived in fear of persecution from the Communists. For the moment, we were not worried about some neighbor reporting us for an unknown violation. Under Soviet rule, we were afraid of our own people. We could trust no one. But with the Germans, though we certainly were not free, we were at least able to talk openly with our neighbors.

During the winter months of 1942-43, we learned that the tide of the war was turning. The Germans had not overrun Russia as planned. The Soviet army dug in during the bitter winter and began to make a counterattack. We heard that in some locations the German army was in retreat. My mother sensed the danger. She seemed preoccupied, wrestling with her options. It was time to do something. Waiting only guaranteed trouble if the Soviets took back our village.

APRIL 1943

Spring was returning. I had just turned seven, and I was looking forward to planting the garden and spending days outside in the sun with nature. The first warm days had arrived when a neighbor came by, carrying two little furry bundles.

"Maria, perhaps your daughter would like these?"

The neighbor held the bundles low for me to look at, and I saw two gorgeous kittens. One was gray with a touch of white; the other was butterscotch, with white patches. It was instant love. I picked one up and hugged her against my cheek. It was only a couple of weeks old. I fervently hoped my mother would let me keep them, but I never expected her to say yes.

To my amazement, mother smiled and agreed. I could keep them! I was overjoyed at these two little pets—worried only that our dog might not appreciate the competition for my affection. But Sjun sniffed at the wiggly balls of fur and, satisfied that they posed no threat, walked off.

I named the kittens Gray and Yellow, and they became my happy friends. As they grew day by day, they darted around my feet and legs, pounced on me from under the bed, or sprang out at me from under the lilac bushes. There was lots of laughter and screaming on my part as we played hide-and-seek. When Gray and Yellow became tired, Sjun amazed us by letting the cuddly kittens sleep in the shelter of her sprawled-out stomach!

I should have realized that something unusual was happening when my mother so willingly gave me the kittens. It kept me from observing that she wasn't doing the normal springtime work in the garden. Instead, she slipped away often to talk with our neighbors and relatives. I should have missed her, but the kittens diverted my attention.

Then one day, a German soldier came to our house. We hadn't seen many soldiers lately, so I watched as he talked briefly to my mother and handed her a slip of paper. As he walked back across the stream and into town, mother stood looking at the paper.

"What's wrong, Mamo?" I asked.

"We are leaving our home," she said, almost in a whisper.

"Where are we going?"

"We are going to Germany."

"Are we going to see Hanusia?" I was excited about that prospect.

"I have written to her. But I do not know if we will see her. We must go to a train in Konstantinovka tomorrow. I do not know anything more than that."

"Is Tarasik going, too?"

"Yes, Tarasik is going."

"Can I take my kittens?"

"No, Dotshitshka, I'm so sorry. We can't take the kittens."

"But Mamo! Who will take care of them?"

Mother knelt down in front of me and gently explained: "We can only take what we absolutely need. I expected we would have to leave, so I already made arrangements with Pashka. The kittens will be better here. Pashka said that she will take good care of them, and she has plenty of milk for them, too." That made me feel better, since we always got our milk from her anyway.

I then asked the question bothering me most: "Why, Mamo? Why do we have to leave? I like living here."

"I like living here, too, Dotshitshka." Mother held me hard in her arms to cover the emotion she was fighting. Then she added, "We have no choice. We have been told to go, so we must go. I do not know where they are taking us."

"Why, Mamo? We haven't done anything wrong."

"Of course we haven't. But that doesn't matter. We must do what we are told."

"What about our home, Mamo?"

"My cousin's family will stay in our house until we come back." And then, almost as an afterthought, she said, "If we ever survive and come back."

I couldn't comprehend what she meant, but this wasn't the time to ask more questions.

"Now, we have work to do," mother said, changing her voice to appear more upbeat. "All we pack has to go in a single bundle. Why don't you help me decide what to take?"

Mother gave Tarasik a big burlap sack. "I want you to put as much dried fruit in it as possible." My brother took the sack and went off to the pantry. Meanwhile, mother spread a large blanket out in the middle of our living room. Everything we took had to fit in this blanket, which we would then fold, tie at the four corners, and carry, along with father's leather portfolio, which contained all of our documents.

There wasn't much to pack. I had one change of clothes. So did my mother and brother. There was a comb that mother and I shared. She picked a towel and a few rags to use for wiping or as bandages in case of an emergency. She also pulled out two colorful ribbons and put them with the comb.

As mother assembled the small pile of belongings, I spotted the doll from my sister lying in a corner. I had left it outside one day when mother was cooking outdoors in the mud stove. A spark flew out and landed directly in one eye of the doll. It instantly melted the beautiful blue eye, leaving a black hole in its place. That was a sad day for us. That doll would stay, I decided. I then set it down and ran outside to find Gray and Yellow, and for the rest of the afternoon, I hugged them and played with them.

As the sun was setting, I placed the kittens down by the shed at the point where the roofline nearly met the ground. It was easy for me to scramble up here and crawl up to the slanted roof of our house. This spot held many memories for me. It was here that mother placed our fruit to dry. I loved to inspect the fruit as it lay on the roof, swat at the flies that swarmed over it, and yell at the insects to go away.

Now life would no longer be so carefree and simple. As I stood on this roof for the last time, I could see above the village to the west. I looked as far as I could, to the horizon, straining my eyes to see beyond where I could see, which was not more than a few miles. I thought Germany was just beyond the horizon, perhaps just a little cart ride away. I didn't think Germany would be much different from Russia.

It never occurred to me that it would, indeed, be very different—that I would never again know the beautiful, serene life of this simple piece of land. Less than an acre. A simple, three-room brick house. A garden. Many fruit trees. A stream. A hill. This was all the world I knew. Soon I would discover a much bigger world—and that world was not nearly so safe or serene.

7

The Cattle Train

Mother was bustling around the house. "Senok!" she yelled, startling my brother, who preferred to sleep a little longer. "Senok, this bag can hold more fruit. Come and fill it now!"

"Mom, I can hardly lift it!" Tarasik protested.

Mother came into the room. "There will be no argument! We must take all the food we possibly can. Now get up and do it!"

Tarasik mumbled something incoherent and stumbled out of the room. I could hear him drag the burlap bag over to the door, then go into the pantry. I slipped off my nightshirt and got into my faded dress, then quietly went past my busy mother and groggy brother to the front stoop. The two kittens were huddled together just inside the door. I picked them up and held them in my lap as the sun announced its arrival, lighting up the clear-blue sky. A slight mist rose from the trees as the dew began to evaporate.

How many spring and summer mornings had I sat on this stoop and welcomed the day? I drank in the sight one more time. *Why did we have to be taken away?* I thought. This was the only home I had known. Apart from a day of war, now over a year past, this had been a peaceful setting. I couldn't imagine life anywhere else. *Would Germany be like this?* I wondered. *Would I make friends there?* I really wanted a friend. The kittens were nice, but they couldn't talk—though they accepted all the love I wanted to give them. And what about nature? Would there be pretty places for me to wander? I loved the smell of flowers, trees, and the dirt. I even liked little wiggly worms and bugs. Surely those things would be where we were going.

Did I know I would never see this scene again? Today I can't be sure what that seven-year-old child was thinking. I know I absorbed every sight and sound as if it were for the last time.

"Emotshka, come and eat!" My mother's voice broke the spell. I set the kittens down, ran inside, and took a few bites from a bowl of kasha, then hurried back outside.

The sound of horse hoofs drew closer and closer. An old friend of our family, Luka Dykyj, was riding out of the village toward our house, his farm horse pulling a little cart. "Brrrrr!" he yelled, bringing the horse to a stop. He climbed out of the cart and turned the horse around so the back of the cart was facing us. Then he walked up to me. *"Dobraye Utra!* Good morning, Emotshka." I looked at him and nodded. "We'll miss you," he said, patting me on the head as he went in the house. I put the kittens down and followed him. I took one more look around the only house where I had ever slept. Tarasik and mother were hurrying around nervously.

"It's too heavy!" he complained, referring to the burlap bag.

"You've got to do it, Senok," she answered. "You're a strong boy!" Yet in fact, he was so skinny you could count his ribs.

I looked in the back room where we slept. It was simple—just a bed for Tarasik, another for mother and me, a third that my older sister once used, plus the adobe stove that heated the house during winter. Turning around, I looked at the simple furnishings in the living room and kitchen. A table. A few chairs. Some shelves. There was a radio that had not been used for some years—ever since they had cut off our electricity. There was a black sofa with a wood frame that had a small mirror in the middle of the back. I loved to peek into it, since we had no other mirror in the house. These furnishings weren't much, but still we had more than other people in our village because of my father's occupation.

"Time to go! Emotshka, come now." My mother never had to yell at me, but this time I hesitated. It was hard to pull myself away. The farthest I had ever been from home was to Stalino, to see my sister when she was in school. That was fifty miles. I figured it was at least that far to Germany.

Tarasik and Luka had gone ahead, and I could see where my brother had dragged the burlap bag of dried fruit down the narrow path. Together they heaved and tossed it onto the back of the cart. Mother followed, carrying a big bundle with our belongings and dad's small leather portfolio, which contained a few photographs plus all of our official papers. No one went anywhere without papers; our birth certificates were the most important documents.

I stooped down to say goodbye to my kittens, then ran to catch up. Tarasik was sitting in front, next to Luka. Mother helped me up and together we sat in the back of the cart, facing the house. The two kittens were fighting and chasing each other, oblivious to the fact that I was abandoning them. I wanted to cry, to scream. But nothing came out. Deep down inside me I could feel an intense knot. My heart ached. I had never experienced such anxiety before.

The cart began to move. Mother took my hand and I looked up at her face. She had already said goodbye to Uncle Alyosha and our other relatives. Her eyes were wet as she looked back at the brick house that had been her home for many years. I, too, looked back. Already the house looked smaller, shrouded by the trees around it. It was strange how I had never looked at the house this way before. Then we rounded a turn, and it was out of view.

Despite the warm morning, I felt a chill as we drove through Drushkovka, our little village. Clinging to my mother, I felt like I was a soaking wet, straggly little animal that was close to drowning in rushing water. Just in time, a piece of driftwood had floated by and I desperately struggled and scrambled to hold on to it. Now we were on our way in whatever direction the current of life would take us. We were roaring downstream with thousands of other pieces of driftwood, each with its own scared occupants. What was this force that was driving us away from our homes? Whatever it was, we were powerless to alter it in any way.

We were in the country again. The wooden wheels of the horse-drawn cart hobbled over the unpaved dirt road. There were numerous dips and potholes and the cart didn't absorb the bumps. We rode slowly past communal farms that showed few signs of life. Once a truck passed us, kicking up dust. But we plodded along and an hour later, we were in Konstantinovka at the small train station.

There was a lot of commotion. A long train consisting entirely of sturdy boxcars stood in the station. The doors were open and I could see people sitting on the floor inside the wagons. *This is how they transport animals,* I thought. On my only other train trip, which was to Stalino, we had sat on benches. *Were we really going on this?* People were milling around the station. German soldiers were patrolling the area, making sure that the people who were on the train didn't go far.

Luka Dykyj lifted me down off the cart, then helped my mother down. Tarasik wrestled the bag of fruit off the cart and struggled to hoist it over his shoulder, but failed. It must have weighed over a hundred pounds.

"Can't someone help me carry it?" he mumbled to himself.

"Please, Synotchok [little son], I beg you, carry it to the train," answered my mother. "It will save us down the road." She said goodbye to our driver, then turned and headed for the train. Whatever our future, she was facing it bravely.

A soldier, with his rifle pointing the way, ordered us to board a certain car. As mother peered in, she could see that there was hardly any room left. It was up to us to make some space. She helped Tarasik hoist the bag to the boxcar floor. He climbed in first, took mother's bundle, then helped pull her and me on board. I could now see that people all around us had staked little areas for themselves against the wall or in the center. They glared at us and didn't move until we started to settle in a small opening. Then they shifted, giving just enough room for us to lie down.

There were no faces we recognized. Everyone seemed similar to us in their coarse appearance. Most were peasants in simple, well-worn clothing. There were two young couples, a woman with her elderly parents, another elderly couple, several single women wearing babushkas (scarves), and a couple of teenage girls. I was the only child. All were simple folk, coarse in language and behavior. Mother winced as she heard the first profanity while trying to establish our area of the floor.

Mother set up "home" quickly. The burlap bag and oversized bundle became pillows against which we could lean. A few minutes later, we had to adjust our space as several others climbed aboard and crawled, squatted, and laid down between belongings and other bodies. Soon our car was jammed full. There wasn't room for us to stretch out full-length—mother and Tarasik had to bend their legs slightly.

Then we waited. Soldiers outside issued orders and shoved people into other boxcars. None of us spoke German, yet somehow we understood. One message was unmistakable: We were slaves, and slaves don't talk back. Slaves bury any hopes, dreams, or rights. We were being loaded like a herd of cows going to market. We were shoved about like pieces of machinery. And the sense was that if one machine broke down, there were others to take its place.

Everything was organized. The soldiers conveyed an arrogance that dictated submission.

Early in the afternoon, the solid-wood doors on our car were shut. We heard a bolt slide into place, locking us inside. Now our only light came from small windows in the top of the four corners of the wagon. We were prisoners. I felt again the pincers of intense anxiety that gripped me during winter, when I was a prisoner in my own house. I clutched mother, trying to drive that feeling away. I thought of my kittens, playing freely by our house. Never had I been so hemmed in by so many people. I wanted to be free, like my friends Yellow and Gray. I gazed up at my mother's face, expecting to see similar anxiety that would reinforce my fear. But instead, she was relaxed, content for now with the fact that two of her children were with her and that we were in this together, able to strengthen and encourage each other by our presence.

"Mamo, I'm hungry," said Tarasik.

Mother opened the burlap bag and each of us grabbed a handful of dried fruit. It was already obvious that this heavy "burden" my brother complained about might prove very useful. I put a dried cherry in my mouth and sucked on it for a long while. Then I ate a dried apple. The sweet fruit soothed my complaining stomach.

A few minutes later, the train finally jerked and began moving. Gradually it picked up speed. Since there were no windows except at the top, I couldn't see where we were going. The swaying of the cars and the click of the wheels on the tracks gradually lulled me to sleep.

I awoke the first time we stopped. It was late; only a hint of light came into the car. The door was opened a couple of feet, a pail of water was set down, and the door was shut again.

The water reminded all of us how thirsty we were. One woman against the far wall scrambled over us to get to the pail. A couple of hands tried to stop her. Several shouted and swore. A babushka near the door immediately took charge. "Patience! Everyone will get a little," she announced, pushing the impatient woman away. Then, using a small cup, she dipped it into the pail and gave it to her neighbor. When the cup was returned, she dipped it again for the next person, and so on until everyone in the wagon received a small drink.

The water reminded me of another need. "Mamo," I whispered, "I need to go. . . ."

One of our neighbors understood my predicament. "You have to use the bucket," she said, pointing to a pail by the door. I shook my head. I wasn't going to do that in front of everyone; I didn't have to go *that* bad. The woman, not unsympathetically, said, "You might as well get used to it. That's all we have." Still, I determined that I would wait a little longer.

Obviously others had a similar concern. How were we going to cope with such a private and sensitive situation? The embarrassment was immense. Finally, one of the women held up a blanket and requested, "Will someone please hold this up for me?" Several others followed her example, using the blanket as a partition.

The train started again. I looked around and in the dim light saw that most of the people were trying to sleep. There was nothing else to do, and besides, if they were at all like my mother, they had worked hard just to survive. This train trip might be a chance to catch up on much-needed sleep, even on the hard, splintered wood floor. And with the hopelessness and uncertainty of our situation, sleep was also a great escape.

Early the next morning, the train slowed to a crawl. I listened and heard the rumbling sounds that we had heard a year before near our house. War! There was fighting somewhere near here. Then the train jerked to a stop, the wheels making a loud screech, and we all slid into our neighbors in front of us. In a corner, one of the men boosted another man up so he could peer out the window.

"I can't see much," he reported. "But it appears that there is damaged track around the bend."

"Partisans! They're at it again," someone commented. We knew that the partisans tried to thwart the German effort at every chance.

The spotter got back down and we waited. An hour or so later, a soldier unbolted our door and opened it halfway. He peered in, then pointed at the two men in the corner: "*Sie, sie. Kommen sie her.*" The two men scrambled out of the car. The door remained open, so several of the women were able to peer out. "They are handing tools to the men," said the woman next to us. "It looks like they have to repair the track."

Some of the occupants used the stop to get off and take care of nature's call. "Here's your chance," my neighbor prompted me. "As long as you don't wander too far, they leave you alone." So mother and I got off the train and quickly took care of our needs behind some bushes. But I wasn't comfortable outside the walls of our wagon. The rumbles in the distance were less muffled and more frightening outside.

After returning to the boxcar, we sat for several hours. As the train started up again, the men who had helped fix the track climbed back on board, exhausted from their efforts. One of them had bloody hands as a result of his labors. A couple of hours later, we stopped and more people were loaded. Every boxcar was now completely full. If any more were packed on, we would no longer have at least some space to lie down.

Our progress was irregular. Sometimes we had to pull over to a siding to let another train pass. Other times we waited as a bridge or track ahead of us was repaired. If we stopped by remote fields, away from any town or village, we were allowed outside. I began to welcome the fresh air of those small outings, for in contrast the air in our car was becoming quite stale. The odor of people packed so close together, unable to bathe, had become more oppressive. Personal hygiene was not available for any women. Perspiration and bad breath made me want to turn my head in another direction. But there was no fresh air to breathe. The community bucket only added to the thick, warm stench. Whenever the train stopped, the first thing off was that miserable bucket.

I began to wonder if we would ever be clean again. Who knew when any of the people in the boxcars had last had a bath? They may have boarded the train already in need of one. Warm water, soap, towels, and toothbrushes were a luxury. The war had stopped all such supplies from reaching the villages. I thought about what it took for us to bathe—something I had taken for granted in Drushkovka. For my family, it started by collecting rainwater in a wooden barrel. Two buckets were filled and brought back to the house. There, a wood-burning stove—if you were lucky enough to have wood or coal—had to be fired hot enough to make the water warm. It was then poured into a portable metal tub. Then the family members took turns taking a bath in the same water. First the babies, then the children, and finally the parents. A bath once a week was the norm. Daily freshening was done at the river or a well.

On the second afternoon of our trip I asked, "Are we in Germany yet?"

"I don't think so," mother answered as she slowly combed my hair and divided it into two long braids.

"We are probably going through Poland, judging by the direction we're heading," said a neighbor.

The name meant nothing to me. "What is Poland?" I asked.

"It's a country between Russia and Germany," mother answered.

"The Germans overran Poland before invading us," the neighbor explained.

For the most part, there was little conversation in our wagon. Suspicion had permeated the Soviet Union for so long that people weren't talkative. There was occasional small talk, like, "Where are you from?" But generally, we got to know each other only by necessity rather than by choice. We were too used to distrusting those around us and worrying about a slip of the tongue that might lead to a knock in the middle of the night from the NKVD. Such fears are not easily broken.

We rolled on through the second night. About the third day, my mother pulled out the comb, undid my braids, and lovingly combed my long blond hair. Then she carefully examined my scalp, picking out anything that didn't belong. She had discovered that someone in our wagon had lice, which spread like fire in close contact with people. She nearly cried when she discovered lice in my clothing and hair. But it was impossible to control; they eventually got to everyone on board.

There were many stops, though we no longer picked up passengers. A couple of times the men were ordered again to help make repairs to the tracks. Mother shared some of our fruit with the people around us. She also exchanged some fruit for a loaf of stale bread, which she split with us. That and water was all we had to sustain us.

On the fifth day, we approached a train depot—we could tell because of all the switching that occurred. We slowed down to a crawl and were shunted from track to track. The men who were our lookouts reported we were coming to some kind of large complex. We went under overpasses and by buildings that cast eerie shadows inside the gloomy car. Then the train screeched to a halt and we heard a jumble of shouting and crowd noises outside.

"I think this is where we get off," observed the man standing on his companion's shoulders.

"Can you tell where we are?" someone asked.

"I'm pretty sure we're in Poland," he said. "But I don't know where."

The door was shoved open and a soldier yelled, "*Alle raus, schnell! Schnell!*" We didn't need to understand the words to know that we were to hurry and get off the train. The soldier waved his hand to indicate where he wanted us to go. I sat on the edge of the car door and someone reached a hand up to help me jump down to the station platform. I grabbed my mother's arm to make sure I didn't get separated from her in this seething and surging crowd.

Suddenly my mother shouted hysterically, "Nyet! Ostanov-ities! No, stop! You have my papers!" I saw a man, running with our leather portfolio, shoving people and dashing away from us through the mob.

Without taking her eyes off the thief, mother gave quick orders to Tarasik and me: "Stay right here! Don't move!" Then defying her weakened condition, she took off after the man.

The crowd parted for her, then swallowed her from view. "Thief!" she yelled. "That's mine! Give it back!"

Terror glued us to the train platform. I tried to keep my eyes on my mother, but in the pushing and jostling of the crowd I lost sight of her. Tarasik stood rigid, holding onto the burlap bag with a death grip. Our large bundle was at my feet and I held tightly onto the top, where it was tied. All our earthly possessions were in these bags. We didn't dare lose these, too! As we waited, I was gripped with a fear that perhaps my mother would not be able to find us. What would we do then?

Guards were already organizing the mob. We were pushed and shoved as the crowd bustled around us. "Schnell, schnell!" the soldiers yelled, motioning with their rifles for the people to move. We had to move—but mother had ordered us to stay!

Who should we obey? An aching fear rose to my throat. I wanted to scream, but I was so petrified that though my mouth opened, nothing came out.

How long I remained in this position I don't know. The picture is frozen in my mind, a stop-action where all of life freezes. Then I saw mother's kerchiefed head emerge from the crowd. She was clutching the portfolio, her arms wrapped around it, protecting it against her chest. In that moment of ecstatic relief I began to cry.

"It's OK, Dotshitshka," my mother assured me. "It's OK. I have the papers. There was no harm done."

I clutched on to my mother, as though by my sheer force of will I could ensure she would never leave me again. As relief calmed my emotions, I also felt a new pride for my mother. I sensed her determination that even though she was from a small

Ukrainian village, she would not be taken advantage of. She had an almost animal instinct for danger—she could sense it and was prepared to take whatever action was necessary to survive and protect her children. It was that instinct, that determination, that imparted some comfort in the midst of this confusing mass of humanity.

The crowd was slowly herded toward a large fenced compound. I looked up and saw soldiers on either side of the entrance, pushing people with the butt of their rifles to make sure everyone stayed in line. We trudged through the gates, then were directed toward buildings that looked like barns. I saw no windows, except high overhead, in a thin row down the center of each building.

The line stopped, and we saw up ahead that the soldiers were dividing the crowd, assigning people to various buildings. As we got closer, I could hear them counting: *"Eins, zwei, drei, vier, funf . . . zehn."* People were divided off into groups of ten and assigned to a barrack. Women and children went one way. Men went another, into an open field.

Inside, the barracks resembled barns designed to hold horses or other animals. The ceiling consisted of wood beams, and the walls, on both sides, had shelves stacked four high. It was on these shelves that people were staking out space. Our barrack was filling up quickly, and mother took the first available plank. The two of us would sleep here on these rough-hewn boards.

In the barrack, the talk was much noisier than on the train. I could sense the anxiety in the room. Why were we here? What would they do to us? Were we going to sleep forever on these rough boards, worrying about splinters every time we turned over? What about food? Surely they would have to feed us. Mother assumed this was just a stopover, since we were in Poland and she knew Germany was our final destination. But no one asked any questions.

As I did on the train, I cuddled close to my mother and drifted off to sleep. The burlap bag was our pillow, and rough wood provided the mattress. As before, sleep was the best escape from our fear.

The next morning we heard soldiers again, ordering us to rise quickly: *"Schnell! Schnell!"* A large barrel of watery soup was placed on the floor in the aisle between the rows of bunks. People lined up to be served and put the soup in whatever container they might have available. As soon as one barrel was emptied, it was rolled out and another one brought in to replace it.

Then we were herded out again, back to the train station, to another cattle train. Tarasik joined us. "I slept well!" he said cheerfully. "How about you?" He explained that the men had been told to sleep on pine branches spread over the ground. "They sure smelled wonderful compared to the stale, putrid air on the train."

Once again we didn't choose our accommodations; the soldiers filled up one car, shut the door, and loaded the next. When it was our turn, we scrambled up and found a place against the far wall opposite the door. "Let's stay out of the draft," said mother. "All we need is for one of us to catch a cold in this misery."

"Does anyone know where we are?" a woman near us asked.

"Beremishl," someone answered. "We're in central Poland."

The soldiers seemed to be in a hurry. They always seemed in a hurry, though we never understood why. After the train was loaded, it began moving out of the station. Soon we were rolling quickly through the countryside. The pattern was similar to the trip out of Russia: We would travel along for a while, stop, wait, then travel some more. Again, in remote areas, the soldiers would let us out for a few moments. On one such stop, Tarasik wandered off a little way, desiring a little privacy instead of being watched while taking care of necessities. Soon after, my mother and I reboarded and the train started moving before the soldiers had closed the doors. I was scared—where was Tarasik?

Soon the doors were shut and the train picked up speed. I was horrified. "Mamo, we can't go without Tarasik!"

She was concerned, too, but hugged me close and said, "He is probably in one of the other cars. He probably jumped aboard whichever car was closest when the train started moving." Mother's explanation made sense, but it didn't calm my anxiety. I cried quietly while she stroked my hair.

My misery lasted several hours, until the doors were opened again. My brother quickly scrambled aboard our car. Mother's conjecture was right—when the train had started moving, he climbed into the car next to ours. How glad I was to see him!

Sometime during the next four days and nights, we crossed into Germany. By now it had been nine days and nights since we had left our home in Ukraine. None of us had washed. One woman near us who was menstruating had no sanitary cloths.

Mother handed her a small rag to cover the embarrassing situation. Everyone suffered from lice. They were everywhere—in the seams of our clothes, and especially in our hair. At home, my mother had carefully washed my hair once a week, combed it, and checked my scalp to make sure I had no lice. But now my hair had gone nearly two weeks without washing. Everyone else had oily hair, too, and many didn't have combs. They used their fingers to scratch their scalps and unknot the worst tangles.

Finally, we reached our destination. The doors opened. Soldiers ordered us out. As we slowly slipped out of the boxcar, it was obvious that we were all wearing down. Lack of food and the degrading conditions had driven life from almost everyone. Nonetheless, my mother firmly clutched our portfolio, hoping to prevent a repeat of the attempted robbery in Poland. But here, people were not rushing about. Most had a haunted, resigned look on their faces. We were like a herd of underfed cattle, waiting to move in whatever direction we were prodded.

First it was *herren* in one line and *frauen* in another. The order filtered through the crowd, and the men and women separated. We were loaded onto large, open trucks and driven a short distance to a base of primitive wooden barracks surrounded by barbed wire. *Why the barbed wire?* I wondered. *To keep outsiders from entering? Or to prevent our escape? Certainly not that! Everyone is too tired and hungry. Who is going to try to escape?*

At the entrance to the camp, we were unloaded from the trucks and walked down a corridor of barbed and electric wire. Just inside the compound, the men and women went separate directions. I watched Tarasik until he was out of sight, but this time I didn't feel the terror I felt when I thought the train had started off without him. At least I knew he was near us in the same camp.

Each person was assigned a number and sent to a barrack, where mother and I left our bundle and the remainder of our dried fruit. Then we were moved into a large hall. Orders were issued in German, and hand motions indicated which direction we were to move. One female German worker began to unbutton her shirt to demonstrate that we were to remove our clothes. She indicated that we were to toss them into piles on either side of the line. Then all the women had to let down and unbraid their hair. Spaced at intervals around the hall were lamps and under the lamps were tables attended by women in uniform who inspected each woman and girl's hair and then sprayed her with some kind of disinfectant.

In the line ahead of us, I heard a teenage girl cry in alarm. A uniformed woman had taken shears and shaved the girl's head. I clutched my head, as if by the force of my feeble hands I might be able to save my own hair. Soon there were others like that girl, stumbling around naked, with shaved heads, dazed and crying uncontrollably.

I felt a hand on my shoulder. *"Komm her, bitte!"* said the voice. A woman was holding a camera, and she wanted to take my picture. Using her hands, she indicated how she wanted me to stand, hold out my thick, long hair, and show how it fell to my knees—much like a natural drape for my frail body. There was a flash and a *"danke"* and I was back in line, wondering what that was all about.

I got tired of standing and waiting, but there was no place to sit. And no choice but to wait. And nothing to do but worry about losing my hair. I could imagine nothing more humiliating than to have my head shaved. Women weren't supposed to be bald!

Finally, my mother and I faced our turns. One woman in a dark blue uniform and short hair inspected my hair strand by strand. She carefully poked around my scalp, then motioned me on to another woman and muttered something I couldn't understand. I awaited my fate, sure I would wind up bald. But the next lady took a pair of scissors, turned me around, grabbed my hair with one hand, and snipped away at shoulder level. I nearly cried with relief—at least one little part of my humanity had been saved! Mother was right behind me. After inspecting her for lice, they let her pass, too. She was able to keep her hair parted in the middle and tucked in a soft knot at the nape of her neck.

We went next to what looked like a shower. Another uniformed woman pumped a handle that released a soft spray of powder over our heads. I closed my eyes, but some particles still managed to get into my eyes and sting them for a few moments.

Then we were pointed toward a huge bin piled full of uniforms. Everyone was to take a dark, khaki-green skirt, and a shirt of the same color. One size fit all. A drawstring on the skirt allowed it to be adjusted to the size of one's waist. Children were pointed to another, smaller table, where we were given an identical uniform in a smaller size. While my family never had much in the way of clothes at home, at least what we had was comfortable. In contrast, these uniforms were rough and irritating to my skin. The itching started as soon as I pulled the blouse over my head.

Next we were issued blue armbands with the German word "*OST*" (meaning "*EAST*") on them. Shoes were issued at another spot on the floor. Like the uniforms, one size fit all. The tops were made of a stiff leather; the soles were wood. There was no way to walk quietly in them. Clop, clop, clop—wherever we went, the sound could be heard clearly. And here in this hall, on the cement floor, the sound of the shoes was deafening.

Once we had our clothes, we were directed to the next table, where we were each issued a small metal pot with a thin wire handle and a plain metal spoon. At another table, everyone was issued two army blankets.

Once we had everything, we returned to our barracks. While they were smaller than the room in Poland, at least they had windows. Along each wall were army cots with mattresses made of straw. Between each cot was a small metal closet for our belongings, but there was barely enough room to turn around between the cots. My mother and I shared a bed.

As soon as we settled on our cot, mother rummaged through our bundle and pulled out the two red ribbons she had saved for my hair. Carefully she wove them into a bow. Then she collected my hair from both sides at the temples, pulled it up and back, and tied it with the bow on top of my head.

"There!" she said. That made me feel so much better. A splash of beauty in a dreary setting!

Then we heard a shrill whistle. Everyone grabbed their pots and spoons and clopped out the door. We followed the camp crowd to another building where a crude mess hall was set up. We could see steam rising from what looked like large garbage cans on the ground, and instantly our stomachs responded to the prospect of a warm meal for the first time in many days. The line moved quickly. When we reached the containers, I held out my dish and a server poured one scoop of liquid into the bowl. The heat from the soup nearly burned my hands, so I quickly lifted the wire handle and grabbed it, trying carefully not to spill any of the liquid. The next server handed out a piece of hard, dark-brown bread.

Mother and I found a place to sit at a long table with other women. I looked into my bowl and my stomach flipped. It was very watery, with a few globs of fat floating on top. I stirred it with my spoon and felt something at the bottom. I fished it out. It was a boiled snail. I dumped it back and wondered how I could possibly eat such revolting food. But my stomach insisted I try. Scrunching my nose, I slowly took a sip of the broth. I gagged at the bitter taste and spewed the water back into the dish.

"Pretty bad, isn't it?" said a woman across the table. She spoke Russian and seemed friendly. "Well, it won't get any better, sweetie. You had better get used to it; if you don't eat it, you won't survive."

"Leave the girl alone," said another Russian down the table. "The stuff isn't fit to feed to a dog." She spit in her soup to show her disgust.

Mother stared at her bowl for a long time, saying nothing. Then she bent over, filled her spoon, and slowly sipped the watery broth. Mechanically, she repeated the process until the bowl was empty.

Back at the barrack, we chewed on some of the remaining fruit. There was enough to supplement our diet for a few more days, then we would have to depend on the camp fare. That wasn't an encouraging prospect. So far, the fruit had saved our lives; already many who had traveled with us had gotten sick and weak. We weren't much better ourselves. Mother was feeling faint, and my brother's ribs made him look like a skeleton.

At 10:00 that night, the guards turned out the lights. Some of the people were already asleep, but mother and I found it hard to sleep in our new surroundings.

"Mamo," I whispered, "how long are we going to stay here?"

She drew me close and whispered in my ear so no one could hear what she was saying. "Not too long, I hope—not too long. We must believe that somehow help will come."

That was our secret hope. My sister, my sister, we need your help soon! We would not survive here for long.

8

Labor Camp

Four o'clock came so very early in the morning. One of the guards poked his head into our room and blew on a shrill whistle. My mother moaned. In just ten minutes, he would again stick his head in the door and yell, "Roll call." Though she was dead tired, mother, with hundreds of other women and men, would have to go outside and stand—often for more than an hour—until everyone was present and accounted for.

I hugged mother hard, as if my intense desire could delay the demands of German authority. Mother tried to reassure me. "I'll be back, Dotshitshka," she said, stroking my hair.

But she didn't understand. I couldn't explain to her the fear that held me in its grip as I waited for her to return from roll call and her work at the factory. I tried to sleep. I wandered around the barracks. But nothing made the time go faster. Nothing replaced the comfort of her presence.

What made matters worse was that mother was growing weaker every day. Her gaunt appearance alarmed me. She needed more food. Sleep was fitful at best, with constant interruptions because of air raids. How long could she last under such conditions before her frail body collapsed completely?

Mother got up slowly off the cot and slipped on her shoes. She staggered to the community washroom adjacent to our room. Then she went outside for roll call. Through the window I watched her line up in the dark along with hundreds of other women. The only light came from a weak bulb hanging from a pole in the yard. It cast an eerie glow in the dismal, drizzly, foggy air.

After a few minutes, mother slumped briefly as though she would faint, but a woman behind her shoved her back up. *Too roughly,* I thought. *If she could just hold out until breakfast!* Though it consisted only of oatmeal, without any sugar, butter, or milk, it would provide some energy. But first was roll call, then a one-hour march to the factory.

The work at the factory was exhausting. The women stood for eleven hours fitting together parts for German bombs. There were only a couple of short breaks, just enough time to use the bathroom. The workplace was so noisy that it was impossible to carry on any conversation. But somehow during the breaks she had learned that this factory was privately owned by one of the men high up in Hitler's leadership. She learned that the name of the town was Fallersleben, and during peacetime, parts for cars, called Volkswagens, were made here.

Finally, roll call was done and the women were ordered to start marching four abreast. My tired body wanted to go back to bed, but I couldn't take my eyes off my mother. I felt tears coming to my eyes as she stumbled again. This time a soldier hit her with the butt of his rifle, and she scrambled back to her feet. "*Mach schnell!* Get going!" he yelled. The women marchers joined with men from the other side of the camp and exited the front gate.

I ran back to my bed and pulled the covers over my head. I wanted to cry, but the tears wouldn't come. I wanted to fall asleep and wake up to find that the last few weeks had been just a bad dream. I wanted to go outside and see the garden by our house in Ukraine and watch the sun rise over the orchard and wander among the flowers and along the stream by my home. Surely this was just a terrible nightmare! But sleep didn't come, and the nightmare was still there when I poked my head out from under the blanket. The barracks were deserted now, except for an old Russian lady and her grandson at the opposite end of the room.

I could hear the woman yelling at her boy, then a slap and crying, and more hitting. I hated those sounds—yelling and hitting were foreign to my home. The horror continued. The woman pulled down the boy's pants and began to whip him unmercifully. He fell to the ground as the old lady pummeled him with blows from her bony hands. I closed my eyes to try and shut out the awful sight. Over and over she hit him. The boy writhed on the ground, but couldn't escape. When she finally stopped, he wasn't moving. I looked over again, trembling in fear, and saw that part of his bowels were protruding. I turned and squeezed my eyes shut for I don't know how long. But the picture would not leave my mind. I was shaking like a thin tree in a horrible wind.

Finally, I put on my shoes and slipped outside. The camp was not designed for little children like me, though there were many of us who came with our mothers when the Germans imported us.

At one barrack door, I saw a little boy. He spoke to me, but I didn't understand what he was saying. I only stood and looked at him. He appeared about my age, wearing a plain green shirt and pants with holes at the knees. Dried dirt on his hands and face seemed to indicate that he had spent time excavating a piece of ground. He spoke to me again. His words weren't German, and though they sounded similar to Russian or Ukrainian, I couldn't recognize what he was saying. I said nothing. He finally shrugged his shoulders and went on his way. I was relieved.

When we had first arrived at the camp, there was no extra food for the children. I was getting used to the growling in my empty stomach. Even for a child who was used to living on little, I felt hungry all the time. Then one day an official ordered a special diet for all the children. We lined up with our little tin buckets at lunchtime and were served a white, cereal-like mixture. A stern-looking woman ladled one spoonful into each of our bowls. Another lady took a plum from a can and plopped it on top of the oatmeal-like mush. I took my food back to my bed and picked at it, eating the plum and a few bites of the mush to calm my stomach. I hid the rest beneath my bed. Mother needed this more than me; I would save it for her. I saved most of my food for her to eat when she came back from the factory, and what she didn't eat she gave to my brother, whose barrack was next to ours but separated by a fence.

That afternoon, I returned to the barrack door to welcome back the workers as they marched back from the factory. They were so tired, however, that every step required superhuman effort. I searched the faces as line after line of weary women passed by. Finally I saw my mother, and could hardly wait to run to her. But I had to restrain my enthusiasm until she was inside the compound and the guards had released the prisoners to go to their barracks. Mother hardly noticed as I ran up to her. A reassuring caress was all she could manage as she limped to our building. When I held her hand, she smiled and seemed to gain strength from my touch.

Once in the door, she collapsed on her bed. I immediately laid down next to her and put my arms around her. Tears started coming now, and I heaved with the emotion.

"Dotshitshka, what's the matter?" my mother whispered. But I didn't answer; I just held her as hard as I could. "It's OK, mother is back now. Everything is OK." She gently stroked my hair and held me until I stopped shaking.

I pulled away, wiped my tears, and pulled out my little bowl of cold mush. "This is for you, Mamo."

She didn't protest. With a faint smile and pity in her eyes, mother ate the cereal. She needed it more than I did. It would help calm her angry stomach when she ate her turnip soup and stale bread at dinnertime. At the end of the workday, as the laborers exited from the factory, they received some bread, but it had to be earned. If a worker didn't fulfill his or her quota, he or she was refused the extra bread. Meat was rationed as well. Actually, it was horse meat disguised with a flavor. Mother often failed to qualify for these rations.

Somehow mother found enough strength that evening to stand in the dinner line and we managed to force down the watery, unflavored soup. Sometimes at supper every person received one or two unpeeled, boiled potatoes. Other days there was a huge tin barrel filled with a liquid that looked like it had been drawn from a muddy brook. To our dismay, we saw boiled snails, still in their shells, floating around. If a person had the stomach, he or she could dig out the meat. I couldn't. No matter how hungry I was, certain things still made my stomach somersault.

After supper, mother went back to her bed while I ran over to the fence that separated the men and women. Earlier, mother and I had made it a habit of meeting Tarasik at the fence each night after dinner. Now mother rarely had the strength even for this important family contact. Sometimes she and my brother spoke briefly while marching to and from work. Generally talk was not allowed, but a short exchange was sneaked in while the guards were elsewhere along the line.

Conditions for Tarasik were even harsher than for me. Most of the men in his barracks were rough, profane, and uneducated. Because my brother was gentle by nature, he found it painful to fit in.

Tarasik was waiting for me when I ran up. "How's mother feeling?" he asked.

"She's very tired," I answered. I didn't say that her weariness scared me, but he seemed to sense my fear and expressed concern for her as well. Mother offered stability for both of us, and we constantly looked to her for encouragement.

"I saw her stumble this morning on the way to the factory," said Tarasik. "The women around her weren't sympathetic. I was close enough to hear them yelling at her, telling her to stop faking it. They think she just wants to get out of work. I saw a soldier push her with his rifle. *Mach mal schneller*," he said. "Move faster!" One woman in back of her pushed her with both hands and said in Russian, "Hurry up. Quit pretending!" She had a most hateful voice. It hurts bad enough to be treated like that by enemies. But to endure that from our own people ... that really cuts deep, more than any rifle butt. We should help each other and stick together."

We knew how hard my mother could work. She wasn't afraid to put in a hard day's labor in the garden or shoveling coal. She had worked hard for many years. But how could anyone work when there wasn't enough food? Add to that the tremendous stress of war, nightly air raids, worry, fear, and discouragement, and it was no wonder that her body had started to collapse from poor health.

Tarasik then added, "There isn't much we can do. We have to survive one day at a time. Are you doing OK, little sister?"

"I'm OK," I said.

"What do you do while we are gone during the day?"

"Nothing much." I shrugged my shoulders. What could I tell him?

"You be careful!" It was obvious my big brother was concerned about my welfare, and I appreciated it. "Maybe Hanusia can help us. We can't hold on much longer."

Mother was already asleep when I stepped back into our barrack. Though there were at least fifteen families in the cramped quarters, it was fairly quiet, for most of the women, like my mother, were too exhausted to do much. I slid next to her and quickly fell asleep, too, and was not aware when the lights were turned out at 10:00.

Sleep didn't last long. A penetrating, shrill sound jerked us awake. "Air-raid sirens!" someone shouted. Women jumped up and scurried to find their shoes and clothes in the dark. There were no lights allowed; they were strictly forbidden. We stumbled in the darkness, trying to find our clothing. Then grouping into a huddle of women and children, we quickly emerged from the building and walked a short distance to the shelter. A soldier threw open the heavy, rough wood door and we went down several steps into a narrow dirt tunnel. There, a weak light bulb hanging by a long electrical cord in the ceiling cast barely enough light to help us see our way to rough wooden benches along the tunnel wall. When we sat on them, our knees touched those of the people opposite us.

No one spoke as we huddled together. None of us ever adjusted to these jolting interruptions which occurred every night, often several times. The first time I had heard the sound of the siren, I continued to shake like a frightened puppy long after the all-clear signal was sounded and we were back in our beds. That fear, though it had subsided somewhat, returned every time the air-raid siren sounded. And even after we went back to sleep, my body remained tense, anticipating that nerve-wracking sound.

I leaned my head against my mother. In the distance we could hear a series of explosions as bombs were dropped on nearby factories. The ground around us shook slightly and dirt loosened from the ceiling fell on us. Mother wrapped her arms around me in a vain attempt to calm my shivering body. Then the explosions stopped and I almost dozed off, only to be awakened by a long, mournful, monotone siren—the all-clear. We stood and slowly made our way back up the stairs and through the dark to our barracks. One might say that we could make this trip in our sleep and it was true, for we were so tired, and it was so pitch-black that it was hard to tell whether we were awake or dreaming. We put our hands out to feel the beds and counted—one, two, three, four—until we reached ours.

Mother fell into bed without removing her clothes. Immediately she was asleep, only to be awakened a few moments later as the sirens wailed again, and we had to trudge back to the shelter. This time I didn't hear the sound of bombs—perhaps it was a false alarm, or maybe the planes just passed over us on their way to another destination. Still, it was half an hour or more before the all-clear signal was given and we made our repeat trip back to the barracks. Two more times that night, the alarm sounded. Two more times, we made our way to the tunnel, then back to our beds. *Why didn't they just leave us in the shelter—wouldn't that have been more restful?* I wondered. In the barracks, we would close our eyes and tell our bodies to sleep, but our minds wouldn't allow that deep sleep, knowing that our rest could be interrupted at any moment.

The next interruption came at 4:00 A.M.—it was time for the women to rise again for roll call and then march to the factories. How could my mother possibly push her body out of bed? "Just a little longer," she whispered, to herself as much as to me. "We must hold on a little longer, Dotshitshka. Any day now, someone will come and rescue us." This was the hope we clung to. It was our only hope. We could not give up before that help came.

*   *   *

One late fall morning during roll call, before the women were marched off to the factories, I heard a soldier speak sharply: "Maria Wasylenko, step out."

I watched as my mother stepped forward from her line. My heart stopped for a moment. Were they sending us to another camp? We had seen women shipped off to work elsewhere, especially after a factory was destroyed by a bombing attack. Though it was hard to imagine harsher conditions than we were enduring, there were whispers and rumors that many died in these other places of starvation and cold.

But there was an even worse fear: If we were transferred, how would Hanusia find us?

Another possibility was that mother had done something wrong and would be punished. Would they take her away from me? Horrors! How would I survive? But that thought fled when she turned toward the barrack and I saw a smile on her face. Something good was happening! I jumped down from my perch at the window and ran to the door. "She's here, Dotshitshka!" my mother said as she came in the door. "We must grab our things quickly."

I jumped up and down and followed mother back to our bed. It took only a moment to collect our things—one simple bundle. We walked briskly to the office; suddenly we were feeling the most energy either of us had felt in weeks! Tarasik was waiting for us at the door. Inside, we were greeted by an attractive, dark-haired young woman. "*Guten Morgen,*" she said. "My name is Hedi. I work for Frau Euler, and she asked me to come and escort you to Göppingen on the train."

"Where's Hanusia?" I asked.

Hedi smiled and assured us we would see her "soon"!

Hedi had the necessary tickets and documents. Mother's papers were examined. We couldn't understand the discussions Hedi had with the officials, but everything must have been in order, for the papers were stamped and returned to her.

Hedi then pulled us to a corner of the processing area and opened up a bag. Inside were clothes. With a grin, she proceeded to give a dress to mother, pants, a shirt, and shoes to my brother, and a skirt and shirt to me. They were used clothes, but they were much better than what we were wearing. I was glad to strip off the horrible green uniform and pull on a navy-blue knit polo shirt with red buttons at the neck. I later found out it was a boy's shirt, but at the time I didn't know the difference. It wouldn't have mattered, anyway. Once the new clothes were on, we were reminded that we still had to wear the blue-and-white armbands bearing the word "OST."

It was early afternoon when we were finally released into Hedi's custody. We walked down to the train station. "We will first stop in Göppingen," Hedi explained. Mother didn't understand, and I was only beginning to understand German words. Hedi was patient as she explained to me and I translated for mother. "You will see Hanusia. Then we will go on to Reichenau."

Why are we going to Reichenau? I wondered. We waited a couple of hours until a train arrived. Finally, we were going to see my sister. I couldn't wait!

The train ride was a delightful change from the cattle cars that had taken us to our camp. We sat facing one another on hardwood benches, Tarasik on Hedi's side, my mother and I on the other. We said nothing, but we smiled a lot at Hedi, communicating our deep feelings of gratefulness for this ray of sunshine that brightened our lives after so much darkness.

Outside, the sun was starting to set and its golden rays cast beautiful shadows across the lush green landscape. Passing by well-kept farms and orchards, it was difficult to remember that a war was raging. There were no airplanes and no evidence of troop movement. The only indication that all was not normal was the blackout imposed after sunset. Lights were not allowed to be on at night. The houses around us were pitch-black, as if deserted. Even within the train there were no lights, so most of the passengers dozed off and tried to sleep.

We rode on in darkness, the only light that of a flashlight carried by the conductor. A couple of hours into the trip, he stopped to check our papers, passports, and tickets. Hedi indicated we were to say nothing. The examination took time. The conductor seemed suspicious, perhaps wondering if we were spies or subversives who intended to bring harm to the Third Reich. Mother, my brother, and I sat still. How could anyone peceive us as a threat? As slaves, we had no rights. We had been ordered around and so intimidated through fear that none of us dared to give an official even a cross look. Anyway, we must have passed inspection, for the man finally returned the papers to Hedi and moved on.

At last, the passengers on the train stirred, reaching for bags and hats that had been put on the shelves above the seats. Many attempted to straighten their hair, which had become matted while sleeping. Hedi picked up the big envelope with our documents in it and put it into her briefcase. She looked official, assured of what she was doing. Our hearts beat faster with anticipation. I looked up at mother. "Are we going to see Hanusia now?" She just smiled a big, sweet smile and I knew this was Göppingen. My sister lived here, making it the most important town in all the world.

The wheels of the train screeched as they came to a stop. Conductors took their place at each exit of the wagon, holding out a helping hand to passengers who stepped down, one by one. Hedi led the way, followed by my brother, then me, and finally mother.

I hesitated at the top of the steps, gazing out over the platform. But it was too dark to see faces clearly. Once on the ground, I peered around people and tried to jump up to see. Mother spotted Hanusia first and picked me up so I could see her. Then we all hugged in an embrace that I wished would never end. Mother cried as we hugged, and Hanusia cried and could only say, "Mamo! Sistlitski!" Tarasik joined the huddle, and we were a family again.

We walked together about ten minutes to the Euler home. Hanusia explained that the Eulers owned a three-story building. They operated a photography shop on the first floor, and had living quarters on the second floor. Hanusia had a small room in the attic, and the third floor was rented to two old-maid sisters.

We entered through the front door and walked through a short hallway. To the right was a flight of stairs that seemed to never end. I had never seen so many steps, and a banister! Everything was polished wood. "I scrub this with steel wool every day," my sister explained. "All the wood must be kept polished."

At the top of the stairs to the right was a big, wide door. Frau Euler opened the door and held out her arm, inviting us to enter. After we went in, Hanusia introduced Frau Euler. We all shook hands politely, as was the custom in Germany, and Frau Euler said, *"Und das ist Uli und Wolfgang"* as she introduced her sons. We understood and smiled.

Frau Euler was a blue-eyed, red-cheeked, round-faced, corpulent lady with her hair permed close to her head. She was taller than my sister, and when she smiled, her front teeth protruded. Uli was exactly my age, seven, and Wolfgang was five. Both boys had jet-black hair and dark-brown eyes. (Hanusia told us later that the boys mostly resembled their father, Major Euler, who had French blood.) The boys stood looking at me. I looked back. None of us talked. Then Uli ran to the stairway, leaned across the banister, and slid down on his stomach to the first step. That looked like a lot of fun, and of course that was what he wanted to show this new girl who was watching in amazement. I couldn't wait for a chance to do the same trick. But Frau Euler scolded her son and told him to come back into the apartment immediately—at least, that's what it sounded like.

Inside the home, I felt like I was stepping on a cloud. This was my introduction to carpeting. The softness continued down the length of the hallway, from which you could go into the living areas. Immediately to the left was a formal dining room, which opened into a living room with several easy chairs and couches. The whole floor was covered with Persian rugs.

I felt like I had stepped into a fairy-tale setting. Everything was beautiful, soft, comfortable, and seemed to say, "Touch me!" After the severe deprivation of labor camp, this middle-class German home seemed to us like a castle for a czar. On the coffee table in the living room sat a bowl of succulent red apples. We had not seen a piece of fresh fruit in over a year. "Go ahead!" said Hanusia. I picked one up and nibbled at it, savoring the sweet flavor. Tarasik was not so shy. He devoured one, and over the course of the evening ate the rest of the apples in the bowl.

While Tarasik munched on the apples, I turned to gaze at a big, brown, stuffed woolly toy bear on wheels—big enough for children my age to sit on and ride. Looking at the boys, I said in my heart, *May I sit on the bear and ride him?* But I stood mute. Uli, however, must have read my mind. *"Hier, du kammst auch mal spielen.* Here, you can play," he said as he pushed the bear toward me. I straddled the soft animal and started pushing myself with my feet along the hallway. Such pleasure! This was happiness! How could anyone ask for more? My pleasure must have radiated over my face, for Hanusia and mother and Frau Euler watched and laughed and shared my joy.

As I rode up and down the hall, my sister slipped away. When she reappeared, she announced, "The bathwater is ready."

"Bathwater!" we exclaimed. We hadn't bathed in months. Only an occasional splashing from the faucets at the camp provided us with any semblance of cleanliness. Hanusia took my hand and led me into a small room. There I watched as a heavy stream of hot water was running into a huge container. *"Badewanne,"* said Frau Euler.

"Yes, we are going to take baths!" said Hanusia. I looked in disbelief at the strange white tub, the smaller basin nearby, and the toilet. I had never seen an indoor bathroom before. What an amazing setup!

Hanusia closed the door and helped me undress. Then I sat on the edge of the tub, dipped my foot in, and pulled it out again. My sister laughed. "It's better to get in quickly," she coached. I slipped into the water and felt the most soothing warmth envelop me. Hanusia sat on the edge of the tub and handed me a soft, pocket-like cloth that I had to slip over my hand. I didn't know what it was for. So Hanusia took it back and slipped it onto her hand, dipped it in the water, then rubbed soap on it and proceeded to wash me with it. The soap had a faint scent of lilac and instantly I was transported to our home and remembering the lilac bushes that gave off a rich aroma in the spring.

"Let me do it!" I laughed with delight and took the washcloth. Soon I was washing myself over and over again. What a heavenly experience! All the dirt and grime from the cattle trains and the camps seemed to slide off, and with it the pain and suffering we had endured over the past few months. I slid into the water until only my head showed, and soaked in the warmth. There was no hurry. I closed my eyes. I felt like sleeping. I opened them, and there was my sister.

"Finished?" she asked. She held up a large, heavy towel. I didn't want this experience to end, but I knew the others also needed to take a bath, so I stood up and stepped out of the tub and wrapped myself in the towel. It felt so soft and warm I could have worn it.

But there was another surprise. Hanusia reached down and pulled a plug in the bottom of the tub and the water ran off without effort. "Where is it going?" I cried.

"It is going down pipes and into a larger pipe under the street outside the house."

"What about mother and Tarasik? They'll want baths too!"

"It's okay, Sistlitski. They will bathe in clean water!"

Frau Euler knocked and entered. "Here, put these on," she said, handing me a two-piece outfit of soft flannel.

I had never seen clothes like this and looked at my sister for an explanation. "They're pajamas," she said. "Clothes to sleep in. Uli had an extra pair." The pajamas felt soft and warm.

Mother was now feeling the full effects of her ordeal. Frau Euler and my sister helped her to the bathtub. She was so weak she hardly had any strength to express her joy at our reunion. I could sense a despondency descending upon her. As she soaked in her bath, Frau Euler and Hanusia talked quietly.

"She isn't very strong," said Frau Euler.

"I'm worried about her. She's absolutely exhausted," my sister answered.

"I suggest that she stay with us for a few days. Let's see if she can regain her strength before she heads to Reichenau."

After our baths, there was a light meal, prepared by my sister, ready for us. It consisted of a homemade noodle called *spatzle* and goulash—heavenly food, compared to the ghastly snail soup at the camp. The excitement, though subdued, energized the table despite the late hour. Tarasik and Hanusia chattered away in Russian. The boys spoke excitedly at each other and to me in German. It was wonderful confusion. Then Frau Euler announced that it was time for Uli and Wolfgang to go to bed, and she marched them off down the hall. Hanusia picked up the dishes, put them in the kitchen sink, and started to wash them.

"How is my Hanusia doing?" mother asked, changing the tone of the evening. "What is your life like?"

"I have an incredible work load," she answered. "But it could be a lot worse. I have a place to live. The boys love me. I have food to eat."

"What do they have you do?"

"Everything. I clean house, wash and mend and iron the clothes, cook, wash dishes, and most important, look after the boys. Frau Euler manages the shop downstairs; you'll see it tomorrow. It's a long day for me, and the hard part is I never get a break. I work every day from 6:00 A.M. to midnight, seven days a week. Fortunately, I like the boys, and they like me. Sometimes we take walks and I tell them stories and we sing songs. . . ."

Mother sighed. Hanusia wiped her hands on a towel, then sat down at the table and took mother's hand. "Mamo, Frau Euler suggested that you stay here for a few days. You look so tired. You can rest here. Then Hedi will take you and Tarasik and Emotshka to Reichenau. It's in the very south of Germany, next to the town of Konstanz."

"I am so glad you got us out of that labor camp," my mother said, fighting tears. "I don't think I could have lasted much longer."

"I didn't do it, Mamo. I'm a slave. But Frau Euler has been happy with my work, and she made the arrangements. I have been called a Russian pig—not by Frau Euler; she doesn't agree with Hitler's philosophy. But I have no rights. The only reason I'm here is because Frau Euler's brother-in-law, Herr Hoffman, is a ranking Nazi official and has connections. He is the one who was able to get me out of the camp so I could come and work here. And he is the one who rescued you and Tarasik. Whenever someone is pulled out of a job, someone else must take his place. So when Herr Hoffman rescued us, he had to put some other Eastern Europeans in our places."

It took a moment for me to comprehend what my sister was saying. Someone else had taken mother's place—other people had replaced my brother and sister in the labor camp. We were out of that hell because others were now suffering in our place. I was grateful and yet horrified.

"What will I do in Reichenau?" mother asked.

"You will work at the Hitler Youth camp—Herr Hoffman is a teacher at the school there. I don't know for sure what they will have you do. Perhaps you will work in the kitchen, or maybe do cleaning. Maybe gardening. All I know is that it must be better than the factory. And you'll be safer. I don't think the war is as serious down there. It's near the Swiss border, and Switzerland is neutral. The enemy planes are careful not to go too close to the border."

"What do they do at this school? Who are these Hitler Youth?"

"I think it's like the *Komsomol* at home. Teenagers compete and are selected for special training to serve the Third Reich. They have camps all over the country. But this is a special school for the elite students."

The two kept talking, but I could no longer keep my eyes open. I was vaguely aware of Hanusia carrying me down the hall and laying me in a wonderful soft bed with sheets below and above me, and blankets tucked in around me. I felt I was in a warm cocoon, surrounded by love, and safe for a while from the horrors of war. Instantly I was sound asleep, and for the first time in weeks, I slept deeply, undisturbed by air-raid sirens.

I awoke the next morning to find my head buried in a soft feather pillow. Light was creeping in around the blackout curtains. I could hear activity in the house, but I lay still, warm in the most comfortable bed I had ever known. The door quietly opened and my sister slipped in and sat on my bed. Stroking my hair, she smiled.

"I've missed you," I said.

"I've missed you terribly," she answered. "I've looked forward to this for a long time."

"Why can't we stay here with you?"

There was a sympathetic look on her face. "I wish you could. But we must be grateful for what we have. There are people who don't have anyplace to stay, who have to live in those awful camps. This arrangement in Reichenau is the best we can do for now. We must make the best of it, and then someday we will be back together again."

"When? Will the war be over soon?"

"I don't know, Sistlitski. I don't know. We must be patient and take it a day at a time."

After a breakfast of soft warm pretzels with butter, we saw the photo shop downstairs. Within two big windows facing the street were posters displaying cameras and other equipment. In better times, the store sold all kinds of photographic equipment. But now, cameras were hard to get and business was slow. Frau Euler mostly sold film and spent time in a lab developing film and making prints.

Outside was a busy street filled with people on bicycles. Only occasionally did I see a car. Next door was another three-story building. On the bottom floor was a hat store for men. Like Frau Euler's store, this shop was low on merchandise. In contrast to our village back home, these buildings were built sturdily with cement walls. Some of the buildings had flower boxes filled with a colorful array of wildflowers mixed with geraniums.

I was intrigued by a peculiar building across the street. It had a tall cone that seemed to reach up to the puffy clouds in the sky. That was a church, my sister said. I wondered what a church was used for. At the base of the cone was a square tower with a huge clock on each of the four sides. Every fifteen minutes a chime would ring, so everyone in our neighborhood knew what time it was. The first time I heard the sound, it felt like someone was hitting us with a big bell. But I quickly got used to it. In the distance I could see another building my sister called a castle, surrounded by many old trees. "Göppingen is an old city," my sister explained. "At one time it had a wall surrounding it for protection from enemies. The castle was owned by the city's ruler. But now it's used for government offices."

That evening, Frau Euler had our family sit together on the living room couch for pictures. We huddled together, Tarasik with his hair still very short—it had been shaved in Fallersleben—and sitting uncomfortably in an old, woolen double-breasted jacket. Mother, Hanusia, and I sat next to him, laughing for joy at this wonderful moment.

There were also gifts. Our hostess brought out a box of clothing. They were hand-me-downs from Uli and other friends and relatives. The quality of the clothes was better than I could remember having at home. Mother received a dress that had been worn by Frau Euler's sister. It didn't fit well, but it covered the body. I received another warm skirt, a pair of boy's pants, and two sweaters. Best of all, I was given a dirndl dress—the traditional German outfit for girls. The dress had a white blouse with puffed sleeves. Over it went a light-blue jumper with two rows of gold buttons. It was laced with a dark-gold cord across the midriff. A matching apron tied at the waist completed the outfit. It was the prettiest dress I had ever seen and I couldn't wait to wear it.

Mother and Hanusia, between her chores, tried to talk, and when they weren't talking, they held hands, as though they didn't want to let go of each other. It was the first time we had really had extended conversation in Russian in months. Mother wanted to know more about Herr Hoffman, our unknown helper at Reichenau. "He's married to Frau Euler's sister," answered Hanusia. "I don't know if you will meet him or not. He has an important position in the Nazi party and he is an instructor at the school. He has six children, and the family lives in the town of Rotweil.

"Herr Hoffman is a decent man—I really don't think, in his heart, that he is a Nazi. But his wife is another matter. Her name is Ulla. She is a proud woman and wants nothing to do with workers from Eastern Europe. You must remember that we're slaves. We have no rights. Hitler has taught the Germans that they are the master race. We are considered inferior. I don't think everyone believes that, but Ulla certainly does."

"Do you know why they hate us?" mother asked.

"That's what they are taught. I don't understand it all, but I think they intend to build what they call a perfect race. People like Ulla believe they are superior to us." My sister chuckled cynically. "You should see her when she comes to visit with her six children—three boys, three girls, all the picture of German

excellence. The boys are blond and blue-eyed and wear tradi-
tional lederhosen. The girls have long braids and wear dirndl
dresses—Emotshka's dress used to belong to one of the girls.
They believe they are the ideal family, and Ulla is proud of that.
She brags about having shaken the hand of Hitler himself—the
way she tells it, one would think she had touched the hand of
God. So how could she possibly consider us simple people from
Russia as anything?

"The last time she was here, she dumped a ton of laundry on
the floor and ordered me to wash it. It looked like she had not
washed their clothes in weeks and was just waiting to get here so
she could have me do it. As if I don't have my hands full already!
But one doesn't argue. I had to go into the basement and scrub
the clothes by hand in a steaming kettle of soapy water. Then I
wrung them out and carried the wet clothes up four flights of
stairs to the roof, where I hung them to dry. And Ulla wouldn't
dream of helping. My mistress at least has compassion when she
sees me work like that. But Ulla considers herself above it all."

My sister also explained that the school we would work at in
Reichenau was once an institution for the mentally ill. "I understand that Hitler's pursuit of perfection was incompatible with
this institution. He emptied the buildings of all the patients and
converted the campus into a school for the best teenage students
in the land."

"What happened to the patients?"

Hanusia held up her hands and shrugged her shoulders.
"No one knows. Where did they go? Rumor is that they were
given 'medication.' Poof! End of problem. They just disappeared. How can you have a perfect race if you have imperfect
people? That's why we don't fit in either. After all, we have
'peasant blood' in our veins. We're good only as servants and
laborers." She shook her head as we tried to make sense of her
words. "I don't know what it all means. Their leader is a mad-
man."

We were in Göppingen for only a few days, but they were a
wonderful relief from the realities of war. Mother rested and was
somewhat revived. As I fell asleep for the last time in that soft
bed, I wondered when I would see Hanusia again. For a few
glorious days, we were a family. But the next morning, we would
board a train for Reichenau. I wanted to cry at the impending
separation; I wanted to laugh for joy for the time we had spent
together. My tired body couldn't comprehend it all, and I slept.

9

Rejection at Hitler Youth Camp

WINTER 1943-44

The scenery outside the train was greener, and there was progressively less evidence of the war as we traveled further south. In the distance, we could see cows grazing. The landscape looked so peaceful and was quite a contrast to the dilapidated labor camp and the destruction in several cities we had passed through.

I fingered the pouch that hung over my shoulder. It was a simple straw basket that Hedi had given to me as I boarded the train. Inside were two little dolls—one a boy and the other a girl. They were my silent friends in this latest trip into unknown suffering. Mother shut her eyes and rocked gently with the swaying train. She was extremely tired. A few days with my sister at Frau Euler's were not enough for her to recover her strength. I was sure she would not have lasted much longer in Fallersleben. But would it be any better where we were going?

Aside from the direction we were traveling, I had no idea where we were. We knew we were going to a youth facility of some kind, but we had no idea what kind of work would be required of us. After several hours, Hedi said we had to get off the train. She smiled and said we were in the community of Reichenau. At the station, we were met by a woman who walked with us the short distance to the school encampment. We entered the grounds and walked down a corridor of trees to a complex of buildings. One of them was apparently an administration building, and we were escorted in there. As we waited for someone to give us orders about what to do next, I looked around and noticed that this office, like the one in Fallersleben, was practical and functional. There were no frills or comforts. It consisted of a plain desk with drawers, a chair, several filing cabinets, and a typewriter. In the corner behind the door was a coatrack built into the wall. On it hung a heavy military coat.

A dour, papier-mâché-faced man wearing tiny round wire glasses and a green military uniform entered the office and reviewed mother's papers. He stamped a couple of them, and handed something to Hedi, who then said goodbye to us and left to begin her trip back to Göppingen. Then a woman in a shabby dress appeared. She introduced herself in Russian as Frau Lola Böshans. Her job was to interpret the German officer's instructions. (We learned later that she was a Jewish woman and she had a daughter named Luisa. We never learned how they got to be in Reichenau.)

First, Tarasik and my mother were given blue-and-white armbands with the word "OST" on them—identical to the ones we received at Fallersleben. "You are to wear this at all times," the dour man instructed us through Frau Böshans. "Slip them on right now, before you leave the building. It is forbidden for you to talk to German citizens unless they speak to you first. When you pass military officers, you are required to salute and say 'Heil Hitler!' like this." He lifted his right arm straight in front of him, then snapped it back down. "Understood?"

Nervously, we all nodded our heads, and the officer continued his instructions. My mother's job was to clean the classrooms, bathrooms, and other facilities in two of the buildings. Tarasik was instructed to report for work at the kitchen. We were forbidden to talk to other Russian prisoners of war. All questions were to be directed to Frau Böshans, who would show us our quarters and workplaces.

The officer carefully studied my brother, then instructed him through Frau Böshans, "You are not in any way to associate or make contact with German girls. You are never to date, flirt with, or even look at a girl. Do not violate this rule or . . ." the official made a slitting motion with his finger across his throat. "Understood?"

My brother nodded that he understood.

"Then sign this!" the official demanded. A document in German, supposedly repeating these regulations, was thrust in front of Tarasik. He signed silently and stepped aside.

Then we were dismissed, and Frau Böshans took us to building 7A, one of the many three-story cement buildings on the campus. I shuddered in the shadows of these cold and lifeless edifices. The interior of building 7A had cold cement walls. I had never been inside a building that sounded so hollow and felt so cold. We started walking up a narrow flight of stairs to the top floor, but mother had to stop halfway up the first flight. She leaned on the iron railing, trying to catch her breath and find the strength to keep going.

"Mamo, what's wrong?" I cried.

"It's OK, Dotshitshka," she replied, placing her hand on my shoulder. "My stomach doesn't feel good. But I'll be all right."

Slowly we continued up the stairs. On the top floor, we entered a large room that looked like an empty schoolroom, with the same cold, gray cement interior. In the middle of one long wall was a bed, unmade but with folded sheets and two army blankets on it. Next to the bed was a chair. Another smaller bed was against the opposite wall. That was all the furniture. I immediately walked over to the dormer window. There were bars across the glass—presumably to keep in the patients who formerly occupied the building. The view consisted of more dreary cement buildings. Cold stone. Hard cement. Iron bars. The message was unmistakable—we were prisoners, and had just replaced prisoners of a different kind.

Frau Böshans gave mother a small alarm clock and showed her how to use it. "You must get up by 5:00 every morning and begin work. Workers eat at 8:00 at the kitchen." A loud ticking filled the room as she set the clock on the windowsill.

Mother sat down on the bed and her head fell back as though she would fall asleep. Frau Böshans looked at her, then at me. She knelt down in front of me and looked into my eyes. "What is your name?" she asked.

"Emma," I whispered.

"How old are you?"

Shyly I looked at her, but said nothing.

"You poor thing. You look about six or seven, but you are so little and thin. This is no place for a child." She sighed. "I have a daughter. But she is closer to your brother's age. I don't know of any children you can play with, since it is forbidden..." she stopped in mid-sentence, then concluded, "We will have to see what we can do."

I liked this woman. It was nice to know someone cared in such a foreign and hostile environment. But she also had to do her job. Turning to mother again, she said, "I am sorry. I know how tired you are. But I need to show you a few other things so you can begin your work tomorrow." Mother pulled herself up from the bed and followed Frau Böshans as she led us down to the second floor, where there was a closet with a broom, a dustpan, a small hand broom, a pail with rags, a mop, and other cleaning items. There was also a clean gray-blue apron hanging on a hook.

"You must wear this while you work. A clean one will be issued each week," said Frau Böshans. She smiled at mother's confusion. "It is unthinkable to work in Germany without an apron," she explained. "Don't ever be caught without one. That is the rule."

Frau said that mother's daily duties were "to sweep, dust, and wet-mop the classrooms. Clean the bathrooms. And make sure everything is sparkling clean. You do not want to make one of the officials angry." It was discouraging to see how many rooms there were in this building, and to know that the next building was the same size. How was mother going to complete so much work every day?

The last stop on our introductory tour was the basement. "Here is where you come when the air-raid sirens sound," Frau Böshans explained. The basement looked spooky to me and I shuddered at the thought of having to go down there, especially in the dark at night.

Mother and I were then excused to go back to our room, while Tarasik went with our guide to the kitchen to learn his responsibilities. The next morning, he left early for his work. And despite feeling faint, mother forced herself to begin work immediately. Unlike the labor camp, there was no guard to awaken us and force the adults outside for roll call. It was tempting to stay in bed after the alarm rang. But that was risky, and even a thought like that was quickly dismissed. What would happen if mother didn't complete her work the way the school wanted her to? It was communicated in no uncertain terms that our masters would not tolerate any laziness.

Mother worked for two hours before we stopped to go to the kitchen for breakfast. I followed her as she went from room to room throughout the deserted building, sweeping and dusting. Each classroom had a slightly different look, depending on the subject taught. One had walls covered with maps—apparently for a geography class. In another were charts with many numbers. Another room had numerous books. I froze at the door of another classroom and refused to go in. "Mamo! What is that?" A chill ran up my back as I pointed.

"That's a skeleton, Dotshitshka. That's how students learn about human bones and the way we are made."

"We are made like that?" I asked.

"If someone stripped us of our skin and everything else, that is what we would look like."

"How awful," I mumbled, stepping back from the room.

"You can come in. It won't hurt you; it's not alive."

Slowly I walked in, but I couldn't take my eyes off this grotesque display propped upright on a narrow metal pole. In fact, it seemed to follow me in my mind when I left the room, especially when I found myself in dark places, or when I was walking up the stairway to our room.

After breakfast at their own cafeteria, the students marched into the building and occupied the classrooms. That's when mother cleaned the bathrooms and swept the halls and stairs. We moved to the building next door and did the same. When the classrooms emptied, she went in to clean them, then returned to our building to clean those rooms as well. It was long after dark before she finished.

The air raids were not as frequent at Reichenau, but they were just as frightening as the ones at Fallersleben. A blackout was in force at night. It was a strict rule: "Do not switch on a light, not even for a moment." We understood that disobeying this rule could get us and many others killed. So we went to bed almost immediately when we returned to our room, setting our clothing in a specific order on top of the chair so we could dress quickly in the dark in case the sirens sounded.

The gruesome sound made by air-raid sirens, *whoo, whoo, whoo,* sounded like the wind of a tornado. It immediately activated a trembling response in my body, as though I was experiencing chills from a high fever. We would dress quickly and feel our way in the dark down the stairs to the basement. I couldn't decide which was worse: being up above, in danger of falling bombs, or down below, in the creepy dark basement, where I was sure the skeleton lurked in the shadows. And if the building *was* hit by a bomb, we had heard that we could be buried under the rubble forever. Those thoughts draped a thick dread over me. While in the basement, we could hear the heavy drone of bomb-laden planes, but they must have had more important assignments than a Hitler Youth camp. The bombs fell on bridges, railroads, or factories around Friedrichshafen, a city on the other side of Lake Konstanz. No bombs were dropped on the compound at Reichenau, though we never knew when they might.

We soon learned the daily schedule of the students. During the day, they marched between classes, always very strict and disciplined. They all wore uniforms and appeared to be between the ages of fourteen and nineteen. The *Bund Deutscher Madchen*, the Hitler Youth girls (BDM), wore wool skirts, wool stockings, and flat shoes. On cold or rainy days, they wore gray wool coats.

In warmer weather, the boys often marched wearing shorts and brown shirts with ties and carrying flags. As they marched, they always sang. As I watched them and listened to their marching songs, I gradually began to understand the words they sang:

> *Ich hatte einen kammeraden . . .*
> I once had a close comrade
> You couldn't find a better friend.
> The drum called to battle
> He walked by my side
> To the beat, stride by stride.
>
> A bullet came flying
> Aimed at me or aimed at him?
> It tore him away
> He now lies at my feet
> As if he were a part of myself.

Another popular army marching song went:

> *Es war ein Edelweiss . . .*
> *Ein schoenes Edelweiss . . .*

It was a lighthearted marching song about a flower, edelweiss, which grows in the Austrian Alps. I learned that the small, white daisy-like flower was considered a trophy to mountain climbers.

At Reichenau, there were special days for parades. On April 20, Hitler's birthday, flags were everywhere. Normally, large Nazi banners always draped the camp theater and the homes of officials. But on this day, there were flags on every building. There was a parade, speeches were given, and tributes were made to the "great Fuhrer." The students were reminded of the greatness of their cause. There was news about successful bombings and victories over the enemies. Listeners were urged to work hard and thus share in the joy of celebration when the great war was won.

Much of what was said was hard for me to understand, but I absorbed the spirit of the school. I quickly realized that to the German women, the greatest sin was laziness. The women rose early, swept the streets, watered plants, and hand-washed their laundry—even their sheets and blankets. They dragged large rugs outside, hung them over a fence or a railing, and pounded on the rugs with a paddle to loosen all the dust. Everyone was required to work.

Posters around the compound urged the young Germans to work hard: "ARBEIT MACHT DAS LEBEN SUSS," which meant, "Work makes life sweet" and "DIE RADER MUSSEN ROLLEN FUR DEN SIEG," which meant, "The wheels must roll to victory."

Besides the exhortation to work, there were constant reminders of the war and how each must do his or her part for the cause. One poster was particularly scary: It portrayed a solid black background and an outline of a man wearing a hat and cape. The only color was two yellow, slit-shaped eyes. This shadowy figure leaned to one side, as though listening, and the words in bold letters warned: "PSST . . . FEINDT HORT MIT," or, "Psst . . . the enemy is listening."

These warnings made me afraid to be alone in dark places, particularly on the stairs of building 7A. I ran as quickly as possible up or down the stairs, taking the steps two or three at a time. I was sure that the skeleton was lurking somewhere in the shadows, waiting for a chance to reach out its bony hand and snatch a helpless child. I would arrive at the top floor breathless and mother would ask me, "What in the world is the matter with you? You look like someone is chasing you." I would just look at her quietly, unable to voice my fears, but comforted by her presence.

One day while running down the stairs, I almost ran over a little boy playing on the steps. I stopped and looked at him. I could tell he was younger than me, perhaps by two years. He had jet-black curly hair and eyes so dark they almost looked like ink. The door behind him was open slightly, and I could see a woman in quarters similar to ours. She looked at me, then opened the door wider and asked me my name.

"Emmi," I answered. My proper name is Emma, but the German people called me Emmi. Since I didn't speak German well enough to object, that name stuck. Besides, it sounded more loving to me than just plain Emma. I knew of no one my age whose name was Emma—for some reason, that sounded to me like a name for an old maid.

The woman pointed to the little boy and said, "This is my son Gunther."

Shyly I smiled. His presence helped relieve my fear of the steps. At least now there was another human being around, and I forgot about the imaginary ghosts. Over the next few days, Gunther and I became friends. I learned later from my mother that the woman was Frau Schirach. Since Gunther was not allowed to stray far from the building, we spent most of our time playing on the steps, in a hallway when there were no classes, or right in front of the building.

One day I happened upon Gunther when he was outside riding a two-wheel bicycle. Although many people rode bicycles around the compound, I had never seen one up close. I watched my friend get on it. Because it was an adult's bike, he was too small to use the seat. So he merely straddled the bike, standing on the pedals. Off he went past me, guiding the bike while standing up. Then he would quickly jump off before it was moving too fast, bring it to a stop, and start all over again. It seemed like so much fun. I studied his every move, craving the chance to try it myself.

Finally, I got the courage to ask, "Can I ride it?" Gunther took a couple more short runs, then quietly he said, "There, you can have a turn."

My heart was pounding. I had watched Gunther closely; surely I could do it, too. Trembling with excitement, I grabbed the handles and did exactly the same thing he had done. At once the wheels started rolling and I was standing on the pedals, rolling faster and faster. I had no idea how to stop! And I was too afraid to jump off. I felt panic. Where was this bicycle taking me? The answer came with a thud as I toppled headfirst into a ditch.

For a moment I was disoriented. I opened my eyes and stared at the sky. Then I scrambled to my feet and realized I wasn't hurt. Brushing myself off, I felt something wrong with my outfit—I was wearing the dirndl dress Frau Euler had given me. I looked down and saw that it was torn from the top to my waist. Apparently it had gotten caught on the bike and ripped. The prettiest dress I had ever had was ruined. Immediately I started sobbing. Gunther peered into the ditch, but I ignored him, scrambled out, and went running back into the building to find mother. What would she say? Would she be angry?

When mother saw me crying, she dropped her mop and wrapped her arms around me to comfort me. There were no harsh words, only empathy. "I'm so sorry, Dotshitshka. What happened? What a terrible accident. Are you hurt anywhere?" There was no physical hurt, but if a torn dress could bruise a little girl, my ruined dirndl did. Mother did her best to mend the tear, but it was never again the pretty dress I loved.

One day I went downstairs to see Gunther. The door to the Schirach's quarters was open all the way. I peeked in and found the room empty. There was no evidence they had ever been there. I went running to my mother with the news.

"Mamo, they are gone! Our friends are gone."

Mother smiled, then showed a look of concern. "Frau Schirach whispered to me recently that they would leave soon. I hope they make it."

"Make it to where?" I asked.

"I don't know. It is better not to know."

"Why didn't Gunther say goodbye to me? Will they come back? Will I see them again?" I started to cry.

Mother reached out and pulled me to her as she said, "I don't think we will see them again. I'm sorry Gunther didn't say goodbye. He probably didn't know what was happening until the moment they left. They were in a hurry. I'm sure he probably wanted to say goodbye to you, but his mother had to catch a train."

There was a pain in my stomach. In just a short time, Gunther had become a friend. Though we talked little, we shared a common situation, and that bonded us in a way I hadn't expected. Somehow we understood each other. Now my first real friend was gone, and I felt an intense loneliness. While in bed that night, I wished I had never met him—the pain of losing a friend was worse than not having one at all.

There had always been a mystery about this woman and her son Gunther. I never asked questions; I knew that it was too dangerous to ask. If someone volunteered to tell about himself, that was fine. If not, that was fine, too. But deep down, I wondered if Frau Schirach and Gunther might have been related to a German official. They were certainly Jewish, and someone was obviously looking out for them. Only much later, with the perspective of history, did I realize that the Schirachs had probably escaped the country with the help of covert sympathizers. Of course, we never knew for sure. Perhaps they had been discovered...

Without my friend, I roamed alone through the school grounds. I walked down a curved road into the central part of the campus. Strolling along, I took my time and looked into the windows of the basements as I passed by the buildings. They were all similar to the ones where mother worked. At one building I stopped and cautiously peeked in. Between the iron bars I could see men who were wearing prison uniforms like the ones we had worn in Fallersleben. They were working at long tables repairing shoes, and in the corner I saw an armed guard keeping an eye on them. I had heard about them from my brother. They were Russian prisoners of war who were doing slave labor for German Hitler youth and staff.

The window behind the bars was open, and one of the men saw me. "Hello, fellow Russian," he said with a big smile. I stared at the speaker, but was afraid to say anything back. We had been told not to speak with prisoners of war. But I felt sad. The men seemed so lonely, locked and isolated behind those small, barred windows.

* * *

Mother worked only a few weeks in building 7A and its neighbor. She was then reassigned to work in the large kitchen that prepared food for the students, faculty, and Nazi leaders. Her job was to peel potatoes and apples, chop onions and other vegetables, sweep the floor, wash dishes, scrub pots, and clean the stoves and ovens. Sometimes she was assigned a temporary job in another building, but she always reported back to the kitchen.

Tarasik was a pickup and errand boy for the school. He would take as many as a hundred loaves of bread at a time, load them onto a wagon that he pulled behind a broken-down old bike, and deliver them to various buildings on the campus. The students ate at various locations, and all the food had to be transported from the kitchen. Tarasik also unloaded delivery trucks and generally helped move things. When he wasn't too busy, he was also used for other various assignments, such as delivering messages or repairing windows.

Tarasik was quite skinny and most of the time his work was too strenuous for him. Yet he quietly tackled every job. He kept to himself, saying little and doing what he was told. One day, he was ordered to go outside and crank up a car for one of the school officials. He did so, and passed out from the exertion. Someone came running back to where we were eating our noon meal and announced that a Russian boy had fainted. My heart was pounding as I ran to the window to see someone leaning over my brother and reviving him. He finally stood up, embarrassed and pale, and smiled but said nothing.

My mother and brother worked every day without a break. The grind wore my mother down, and at night, when I asked if she was OK, she often had a slight headache or pain in her stomach. She wrote short letters to my sister, and mentioned several times that she was finding it increasingly difficult to fulfill her duties. One morning, she simply couldn't force herself out of bed.

"Please go tell Miss Stortz that I am not feeling well today," she said. I walked down to the kitchen and told Miss Stortz, the woman in charge, that my mother was sick. At first she grunted and muttered something about how she would get her work done. But then she pointed to some food and instructed me to take it back to mother.

Frau Böshans came by later that day. "This is very dangerous," she soberly warned my mother. "The rule here is that every job must be done, and every task is assigned to a specific person. If you can't do it, someone must take your place and perform your duty. The Nazi officials must not find out about your condition. They care less about a person's health; they just want things done. They are not sympathetic; they will make you work no matter how you feel."

The next day, mother returned to work and tried to complete her tasks. But her body wasn't strong enough, and she faltered through her chores. By this time, my sister had been able to take action on behalf of mother. Hanusia totally surprised us by showing up at our room late one afternoon. Happily we embraced her in a wonderful reunion hug.

"I'm here to give you a break, Mamo!" she announced. "Frau Euler and I talked about your health. She said I have been a good and faithful worker, and I have never had a vacation, or so much as a day off. She made arrangements through her brother-in-law and I am here for two weeks. I will work in your place while you rest and get well."

Mother wept and hugged her daughter again. Just having her here was an encouragement!

Hanusia was assigned the task of washing windows with a short, stout, blond Russian lady named Aksiuta, a bouncy, fast worker with a happy attitude. I made sure that mother got her meals; each day I went and picked up the food from Miss Stortz and carried it back to mother. Then I hung around my sister and Aksiuta.

One evening, my sister commented about her working partner. "Her attitude will carry her through tough times," she told me. "Remember that, little sister. If you are droopy and down and sour, it will be harder to survive. But if you will yourself to have a good attitude, it will give you strength and help you survive."

"Our Mamo has a good attitude," I noted.

"Yes, she does. But her body is weak. She has worked hard for many years without any rest. I am hoping that two weeks of rest will revive her."

Mother's health did improve dramatically and when she returned to work, she was assigned to clean the bakery, a building near our living quarters on the south side of the compound.

One day as mother opened the door to the broom closet and put on her apron for work, a young Russian man cracked open the door at the opposite end of the corridor and smiled at her. It was obvious that he was a prisoner of war, so of course, we were not allowed to talk with him. But he knew that she was Russian, too, and they communicated with a smile or nod once or twice a day whenever no one else was looking. It was dangerous, for we were forbidden even to smile at each other.

A couple of days after the first glimpse of this man, mother went to the closet to get her coat at the end of the day and found something jammed inside her sleeve. When she investigated, she discovered a sack of hard-boiled eggs. What a surprise! How in the world did they get there? A few days later, a loaf of bread was in the other sleeve. Mother remembered that smile and guessed instantly where the food was coming from. These gifts were a critical supplement to our meager diet. We were greatly encouraged to know that someone cared for us and was willing to take such a big risk to help. The next time mother caught sight of him, she acknowledged the gifts by stroking her stomach with a smile.

Despite the amount of work mother did in the kitchen or bakery, we still had barely enough to eat. However, the food was more substantial than it was at the camp in Fallersleben. We ate potatoes and vegetables that were grown at a nearby garden that helped support the compound. We also received a piece of bread and a pat of butter, usually at breakfast. That was my favorite food. However, there were no snacks between meals.

By hanging around the kitchen and hearing the people talk, I absorbed more and more of the German language. Often as my mother worked, I sat on the front step and played with the two little dolls in the straw bag Hedi had given to me. One day, two German girls about my age approached. Apparently they weren't aware or afraid of the regulations about talking to foreigners, or perhaps they thought I was German. Shyly they came toward me, staring at my dolls.

One of the girls finally pointed and asked, "*Wie heissen deine puppen?* What are your dolls' names?"

She expected me to answer like a German child would, by stating their names. I understood their question, but I did not yet know how to converse properly in German. I thought for a moment, then answered with words I knew: "*Das ist grossvater,*" I said, pointing to the boy doll. "*Und gross mutter,*" I added, pointing to the girl doll. "Grandmother and grandfather."

They looked at each other and started to giggle. "You're funny!" said one girl.

"The way you talk," said the other. "It's funny."

Embarrassed and uneasy, I smiled but said no more. But something clicked in me: I thought maybe they were amused not because of what I said, but because I *was* funny. They smiled back and hung around for a couple of minutes, then went on their way. But already I felt some kinship with them. They were about my age, and I wanted to see them again.

They came by the next day and said hello. Then I found out their names: One was Christa, a dark-haired girl. The other was Anne Marie, a reddish-blond girl with freckles across her nose and cheeks. They both had long braids. All the German girls seemed to have braids, and I wanted to look the same way. How I wished that those people at Fallersleben hadn't cut off my hair! Then I would have been able to braid my hair like these girls did, and they would not have thought I was funny or different.

The girls came by often to visit and talk to me. Conversation in German quickly became easier and fun. One day, Christa invited me to follow her to her home, which was a house only a couple of buildings away from the kitchen. Her parents were gone. She took me into her room and there I gazed at the most wonderful assortment of toys. There were dolls with changes of clothes, a little doll buggy, and other playthings. I had hardly ever seen so many toys. How could a child choose what to play with? I was overwhelmed with awe. Christa invited me to play there again, and I enjoyed playing with her and Anne Marie.

But one day my friendship with Christa and Anne Marie came to a sudden stop. They didn't come by to chat and giggle with me anymore. I often walked by Christa's house slowly, hoping to be invited back in if she saw me. One time I saw her peer out the window at me, then close the curtain.

What was wrong? What had I done? Didn't they like me anymore? Apparently Christa's parents objected and cut off the relationship for political reasons. The feelings of rejection that I had felt when Gunther left without saying goodbye returned. I hated the pain, but there was nothing I could do to make it go away. It lodged tightly in my chest, as though I had swallowed a rock.

Next door to Christa's house lived Herr Krieger, my brother's supervisor, with his wife, daughter, and parents. One morning after it had snowed, I walked by the house and saw Grandfather Krieger pulling a sled. On the sled was a cute little blue-eyed girl who looked about three or four years old. "Would you like to ride on the sled with Siegrun?" he asked. I joyfully climbed aboard, and we had a fun ride.

On several other occasions when grandfather and grand-daughter took a walk, they invited me to walk with them. Siegrun and I enjoyed being together, though she was quiet and shy. So most of the time we walked together in silence. Then one day, with no announcement or explanation, the walks stopped.

Later it became apparent to me by the man's tense and sad face that someone had warned him about associating with a low-life Russian girl. Nazi orders were the same for every German—do not mix with slave workers. He could no longer risk my presence, or his family would face harsh consequences.

Again, I felt the pain in my chest and my stomach. I couldn't eat. What was wrong with me taking a walk with an old man and his granddaughter? I couldn't understand. It didn't make sense.

Frau Böshans was one person who wasn't afraid to help me. I could feel her love. "You should be in school," she said to me one day. "What a waste of time for a young child like you to roam aimlessly, killing the day." Despite the restrictions on foreigners, somehow she managed to persuade people in charge of the local school to enter me in kindergarten. Reichenau was such a small community that the school was only a short distance away, and Frau Böshans took me by the hand and walked me there the first morning.

As soon as I walked into the classroom, I knew I had entered heaven. The room had little tables and chairs for about fifteen children. On one side, coats were hung neatly on wooden hangers that were decorated with colorful paintings of German flowers—enzian and edelweiss. The backs of the chairs were also painted with scenes from fairy tales. One wall was covered with pictures—some drawn by students, others taken from magazines. Another wall had a blackboard, and above it was a beautifully scripted alphabet. I had never been near a school, and I was overwhelmed by the new building, new language, new everything. It was mind-boggling. I was thrilled and excited and loved it all, and was eager to learn everything possible. Being here gave me a feeling of warmth and a sense of finally belonging and being included.

After enduring so many winter days with nothing to occupy my mind and attention, school was a feast for my senses. A beautiful woman in a red-and-white dirndl outfit told us stories. We drew pictures. We sang songs. We played games—sometimes in the classroom, sometimes outdoors. I found I had learned a lot of German just by listening to people, and I was already quite proficient. So I understood and learned easily and mingled well with the other children, most of whom were a year younger than me.

One day the pretty lady led the class into the courtyard of a building where my mother was cleaning that day. We played a game where we held hands in a circle around a single child who was the princess, then danced around her as we sang a song. I searched the windows, hoping to see my mother looking out and watching me. Then it was my turn—I was the princess in the middle! As my classmates danced around me, my only thought was, *Can mother see me? I got to be a princess for a moment. Oh, how I hope that she can see me through the window!* All this while, the children sang, *"Dornroeschen war ein schoenes kind, schoenes kind, schoenes kind.* Sleeping Beauty was a beautiful child, beautiful child, beautiful child."

I could not wait to ask mother that night if she had seen me from the window. She smiled and said, "I watched you from the far window on the second floor. My Dotshitshka was standing in the middle, and the children were dancing around her!" How happy I was that night!

There were also some confusing moments during school. One day the teacher asked me, "Emmi, when is your birthday?"

I looked at her with a blank expression. *What is a birthday?* I thought to myself.

"That's the day when you were born," the teacher said. I still did not understand. "We're celebrating Ilsa's birthday tomorrow. Why don't you ask your mother when your birthday is so we can also do something special for you."

This was the first time I had ever heard about birthdays. I had no idea what one was, or if I even had one. But there was one way to find out. That night as we were preparing for bed, I asked mother, "Mamo, do I have a birthday?"

She chuckled and answered, "Of course you do, Dotshitshka! You wouldn't be here if you didn't have a birthday."

Obviously, I hadn't thought too deeply about when and how I was born. "When is my birthday?" I asked.

"You were born on February 25, 1936."

The next morning I walked up to my teacher and told her the good news. A few days later, she handed me a beautiful, thick white candle covered with red ladybugs. All the children joined in song: *"Wer hat denn heute Geburtstag. Die Emmi hat Geburtstag. Fa la la la la!* Whose birthday is it today? It's Emmi's birthday!" It felt special to have everyone sing to me.

A few days later, a woman came into the classroom and spoke quietly to the teacher. The woman glanced at me a couple of times, and I felt uncomfortable. My teacher was clearly disturbed. The woman left the classroom and a few moments later, as we busily drew pictures, the teacher gently touched my shoulder and motioned for me to follow her. We stood outside the classroom door, and she looked down at me with sad eyes. "I'm very sorry, Emmi, but you can't be with us anymore."

It took a moment for the news to register. No, this couldn't be! I loved it here. I was a good student. There was so much to learn. I just couldn't stop now!

The teacher knelt and looked into my eyes, now filling with tears. "I know you like school. You're a smart little girl. But one of the parents said you shouldn't be here. She says you are not German, and insists that we follow Hitler's policy that foreigners not mix with Germans. I'm very sorry, but there is nothing I can do. It's too dangerous. . . ."

I felt as if someone had stabbed me in the heart. Though there was no physical reason to hurt, I had never felt such pain. I couldn't understand why I wasn't wanted. I got along well with the other students. Why didn't the parents like me? The teacher was at a loss for words. All she could do was pat my head, then take my hand and lead me out of the building. I walked slowly down the steps, then started running. I ran past a group of officers but didn't stop to salute. I dashed past students, tears now blinding my eyes. When I reached our building, I tore up the stairs, burst into our room, slammed the door, and fell on the bed and cried. When I couldn't cry any more, I fell asleep. But when I awoke the pain was still there. The hurt wouldn't go away.

Nothing could have made me feel more rejected. I could not understand what made me different from other children. Why didn't they like me? I wanted to be friends with people; why wouldn't they let me?

That night mother and I had a long, heart-to-heart talk. She cried with me; I think the news hurt her even more than it did me. "My little girl," she said over and over, holding me and rocking me as I cried in her arms. Of course, she understood. Rejection belted us from all sides, from our own people, from German officials, and now from strangers who would impose their prejudice upon children.

"Dotshitshka, these people don't know what they are doing," my mother said as I cried in her arms. "Wartime makes them do things that they might not do when there is peace. We just have to wait. Someday it will be better." At that moment, I couldn't imagine our circumstances getting better. Besides suffering from the pain of this rejection, I suddenly felt again the previous ones—Gunther, Christa and Anne Marie, the Kriegers. Combined, they crushed me until I felt I couldn't stand to live. It didn't matter what their reasons were. No explanations could alleviate the pain.

I didn't understand hatred and discrimination, but I sure felt it. I'm sure it would have been easier if someone had hit me. At least that pain would eventually die away. The pain of rejection didn't. It was still there the next morning when I got up, and the morning after that.

The only time I felt better was when mother would cuddle me. She tried to express hope. "It will be better someday," she said often. I don't know how much she really believed it. I know that the hurt stayed with me for a long, long time, like an oozing wound. It left an invisible scar deep within me that would turn to deep-seated resentment as I grew older.

10

Friends Among Enemies

1944

Once again I was left alone. Usually I went with my mother to the kitchen. Then while she worked, I roamed the campus. There were no playgrounds; no places for a child to stay busy. When weather permitted, I would wander into a meadow next to the kitchen. It led up a hill into a cemetery. I never met any people there, yet I could still see the kitchen where mother worked, so I didn't feel totally alone. It was such a peaceful place and reminded me of the outdoors I had enjoyed back home. The grass was perfectly groomed. Pansies were popping up all around, and other flowers were carefully placed by some of the gravestones.

Sometimes I wondered about who was buried here. My sister had speculated that these were the former patients of the asylum that was now the school—the mentally ill. Hitler had simply eliminated them. I shuddered to think of the cruelty. But I didn't mind being there. I had something in common with these people. I, too, had suffered under Hitler's cruel edicts. Only now they had found peace. They were no longer suffering. And for a few moments, standing in their midst, I was also at peace.

I wandered through the labyrinth of walkways and neatly trimmed bushes, letting the outdoors soothe some of the sting of rejection. Birds sang, as though ignorant of the horrible fighting going on to the north and the sufferings of refugees and slaves and prisoners of war. I sat on a gravestone and felt the sun warm my face, and remembered that feeling on the step of my house in Ukraine. What had I felt then? Loved. I knew I was loved. Yes, my mother loved me, but there was something even more. I sensed the love of another, someone out there whom I could not name. He let the sun shine and warm me to let me know that someone loved me when I was all alone. Maybe someday I would meet the source of that love. Before heading back, I knelt down and picked some field flowers to take to mother.

Some nights later there was a light knock on our door. It startled us, for apart from Frau Böshans, we never had visitors. Tarasik opened it, and there stood a pretty girl in her pajamas, beaming as she said in German, "My name is Dolly. May I come in?"

Of course we let her in. We were too conditioned to obey every command or request by a German. However, we could tell she was one of the students on campus, and we knew the rules about fraternizing with them. We stood awkwardly for a moment. Dolly giggled. Tarasik mumbled, "Are you supposed to be here?"

"I just wanted to meet you!" she answered. "I sneaked out of my dorm. No one saw me."

Tarasik blushed, flattered by the attention, and also scared by the implications. If this was discovered, wouldn't he be blamed? They could execute him. Yet there was also a vicarious thrill at this brief rendezvous.

"Why?" my brother wanted to know.

"I saw you yesterday during dinner." She giggled again. "I have been noticing you for some time."

Tarasik didn't know what to say. I snuggled next to mother. She didn't understand what was happening. There was a certain curious horror to this encounter. We didn't want it, yet we couldn't avoid it. She was such a cute, friendly, naive-acting young girl.

My brother finally broke the awkward silence. "Do you know we are from Russia?" Tarasik's German was improving, but his accent was still evident.

"I know," Dolly answered coyly. "I have never met a boy from Russia. But now I have!" She proceeded to tell us about her background. "I'm from Hamburg. My parents live there, and my brother. My father runs a big factory. I was the only one in my school chosen to come here. This is my second year in Reichenau."

She smiled again, then said, "I had better go now, before I'm missed. Maybe I'll pop in again sometime." With that, she slipped out the door. I was tempted to pull up the shade and watch her leave the building, but it was dark outside. Deep inside, all of us were frozen with fear by this encounter. What did it mean? Was that girl genuinely attracted to my seventeen-year-old brother? Or simply curious? Or was she acting on a childish dare, uncaring of the terrible danger she could place us in? She obviously had a big crush on my brother—it was written all over her face as she gazed at him.

Dolly visited again a few nights later. The scene was repeated two or three more times. Tarasik was both terrified by the visits and flattered by Dolly's interest. The visits were always after curfew and lasted just a short time with only a few kind words exchanged. Maybe this young girl was rebelling in her own way against the oppressive regimen she faced each day. Maybe she had to find out for herself that we were real people, no different from Germans. Unfortunately, we never could learn more, for the rules were strict and the dangers too great for more frequent and lengthier contacts.

The last time Dolly visited, she handed my brother a slip of paper. "This is my home address. If there is an opportunity after the war . . . I mean, after things change, please come and visit me." Shortly after that, she left the youth camp. We never learned why. Could it be that a friend may have tattled on her?

* * *

Frau Böshans was always a special friend to us. She encouraged me to call her Aunt Lola. Even as well as we got to know her, there was a mystery about her. Was she Russian? Or was she German? She had a teenage daughter who also worked on the premises. She and her girlfriend took a liking to my brother, casting glances at him and trying to make contact with him by flirting and teasing.

Once Frau Böshans told me to get dressed in my warmest clothes and we walked to the town of Konstanz—about three or four miles. In the downtown area, there was a whole row of neatly decorated shops. My face pressed against the glass of each store. A few were closed and empty, but others were filled with many different products. I had never seen such stores before, with clothing, shoes, flowers, books—all kinds of merchandise.

"This isn't like it used to be before the war," said Frau Böshans. "Then, the shelves were full. You could get almost anything you wanted. But now, it is hard to find things. The only reason these stores have so much is because we are near the Swiss border and so many of these items come from Switzerland."

I listened as my eyes took in the wonders of the stores, not really comprehending her explanation. I didn't understand what Switzerland was, and why it could produce such things and Germany could not. But that didn't matter to this eight-year-old child. Frau Böshans took my hand and led me into a department store. It was filled with wondrous things—dolls and figurines and china cups and beer steins and jewelry. She led me to a little glass case filled with a display of colored objects made of a plastic-like material. They appeared crafted to capture a child's eyes—birds, kittens, bugs with colored stones for eyes.

"They're pins," she said. "You can put them on your coat and wear them as a decoration. Which one would you like?"

Carefully I examined all the pins in front of me. I pointed to one that looked like a little Scottie—a cute little dog. There was a painted eye on it, and a red collar around the neck. Frau Böshans asked the clerk to take it out and she proceeded to pay for it and pin it on the lapel of my coat. "It lights up in the dark," the clerk said. She cupped her hands over it and had me peek in so I could see that it indeed glowed in the dark. I loved it and couldn't wait to get back and show it to my mother. I was proud of that little pin, which was noticed by others, and, for the first time ever, I heard people make compliments about something I owned.

We continued to wander around the shopping square, just looking at and admiring everything. We stopped at a fun house that featured several mirrors. We laughed together as we made ourselves fat, then skinny, and other funny shapes depending on the mirror. Then we walked over to another building and Frau Böshans went up to a little booth and bought two tickets. I took her hand and followed her into a dark auditorium. I was a little scared because I couldn't see where we were going; I didn't know where she was taking me.

We sat down in a row of chairs and soon I found myself laughing in wonder. In front of me a picture moved across the wall, and there was music and speaking. This was my introduction to movies. It was like another world of magic coming to life before my eyes. It was a most memorable day for a little girl who had grown up without a single toy, who had been forced to stay in bed during the winters, and who now had to spend most of her days roaming the grounds of a community alone. I would always hold a special place in my heart for Frau Böshans.

About the time that I felt like I could never have another friend, I met another German girl. My brother was frequently sent to a greenhouse to pick up vegetables, lettuce, and other foodstuffs for the kitchen. The man who operated the greenhouse had a daughter named Ruth. She had dark hair, a dark complexion, and was about my age. Ruth never made me feel like I was a foreigner or different from her. She never seemed concerned about being seen with me. Why, I don't know, but perhaps it was because her parents weren't concerned. Still, I was more cautious about this friendship, wary of getting too close and then experiencing rejection again.

One day Ruth took me to the community dump, which was at the far edge of Reichenau. We climbed the pile of rubbish looking for things we could play with. I found two tiny beer steins that were meant for a dollhouse and took them back to our room. In order to try and occupy another day, I went back to the dump on my own. I took my time rummaging through the messy heap and found a tiny tin cup with a handle on the side. It looked like a toy; maybe it had belonged to a little girl for her doll. I picked it up and put it in my pocket. That night, mother washed it out and with a gleam in her eye, told me to close my eyes for a moment. "We are going to play a game of hide-and-seek!" she told me. "But it won't be the regular way. We'll hide and seek this little cup."

This was going to be fun! Mother hid the cup in the bed and told me to open my eyes and find it. I looked all over and found it tucked underneath the pillow. We laughed and she hid it again. We repeated the game several times, until finally I couldn't find the cup. I searched all over the bed. I climbed under the bed—it wasn't there. I looked inside the pillow—it wasn't there. I looked in her hair—it wasn't there. Mother laughed and pointed and said, "It's at the very tip." I looked in the direction where her finger was pointing but couldn't find the cup. "It's at the very, very tip!" she said again, emphasizing "very" by pointing up at the ceiling. I looked even harder, and soon she was laughing and shaking so hard she had tears in her eyes. "It's at the very, *very* tip," she repeated. I scoured every inch of the bed and searched and pawed all over my mother. She was laughing so hard she had to lie down. Then she held her hand up in front of my face. There, on the tip of her ring finger, was the cup! I had been looking in the direction where she pointed, not at her fingers. I laughed and snuggled next to her. Years later, mother or I would often say, "It's at the very tip," recalling a brief but intensely happy memory in the midst of war.

Our game was a rare moment of joy and it seemed to further soothe the pain of rejection. We really had only each other. Each night, after we were in our nightshirts and lying in bed, we would share an intimate moment. Sometimes my mother would let me undo her pinned-up black hair and comb it, then practice braiding it in a new hairdo. Another night, she made a paper clock and taught me how to tell time by moving the hands on the numbers and asking me what time it was. Sometimes she would lightly scratch my back until I fell asleep. These were our simple moments of pleasure, our escape from a dreary life. It didn't take much to make us happy. Just each other, and sometimes a little possession, such as a tiny, discarded, thimble-sized tin cup.

Tarasik, now eighteen, had been given a room of his own next to us. He didn't like being indoors and frequently spent his free time sitting on the steps in front of the building after work, watching people go by and wondering about our future.

Most days, I either sat on the steps in front of mother's workplace or wandered around wherever I wanted to investigate, though never too far away from mother. I always made it back in time to eat with her. It was critical to show up for mealtimes because there was no other resource for food. The workers were allowed to eat after the main meal was served to the students and faculty. Yet the food was so different from how mother fixed food for us, and I found it impossible to eat everything I was served.

Eventually, ugly red sores broke out on my hands, especially on and between my fingers. The sores filled up with pus, itched, and looked awful. One day, one of the kitchen staff took me to another building where she had contacted a nurse. There, in a small clinic, a pleasant young lady with red hair and thick glasses examined my hands. Tenderly she turned them over, then put them in a basin of water and gently washed them. From her cabinet she brought out a jar of ointment and smeared some on each sore. Then she unwrapped some gauze and carefully wrapped it around my hands and fingers. She smiled at me and ordered me to open my mouth. I obeyed, and she popped a large white tablet on my tongue. It had a delicious, sour taste that I liked. It dissolved quickly and I swallowed it. "I want you to come back every day about this time and I'll check your hands. OK?" I nodded my head.

Each day for the next few weeks *Schwester Liesel*, Nurse Liesel, washed my hands and redressed them and gave me another white tablet. "What is that?" I asked her one day. "Vitamins!" she answered. "You aren't getting enough nutrition. These vitamins will help you get better."

When I hung around the kitchen, I was not allowed inside where the adults worked—only in the entry and narrow hallway. Frauline Stortz, the woman in charge of the kitchen, was a tall and thin lady with a severe look. She wore wire glasses and had her dishwater-blond hair parted down the middle and pulled back in a bun. She always wore an apron and clunky black shoes. She was a stern-looking woman—I never saw her smile.

One day shortly after my hands were bandaged, she pointed at me and said firmly, "Come here!"

I was certain I was in trouble but was too scared not to follow her. Frauline Stortz marched outside the door to the small entryway. There, on a ledge, was a tin cup full of milk. She pointed at it. "That is for you. It will be here every morning. You come and you drink it." Then she marched back into the kitchen. I reached for the cup and slowly sipped the milk until it was all gone. Then I placed the cup back on the ledge.

The next morning, the cup of milk was there when my mother arrived for work. And every morning for the rest of the war, that cup of milk was always on the ledge waiting for me. No one ever disturbed it. With the help of the milk and the vitamin tablets, I began to feel stronger and healthier, and the sores on my hands started to clear up. After several weeks of treatment, Nurse Liesel removed the bandages from my hands for the last time. "You are all better," she said as she gave me a hug. "You do not need to come back anymore." Before I left, she gave me a little present. It was a scissor-cut picture of a boy and a girl, matted with green satin, and framed with a hand-carved black frame. Mother and I hung it on the wall by our bed. It was the first decoration we had obtained for the large, cold cement walls.

Periodically, mother was given special tasks to do. For example, one day she was told to report to the gymnasium to clean the parquet floors. While she was scrubbing, I wandered into the large gym. The room had huge windows and was bright and sunny. It gave me a wonderful feeling of freedom after being confined to our "prison cell" room. I ran around in the gym and listened to the sound of my footsteps echoing off the walls and ceiling. It seemed that everywhere I went around the compound, there were restrictions: Do not enter; do not talk to fellow Russians who are prisoners of war; do not go anywhere without permission; do not ask for anything. But here in this room, at least for a few moments, I was free to do whatever I wanted. No one said I couldn't play. I played on a metal pole, a climbing rope, and the parallel bars. How I wished my mother worked here more often so I could come and run and do cartwheels and climb all over the gymnastic equipment!

*   *   *

We had been in Reichenau about a year when my mother was called to the administrative office. When she returned to our room, she was carrying a travel permit. She told Tarasik and me that the officials had told her we had to go on the train to a certain town to get some documents renewed.

Early the next morning, we boarded a passenger train heading north toward Freiburg. The train filled up quickly, mostly with people in uniform. We felt conspicuous wearing the mandatory blue armbands that announced we were from Eastern Europe. But we were ignored. It was a beautiful fall day. The sun was just beginning to rise. The air was clear and cool and I enjoyed looking at the farmland, which was a lush green from the recent rains. We made a few stops in small towns, and continued north. Steam from the engine puffed up in the sky. We were in the middle wagon of the train, so when we went around a curve, sometimes I could see both the engine and the last car.

A sudden murmur from across the aisle startled us. Everyone's attention focused on one of the soldiers who yelled, "Over there!" and pointed at the horizon. In a moment I saw them— two planes flying overhead. But whose airplanes were they— German or enemy? The military passengers seemed to realize they definitely were not German. But they were so high in the sky that they appeared to be passing over us.

Suddenly the planes turned around, dove downward, and came flying back toward us like lightning. Bursts of flame spat at us. "Everyone get down!" someone shouted. Passengers instantly slid off their seats, fell flat on the floor, and covered their heads.

The train didn't slow. The planes leveled off at just a few yards above the ground and headed toward us. Again they shot at us. I felt mother's hand on my head. She pushed Tarasik and me to the floor and hovered over us like a bird protecting her young ones under her wings. My heart was pounding so hard I felt like it would burst out of my chest.

There was a squeal of brakes and our bodies slammed into the seat in front of us. Windows shattered, splintering glass over us like rain. Wood cracked as bullets tore through the wagon's walls. Someone moaned. Others screamed from fear or groaned in agony. My heart was racing, wondering if our lives would end.

The train jerked again, stopped, and listed to one side. There was a moment of dead silence, then a mixture of sounds, of terrified voices and pain and grief. Someone in the front got up and scrambled off the car. Immediately, everyone got up, attempting to flee the carnage in case the planes returned.

Mother rose, grabbed our hands, pulled us up, and lined up with the crowd leaving the train. As we stepped down onto the ground, I looked straight ahead and there, just a few feet from the train, was a huge bomb embedded in the mud of a ditch. Now we had even more reason to move. Miraculously, the bomb had not exploded, but if it had, it would surely have blown up the entire train.

Behind us were several of the wounded. One man collapsed, crying and panting from pain. I looked at his leg and saw blood-covered trousers. Quickly, mother went over to him, pulled a small towel from her bag, and pressed it over the wound to try and stop the bleeding. A few others tried to help the injured while nervously searching the sky to see if the planes would return. A woman who appeared to be a nurse was administering first aid to one of the injured. My mother looked around wondering how she could help. But she had no medical training, and no tools or bandages—just the one towel she had used for one man's leg. There was nothing more she could do. So she grabbed our hands and we began running behind others who seemed to know where there was shelter.

Most of the crowd headed toward a small train station a short distance ahead. We passed the engine of our train, which was flipped over on its side and still belching steam. Three cars behind it were also derailed, and several more cars were leaning precariously. The engineer was slumped over at his post. "He's dead," I heard a soldier say.

As we reached the run-down station, it was obvious it would provide little in the way of shelter. All of us were shaking from the trauma. Then our group's attention was drawn to an old man, balding, skinny, with eyes bulging as though he was insane. He cried out in a loud, haunting voice, but no one could understand what he was saying. A woman, perhaps a wife or daughter, tried to hold him and calm him down. I clung to my mother and she pressed me closer to her. "Everything will be all right," she said. "They will calm him. Don't be afraid, Dot-shitshka."

A couple of men came to the woman's aid. Each grabbed an arm, and though the old man cursed and shouted and struggled, the young men led him away. But his shrieks remained in my mind and scared me even more than the attack on the train. What had made him go so mad? Was it constant fear and stress that finally caused him to break?

One observation I must make about the Germans is that they are very efficient. Despite the chaos during the initial minutes after the attack, order was somehow restored quickly among the people. The injured were attended to. Soldiers cleared the tracks. Another engine arrived. By early afternoon we were already back on the train and we completed our trip.

The rest of the day was a blur. We found the office, my mother did her business, and we returned to Reichenau. The next day was another workday for my mother and brother. There was no time to think about what we had been through. That evening we lay in bed completely exhausted. Mother gave me her comb and allowed me to comb her hair. I loved to do that, and I chattered away as I stroked her hair. After a while, she took the comb and began to do my hair and separate it to make braids. My hair was finally long enough to braid, and I wanted to look like my friends Christa, Anne Marie, and Ruth.

"Ouch!" she exclaimed, stopping for a moment.

"What's the matter, Mamo?"

In amazement she shook her hand, looking at it and saying nothing. I pulled her arm down and looked at it myself. Across her wrist was an ugly red mark, like a streak made by a burn. What could have caused such a mark? She tried to think back over the day, then further back. Slowly she reached up her hand and gently took hold of my head and cradled it against her chest, still looking at the burn.

It dawned on both of us simultaneously. She had cradled my head on the floor of the train car during the air attack. The streak was the burn mark of a bullet! During the attack, one of the bullets had grazed her wrist, just an inch from my head!

An awe settled on us that night. Our lives could easily have ended in that attack. That bullet could have penetrated my mother's arm and killed me. The bomb could have exploded and killed us all. Any one of hundreds of bullets could have claimed us, and we would have been two more of the millions of casualties of the war. Who would have known or cared? But for some reason, that bullet sped one inch to the right instead of one inch to the left. For some reason, that bomb didn't explode. For some reason, we were spared.

Was this simply chance? Or was there a power greater than the war protecting us?

11

War's End

The older I got, the more aware I became of discussion among the adults and of the news on the radio. While we didn't have a radio in our room, there was usually one playing in the kitchen eating area where all the employees and workers had their meals.

The propaganda on the radio was always upbeat and positive. The announcers said that the German army was going to triumph. Of course, they had just suffered a defeat, but that was only a temporary setback. We were assured that there was always an endless supply of troops waiting in reserve, ready to come in and rescue the nation. Germany would never capitulate. The enemies of the Third Reich would pay dearly for their opposition.

But on this compound of Hitler Youth, there was evidence that the confidence was not universal. The edginess wasn't overt; the students still marched and drilled and went to classes. But there were also rumors. The war wasn't going well. Something was seriously wrong. We heard that the English and Americans were pushing the Germans back from the west. And the Soviet army was advancing toward Berlin from the east. The defense was cracking. There weren't enough troops. Hitler was calling up any and all able-bodied men. Still there weren't enough men. All that remained were the Hitler Youth. But these were just kids. Nonetheless, they might be called. Almost daily, the teachers and

151

instructors made sure that these young people were ready to sacrifice their lives for the fatherland and the Fuhrer. No sacrifice was too great. There was no greater glory than to die for the Reich.

In the spring of 1945, most of the young men suddenly started packing up. I watched from a sidewalk as they lined up in formation, as they always had, but this time they were leaving to be trained and outfitted for war. Many of them were only fourteen or fifteen years old! Despite the optimistic radio broadcasts, we knew now that the situation was grave and uncertain.

That evening, Tarasik burst into our room and blurted, "Mamo, they have ordered me to line up with the next load of men to go to war."

Mother could only stare at him.

"I've been drafted. I have to leave right away, and I . . ."

He choked up and embraced mother. Then he stepped back and looked at her with an expression that said, "What am I going to do?"

Tears streamed down my mother's face as she looked at her eighteen-year-old son. I was horrified that my brother was being used this way—an additional body in a hopeless situation. How could he be commanded to fight for the Germans when he wasn't even a German?

My mother managed to choke out a question: "Where are they taking you?"

"I don't know," Tarasik answered. "I believe we are going to get some training first. I don't know where. After that . . . they say everyone is being sent to Berlin. It's desperate. The Germans say if Berlin falls, the war is over."

It sounded to us like a death sentence. They were throwing an innocent boy into the war to be used as cannon fodder. Again, he hugged mother. "Remember, Mamo," he whispered, "good-bye is not forever."

Then he bent over and hugged me. He hurried out the door and I ran to the window and watched as he dashed off to join a collection of young "soldiers" who were marching off to war.

Mother went immediately to bed and buried her head in the pillow as she wept. I stood at the window, unable to move for several minutes. Then I climbed next to my mother and we clung to each other.

Mother didn't get up the next day. Her nerves were stretched like a tight rubber band. Was she ever going to experience a halfway normal life? How much longer could anyone endure such heartache? She complained of headaches and pain in the upper part of her stomach and wouldn't eat. She didn't have to say why. I, too, quietly worried about my brother. There was a sense of utter helplessness. Everything had been taken from us. There was nothing we could do. There was no one to turn to. A noose hung around our necks, and all we could think about was how to keep that noose from tightening its hold on our throats. Already we felt like we were beginning to choke.

A few weeks later, I listened to the radio in the kitchen with all the employees and workers. Suddenly there was a news bulletin with a speech by an Admiral Dönitz: Adolf Hitler was dead. He, Dönitz, by the will of Hitler, was the new Fuhrer who would lead the nation to its final victory.

Almost immediately there was a flurry of activity on the compound. Officers, faculty, and the few remaining students hastily packed and took any means of transportation available to escape. Even to a simple Russian girl, this was no sign of a nation rising up for final victory, but rather a scared people escaping to save their lives. Most of them headed in the direction of Switzerland.

By the end of the day, the compound was almost deserted. On my way back to building 7A, I passed the building where the Russian prisoners of war were housed. The basement was empty; the prisoners were gone, too.

Mother and I went to the kitchen the next morning. Frauline Stortz was there along with a few other workers, but there was little to do but feed ourselves. Several foreign workers sat around listening to the radio. Two prisoners from Holland, who did much of the painting around the compound, talked noisily.

"The war is all but over," said one. "It's just a matter of time. Germany has lost, and they know it." Frauline Stortz and the other German women in the kitchen said nothing.

It was hard to tell from the radio reports what was happening. We heard rumors that Hitler had committed suicide, then we heard that he was safe in a secret bunker in Berlin. We heard that he had escaped and sought asylum in another country. We heard Berlin was surrounded and about to fall. There were reports of various elements of the German army surrendering. The Allies would soon occupy Germany. We had no idea what any of that meant for us.

Finally the announcement came: The war was over. An armistice was signed. The various Allied troops were occupying Germany.

The men from Holland talked about how black men were among the conquerors. My ears perked up. One of the men saw me listening and put his finger to his mouth, as though he was about to tell me a secret.

"Have you ever seen a black man?" he said.

I shook my head.

"They are going to come in, with knives in their mouths. They love to carve up little girls!"

The man's friend started laughing. I was startled and went running to find mother. I was just sure that among these Allied troops were savages and that certain destruction, worse than our forced slavery, would appear at any moment.

"What are we going to do, Mamo?" I cried.

Mother held me close. "We are going to be all right, Dotshitshka. They were just teasing you. Don't worry."

For the first time in two years, the light in our room was on at night and the blackout shade raised. It felt good to leave the light on, and I was in no hurry to turn it off. There was no fear of air raids that night, but there was an intense feeling of loneliness mixed with foreboding. Most of the buildings on this large compound were deserted. Our documents were in German. Our passport was Soviet. Would those papers save us or convict us? Who was in charge now? And what did that mean for us?

"I don't think there is anything we can do right now," mother said quietly. "We just have to wait."

"I wish we were with Hanusia."

"So do I. But we have no way to get there. And only God knows what is happening in that part of Germany."

Neither of us spoke about Tarasik, but I knew mother was thinking about him constantly, wondering where he was. Had he been forced into battle? Was he alive or dead? Was he captured by the Allies? Or, maybe he was wandering around in the confusion of the war's end. I tried to imagine what he might be experiencing.

We lay awake for a long time that night, drawing strength from each other for another day of uncertainty.

The next morning Ruth and I played together while the adults sat by the radio, eager for any shred of news. "It's OK to play with you now," Ruth said. I hadn't yet thought about how the harsh German rules were no longer in force—at least for the moment. Later that day, I saw Siegrun and her grandfather and they greeted me warmly for the first time in months. I began to realize that not all of the Germans were evil. There were many people who didn't agree with our subjugation, who quietly resisted—at least until their own safety was threatened. There were numerous examples: Frau Euler, Frau Böshans, Frauline Stortz, Nurse Liesel, my kindergarten teacher, and others. And that was in the midst of one of the most prestigious German institutions! The rules were clear—no mingling with foreigners. Yet these good people risked the wrath of the authorities to show us kindness. That realization removed some of the sting from the pain I had felt from earlier rejection.

The announcement of the war's end left us feeling like we were suspended high in the air, wondering who would cut the rope and if we would fall—maybe to our death. But nothing happened. The uncertainty seemed even greater than ever before!

SUMMER 1945

A couple of days later we heard they were coming: the conquering troops. Curiosity pulled the children outside the buildings. We stood waiting in front of the building that housed the kitchen. For what? Then around the bend we saw them march. Row after row of soldiers in khaki-green uniforms, carrying packs on their backs, marched toward the youth camp.

A man shouted, *"Arrete!"* and the troops stopped. Other orders were given, and some of the men headed in various directions to check out the buildings on the compound. Most of the others relaxed, some of them sitting on their backpacks waiting for instructions.

"What did he say?" someone whispered.

"I don't know," another spoke.

"I think they are French," said another. "It sounds like they are speaking French."

"Yes, they are French," one of the Hollanders agreed. "Let's ask Teresa." Teresa was a young French woman who worked with mother in the kitchen.

The leader came up and looked over our ragtag group of people and children. *"Est ceque quelqu'un parle Francais ici?* Does anyone here speak French?" There was silence for a moment.

Then the kitchen door opened and Teresa came out. They talked for a few moments and I tried to follow this strange new tongue with its nasal tone, which stood in contrast to the harsh and almost guttural sounds of German. After a few exchanges, Teresa turned to us and said, "The men are hungry. We are requested to feed them. They are going to barrack here for a while."

Frauline Stortz and the rest of her crew filed back into the kitchen. Ruth and I and several German children stood looking at the men. None were black, and they didn't appear to be savages. They looked tired, but they didn't seem to be terribly harsh. Some were lying down, leaning their heads on their backpacks with their eyes shut. Others picked rations out of their packs. Cautiously we walked toward a couple of soldiers for a better look. One of the men looked up at us and smiled. Holding up his hand, he said, "J'ai quelque chose pour toi. I have something for you," and then rifled through his pack. He pulled something out and held his hand open for us to see. It was candy. "Nes pas peur c'est bon! Come on. It's OK!"

Candy does wonders for breaking down fear in children. Ruth and I accepted the gift and then moved aside and let the other children have their turn. The candy had a colorful wrapper and an aroma unlike any I had experienced before. (We later learned that it was American candy.) Carefully we put the sweet stuff in our mouths. For me, it was the first sweet treat I had enjoyed in years. I looked around and saw that other children were befriending the soldiers. Though we couldn't communicate in words, we knew instantly that these men were our friends.

Ruth got excited as she finished her candy. "Komm!" she said, pulling on my arm. I followed her as she ran down the street to her home and went into her father's greenhouse nursery. There, we arrived at a large flower garden. Giggling, she explained to me her plan. "Let's pick flowers for the commander!" she said. "Maybe he will give us more candy!" She immediately picked some carnations, and I followed her example.

After we had assembled two beautiful and aromatic bouquets that were too thick for our small hands to reach around, we walked back to the kitchen. The man in charge was talking to several of his men as we approached. He turned and saw us and smiled, and I thought, Wow, he is nice looking!

Ruth stood on her tiptoes and handed him the flowers.

"Ooh, Oui! Merci bouque!" he said and bowed. Ruth curtsied and backed away.

I stepped forward and shyly held out my bouquet for him. My cheeks felt hot. I curtsied; he bowed, then indicated by his hands that we were to wait. He went into the kitchen and emerged a moment later without the flowers. In his hands were two chocolate bars!

"We curtsied again and said, "Danke!" as we backed away, giggling happily at our success. Then I turned and ran to find mother and show her this great prize. She smiled as I asked, "Can we share this together, tonight?"

"Of course, Dotshitshka!" she answered, and knowing that this made my mother happy made me even more excited.

That evening, we divided the chocolate. Apparently my taste buds had matured since the time the German officers, while billeting in our home, had given me my first taste of chocolate. There was an unusual sense of contentment as we silently let the chocolate melt in our mouths. For as long as I could remember, our family had never eaten or even tasted something without sharing it with the rest of the family—even if it meant each person received only one bite. Sharing this candy with mother made it taste even better.

The next afternoon, Ruth and I repeated the ceremony, picking flowers and taking them to the French leader in the kitchen. He came to the door of the cafeteria, and with a smile, accepted our gifts and gave us each another chocolate bar. Thus we established a little ritual as nearly every afternoon, about 4:00, we gave him flowers and he gave us chocolate or some other treat. The Frenchman was always friendly, and obviously amused by our daily visits. We felt that he liked us, and we certainly liked him.

But even though the French were friendly, we remained in suspense concerning our future. Hanging around the kitchen, I quickly picked up French words and phrases. Between overhearing conversations and listening to news on the radio, I began to realize that Germany was now divided into four sectors—French, where we were, and American, English, and Russian. I also figured out that Göppingen, where my sister lived with the Euler family, was in the American sector. And of course, we had no idea where Tarasik was. At night, mother agonized over the whereabouts of her son. Where was he? Was she going to see him again? Did they send him to the front lines to be killed? Or was he captured as a prisoner and holed up in a detention camp somewhere?

The question for mother and me was, What did our situation mean? Would we be required to go to the Russian sector? Or would we be allowed to go to Göppingen and reunite with Hanusia? Or, did we have to stay put and serve the French? If so, how long would they be here? Would they eventually turn the area back over to the Germans? We speculated, but no one knew the answers. So we waited.

One morning, two men in Russian army uniforms arrived. We had no idea where they had come from. I saw my mother's body stiffen as we looked outside the cafeteria window and watched them announce themselves to the French commander. We had left the Soviet Union over three years ago, but the fear was still there, deeply rooted in our souls. What was mother thinking? Was she remembering my father—now perhaps dead? Was she recalling the humiliation of looking for work and being rejected just because her husband was in prison? Was she reliving the fear of Stalin and how one poorly chosen statement might lead to her being arrested? I had to wonder where home was for us. Would we ever know a settled, peaceful life?

Mother went back to work, but not long after, she and all the other Russian workers were called to go to a room for a meeting. I went with her as we met the two officials.

"*Dobre Utro!*" the men greeted us. "Good morning! Sit down, please!"

We sat down and one of the men warmly announced, "Dear citizens, we have come to take you home! The war is over. Our army has bravely resisted the fascist invasion. We have driven the enemy from our land! Now, dear citizens, you are free!"

The partner chimed in: "We know you and many others like you have resisted the enemy. You have endured humiliation and ill treatment. We want to gather you up and take you home to your families and to your people, where you belong!"

After years permeated with suspicion, mother listened carefully. Was this an invitation? Or was it a demand? And if we were required to go with these officers, what did that mean? Could it be that things back home had changed? There were many questions. A woman near us calmly asked, "Will we be going straight to our homes?"

"Of course!" came the answer. "First you will go for a few days to a camp where we are bringing together all our people from around this area. We have a nice place for you to stay until the plan is complete and everyone is ready to travel back home.

Then we will take you back to our beautiful Russia, and all of your homes and all of your rights will be restored. We have driven out the Germans and squashed every one of them! There is nothing to fear. You may go to your homes and live in peace."

Someone else hesitantly asked what was on all of our minds: "Sir, excuse me. How do I say this? It is hard. But . . . please, what will happen to us?"

It was an awkward attempt to determine whether we would be treated as traitors. The officers smiled and reassured us. "Nothing will happen to you! You are citizens of the Soviet Union. We have come to take you home."

The other officer seemed to understand. "There were some difficult times before the war," he said. "Comrade Stalin required sacrifices from all of us. But it was for our good. Now that the war is over, things have changed. You will see! Things will be better."

It sounded too good to be true. But maybe . . . maybe Russia had changed. It was about time; for too long it had been strangled in the grasp of fear and distrust. Yet the promise was said so quickly, so surely. The implication was clear: Things would be different. We would be free. Yet nothing *specific* was promised. What were we to make of this invitation? Should we ignore the distrust that was so ingrained in our souls?

"There are many other people like you scattered throughout Germany," the officer said. "We are making plans to pick you up next week on Monday. You will want to get ready and pack your things. We will leave Monday by 10:00 in the morning. We will bring some trucks on which you and your belongings will be loaded. We have prepared a nice temporary place for you, where you can go and wait until all the arrangements are made for you to return home. You will be there only a few days." Then the officer rose and smiled. The conversation was over. That was the invitation. It wasn't an order. Or was it? The French remained silent; they weren't giving us another option. Apparently they were cooperating and letting the Russians do whatever they wanted.

The following Monday, at 10:00 A.M. sharp, three trucks pulled up and parked outside the kitchen. All the people from Russia were already waiting outside on the sidewalk with their belongings. Long benches were on each side of the truck bed. Two men helped us climb up. Baggage, what little we had, was piled into the center of the flatbed. When our truck was full, the back rail was put up and fastened on each side. The drivers, Russians, then took their places and we pulled out onto a country road. Eventually we reached a main highway and drove in a convoy for several hours.

We slowed down near the town of Singen and pulled up to a long, one-story wooden building. It looked like an unoccupied barrack of some sort. The people on our truck were put in a large room that had cots lined up on either side. Most of the women in the room we had not seen before; apparently they had been brought here from elsewhere in Germany. Sheets and blankets were placed on the mattresses. A man read off a list and pointed with his pencil to the spot where we were to sleep.

We entered the room through a blanket that hung on the doorframe. Suddenly mother realized that nothing had changed. The building was shabby and run-down. This was a "nice" place? Our leaders were full of promises, but their promises were empty. We could see that the officials around us were disorganized and confused. People around us were rattled, alarmed, and began grumbling.

"What kind of a 'better place' is this?" shouted one woman.

Another woman chimed in: "You told us that we were going to be treated decent, not like animals!"

"Look at this filthy place!" shouted another. "Do you think that we are pigs?"

An official lifted both of his hands. "Calm down! Take your cot and be patient. When we get back home, things will be better. You know that this is only a temporary holding spot."

"Why should we believe you?" said one of the women.

"Quiet down! You will get in trouble," said another.

"I won't quiet down. They have lied to us, just like they always lied to us. Nothing has changed."

Mother silently watched the scene. The expression on her face told me she was deeply troubled. I squeezed her hand, trembling from the turmoil around us. I felt threatened, wondering if people might begin hitting each other.

That night, almost immediately after the lights went out, the war began. It started with a shriek as a woman jumped off her cot and began flapping her blanket against the mattress. Another woman grabbed a shoe and started hitting her mattress and the walls above her pillow. Mother and I soon joined them. The lights came back on and we saw we were fighting against big red bedbugs. It was hardly a night of rest; the lights switched on and

A picture for Daddy: Amy is looking for the birdie.

Fyodor (second from right), age 6, at his father's funeral with two uncles and a grandmother. Note the crutch under Fyodor's left arm.

Amy's father,
Fyodor Philipovich Wasylenko,
when he was twenty-three years old.

Amy's mother,
Maria Denisowna,
when she was nineteen years old.

Amy's mother and father shortly after their marriage: Mother hand-embroidered the shirt father is wearing.

Amy's family in 1940. This picture was sent to Amy's father in Siberia.
From left to right: Maria, Tarasik, Amy, and Hanusia.

A picture Fyodor sent to his family from Siberia in 1939. On the back of the photo, he wrote:

"[Since] my childhood homeless, hungry, cold . . . [now] jail, and eternal torture in my older years all because of my sheep-like, without-guile honesty. . . . Not needed by anyone—I am suffering, but not weeping."

Fyodor and Maria's brick house on the out-skirts of Drushkovka. Most of the homes in the village were made of mud and straw.

Tarasik, Amy, Maria, and Hanusia in front of their house in 1942.

The family is reunited in Göppingen after several months
in a German labor camp, and soon all but Hanusia
will travel to the Hitler Youth camp in Reichenau.
Left to right: Tarasik, Maria, Amy, and Hanusia.

Amy at age 7.

A from-the-air view of the Hitler Youth camp in Reichenau.

A photo of Amy at the Hitler Youth camp in Reichenau.
Someone gave Amy the cap, which was worn by
Hitler Youth girls. Amy was so proud of the Scottie lapel
pin bought for her in Konstanz by Frau Böshans.

The Euler camera shop: The Euler family lived on the second floor. The Langs were next door to the right.

Frau Euler

Left and below:
In 1976, Bob and Amy
visited Göppingen and
saw the attic where she
and her mother hid for
a year.

The Lang family at Christmas.

*Above:
Frau Euler's Hinterhouse
("house in the back") where
Amy's family lived after
becoming "stateless."*

*Right: Maria working in
the tiny kitchen in the
Hinterhouse quarters.*

Maria, Amy, and a friend in 1948.

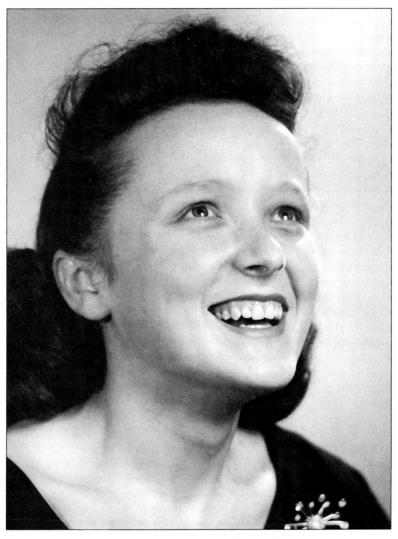

Amy as a young woman at age nineteen.

Bob George (right) with army buddies in Göppingen in 1956.

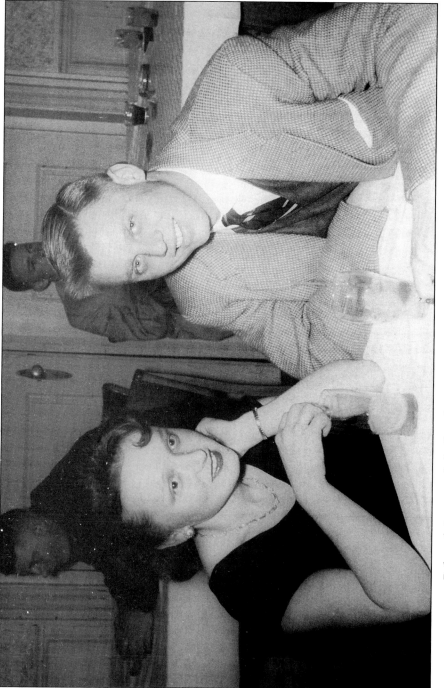

Bob and Amy on their first date at the EM (enlisted men's) club, November 1956.

*Frau Euler and Maria congratulate Bob and Amy
upon the announcement of their engagement.*

*Bob "borrowed" Amy's confirmation ring to size her
engagement ring, which he gave to her on her birthday,
February 25, 1957.*

The new Mr. and Mrs. Bob George, 1957.

Debbie, Bob, Bobby, and Amy in 1963.

Amy, Debbie, Bobby, and Bob at Bobby's wedding in 1990.

Reunited with father in May, 1977!

*Fyodor and Bob enjoy Dairy Queen
ice cream.*

The first family portrait, taken in 1977, forty years after father was arrested and taken to Siberia. Left to right: Hanusia, Amy, Fyodor, Maria, Tarasik.

Amy with her mother in 1988, one year before she died.

Amy's father in America, May 1977.

off as one woman or another jumped up to combat the biting pests. The next morning, there were red stains all over the walls where bugs had been splattered by shoes, and we were all tired and irritable.

It was impossible to sleep over the next few nights. The room was a clamor of emotion. Women were frustrated and angry. The nights were filled with cursing and whispered hisses and shouts of frustration.

One heavyset woman seemed oblivious to the commotion around her. She arrived at the camp carrying a little baby boy no more than six months old. She kept to herself in one corner, saying nothing, obviously in a deep depression. A few mornings later we saw the women in our barrack swarmed around the heavyset woman, cursing her and angrily denouncing her. "Why did you do it?" I heard one woman scream. I clung to my mother while a neighbor explained in a hushed whisper, "She murdered the baby. She took the drawstring of the baby's gown and wound it tightly around the child's neck." But the woman said nothing to her accusers. She just laid there, staring at the ceiling, saying nothing. Eventually, the other women moved away from her in disgust, leaving her alone in her misery. There was no arrest. No justice. If only it had been just a bad dream!

Several men stayed in the room next door. Soon one of them was making regular visits to a certain lady in our room. A blanket was hung on some wire for privacy as the man and woman proceeded to romance on the bed. I could hear whispers from the couple, but I could not understand what they were saying. The other women in the room did not approve of the situation, but no one had the authority to do anything about it.

Everyone was disgruntled by the sleepless nights. So much for the nice accommodations that had been promised as we waited to travel home! If the officials had lied about the holding camp, what other lies had they told? We couldn't tell how much we heard was rumor and how much was fact. But we did hear that the Communist party was still firmly in power and that things had not changed back home. We heard that arrests, similar to my father's, had continued throughout the war. Soldiers who had been captured by the Germans and escaped back to their own lines were arrested and charged with spying for the enemy or treason. The attitude of the Soviet government was that one should die for Stalin rather than be captured by the enemy, ignoring the deepest instinct of man—survival. Prisoners of war were being returned to Russia, and rumors said they were being executed. And people like us, who were carried away as slave labor, were considered traitors to the motherland. Someone whispered to us that a load of refugees had simply been dumped in a wilderness area and left to fend for themselves.

We had no way of knowing what was true and what wasn't. But we knew our country, so we knew some of the stories might well be true. That was frightening news, which started all of us thinking about possible alternatives.

One night, a woman tore into our barrack. "Where is that lousy, no-good husband of mine?" she screamed. Seeing the blanket on the wire, she ripped it down and found her husband and the woman hurriedly fastening their clothes. "How could you!" she yelled, grabbing the man.

"Get your hands off me," the man said.

"I will not! I plan to tear you to pieces, you no-good, ungrateful, pitiful pig."

The man jumped off the bed, balled up his fist and swung at her. She ducked, but he attacked and started pummeling her as she cried in anger and pain.

"Mamo, let's get out of here!" I shouted in horror. I grabbed my mother's hand and pulled as hard as I could. "Mamo, let's go," I pleaded.

"No, don't be afraid. They won't bother us, Dotshitshka. It doesn't involve us. They are not going to hurt us."

"Please, Mamo, please!"

I pleaded and pulled. Mother reached out and gently pulled me into her arms. I cried and shook as she tried to soothe me. Soon some of the other women broke up the fight, and things calmed down for the night. But my mind was not calm. I continued to tremble at the memory I could not turn off. In my fitful sleep that night, I saw the man striking the woman in the face, and I cried again.

The next day, mother took my hand and we walked outside. She had to think. We walked for a long time without saying anything, noticing only the squalor of our surroundings. There were people milling around aimlessly and down in spirit. They were angry, disillusioned, frustrated. The area was messy. Papers swirled around in the breeze. Food carelessly dropped by the occupants had been left to spoil. Germans never allowed messes like this. There was an attitude of indifference evident everywhere we looked. This was most certainly not a camp of happy people liberated from their oppressors and eager to go home.

"Nothing has changed!" mother finally stated. "They have lied about this camp. I must assume they have lied about everything else. If we go home, we're in danger. We most likely will not see our home again. We housed German soldiers. And the old label on us from your father's arrest makes us doubly suspect. We are marked people. Your father . . . maybe he is still in prison, or maybe he is even dead. We are not free. I can't put my finger on it, but something is definitely not right. We have to find a way out of this mess."

I listened. There was no need for me to speak.

"We must see how we can get in touch with Hanusia," mother announced. "Certainly they can't make us go back until our family is together. And we aren't together. We must also find Tarasik—it is hard to know where they took him. But first we need to contact Hanusia."

There was a new determination in my mother. She was convinced that we could not return home without Hanusia and Tarasik. Her personality took on a new strength. Instead of the tired, meek lady who went about her work without resistance, she now was quietly alert, looking, listening, thinking of a plan to accomplish the goal of reuniting her family.

Because the camp was only loosely controlled, Germans who lived in the neighborhood could come and trade with the Russians. Usually they bartered for food. Occasionally someone had the good fortune of obtaining a package of American cigarettes (usually Lucky Strikes or Camels). They were worth more than money and were eagerly traded. Mother and some other people also collected the leftovers from our cafeteria food and used them to barter with the Germans.

Mother met a German lady who raised some rabbits and came daily to our camp to scavenge for leftover food—usually stale bread or wilted vegetables. After seeing her a few times, mother started trying to talk to her in very broken German. The women quickly became friends, and we were invited to come and visit her.

Since the lady's home was nearby, mother and I would walk over to her home, bring her some leftover food, and talk briefly. We learned that she was a seamstress, and that her husband was a truck driver who occasionally drove into the American zone. With that information, mother began formulating a plan. She told no one about her intentions.

One day, mother asked her friend, "Do you know where Göppingen is?"

"Sure. Why do you ask?" the woman answered.

"My daughter is in Göppingen." With my help as an interpreter, mother quickly proceeded to tell her the story about Hanusia and how we wanted to be reunited as a family. "Here we are in the French zone, in a Russian holding camp. But my daughter is in the American zone. I do not know how we can get back together. I cannot go back to Russia and leave my children behind."

The woman seemed to understand mother's dilemma. "Göppingen—that's near Stuttgart. My husband drives through Stuttgart about twice a month. When he gets back in three days, I'll ask him about the possibility of taking you there."

A few days later, the woman came by and asked us to drop by her house and meet her husband. We walked over to their home. The man was lithe, had blond hair, and said little. He sat back in his chair, his blue eyes boring into us, as though evaluating the risks of accepting an extra load.

"I have very little money," my mother said, holding out a few marks my sister had given her more than two years before.

"They're worthless!" he said.

"What do you require? I will give you whatever I can," mother answered.

The couple talked briefly in whispers. Then the woman escorted us to the door, saying she would give us an answer the next day.

That night it was impossible to sleep. This time it wasn't the bedbugs that tormented us, but the uncertainty. Would the truck driver agree to take us? If not, what then? This seemed like our only opportunity; did we even dare to think that this plan wouldn't work? But we kept our turmoil private. No one was to know any details about our thoughts or plans. The next day dragged by slowly as we waited for the woman to make her late-afternoon visit, after the food rations had been distributed.

The lady arrived at the usual time, and winked at us with a slight smile. As mother handed over some leftover bread and potatoes, the woman said, "Make plans and get your permit.

He's making a delivery next Monday." That was five days away, the last Monday in August.

Four days later we went to the makeshift office in the front of the building. In a polite voice my mother told the officer in charge, "My daughter lives in the American zone in Göppingen. I really want to go back home, but first I want to have all of my family with me. My oldest daughter needs to be released from her work. May I take a few days to go and bring her back here so we can all go back home together?"

"Name?" The official had his pen poised over a form.

"Maria Denisowna Wasylenko." She spoke slowly, emphasizing each syllable.

She handed him our passports. He looked at my mother's passport and copied the information. "Daughter's name?"

"Ann." Mother gave the Russian version of my sister's name, rather than the Ukrainian variation, Hanusia.

"What is her address?"

"Hauptstrasse 36."

"Where is Göppingen?"

"Near Stuttgart."

The official consulted a map, located Göppingen, and wrote some more information down on the form. Then he wrote down dates, signed the form, and stamped it. He handed back the passport and the form.

"This is a five-day pass to the American zone," he explained. "You must be back by noon Friday. We will be waiting for you. If you do not return by then, you will be in breach of our regulations and we will come and find you!"

We knew we had transportation to Göppingen. As far as the return trip . . . we had no intention of coming back. Mother and I didn't talk about it; we simply understood that this was our one chance to escape. We had no idea what we would do after we found my sister. We would worry about that later.

That evening, we picked up our bread rations and carried them to the woman's home. "Did you get the pass?" she asked. Mother showed her the paper. "Good. My husband is leaving for Stuttgart in the morning. He said he would pick you up outside your barrack at 4:00 A.M."

"You never told us how much it will cost," said mother.

The woman simply looked at our bread and nodded. Mother didn't argue. She handed the two loaves to her friend. She had already made a couple of sandwiches for later, and she was more than willing to give up our remaining food for a chance at freedom.

"Do you have any money?" the German woman asked.

"No, nothing," mother answered through me.

"Then let me pay you for the bread. You will need money for train tickets after you get to Stuttgart."

Mother tried to thank her, but the lady waved us off. "Pay me back when you return."

We gathered our belongings into a couple of small bundles and left the camp very early the next morning. We waited outside the gate and stood patiently. Soon a truck with a canvas cover lumbered up. The driver, the woman's husband, stuck his head out and whispered, "Are you ready?"

"Ja," my mother answered as she grabbed my hand.

He climbed out and led us to the rear, pulled back the canvas flap, and helped us aboard. He shut the flap and we groped in the dark for a place to sit. There were many crates and boxes of various sizes. We felt around for a flat spot on which to settle as the truck jerked and started moving, throwing us off balance. Finally we settled down and I leaned against my mother. We were so exhausted from the secret preparations that despite our uncomfortable setting, we quickly dozed off. At least in the truck there were no horrible bedbugs to bite us.

As we slept, the truck bounced wildly at times, bumping over potholes and other rough spots on the road. The ride seemed to symbolize our lives the last few years—rough and unpredictable. I knew that mother had no intention of coming back to the French sector. But where were we going? After we linked up with my sister, then what? Would they let us stay in the American zone? The British, Americans, Russians, and French were one big happy family of conquerors. Were they in agreement on everything? Would they make us go back to Russia?

There were so many unanswered questions. We would learn the answers eventually. But for now, sleep was sweet.

12

The Hiding Place

We had no idea what time it was. With the canvas firmly fastened over us and the boxes, it was completely pitch-black. There was one stop and we heard voices briefly. Instantly I tensed up, wondering if we would be discovered. Then I realized that it was probably a checkpoint between the French and American zones. The driver had made this trip many times; the soldiers let him pass without searching the truck.

The trip continued, along with doubts about whether we would reach our destination. Could we really trust this man?

The truck stopped again and we saw daylight creeping in between the canvas flaps. The driver opened the back. "Stuttgart," he said. "Time to get off." He offered a hand and helped us jump to the ground, then lowered the bags containing our meager possessions.

We blinked our eyes at the bright sun and tried to orient ourselves. "This is the *bahnhof* [train station]," he said to me in German. "From here you can catch a train to Göppingen."

"What did he say?" mother asked, still having great difficulty understanding German.

"He says we're at the train station."

"*Aufwiedersehen*, and good luck!" said the driver. He climbed back into his cab and drove off.

The warm morning sun felt good on our sore and stiff bodies. But the scene before us was depressing. All around us, and as far as we could see, were gutted buildings and rubble, as if a giant had destroyed the city and stomped it to tiny pieces in a fit of rage. There was also an eerie silence. We felt like aliens dropped into an ancient and ruined civilization. It took a few minutes to realize that we were standing next to what had once been a large train depot. There were at least a dozen railroad tracks and platforms in various stages of disrepair. Some of the tracks were twisted, as though a washerwoman had taken them and wrung them like wet rags. The main station consisted of a couple of walls and a heap of stones and dust that towered above our heads. We wondered how any trains could possibly run in such conditions. But as we looked more closely, we did see that a couple of tracks had been repaired. Perhaps they were in use.

There were no boards with arrival or departure times. No conductors were available to answer our questions; in fact, there was not one human being to be seen. For a while, we wondered if we might have to walk the thirty miles to Göppingen. But it was still early enough that it seemed likely a train might come by sometime during the day, though there were no clocks to tell us the time.

We found some stones to sit on near the tracks. Some empty passenger train cars were parked on a siding behind some rubble, several yards away. There were eight or ten wagons connected, but no engine. Would this be the train taking us to Göppingen?

Time seems to pass slowly when a person is stranded in desolate rubble. My eyes, now adjusted to the brightness, searched for any sign of life. Nothing! Not even a bird or a rat—just a few flies that buzzed here and there and pestered my ears.

Finally in the distance we saw a man slowly wandering toward the train tracks. He wore what appeared to be a ragged uniform— perhaps that of a train conductor or postman. He picked his way through the rubble, and appeared to be in no hurry to go anywhere in particular.

"Emotshka!" said mother. "Please go ask that man when there will be a train for Göppingen."

Despite my shyness, I forced myself to approach the man.

"Excuse me, please," I said. "We need to go to Göppingen. Is there a train going there today?"

The man looked at me kindly and said, "Yes, young lady, there should be a train to Göppingen on track fifteen."

He pointed in the direction where I had spotted the empty passenger cars, so I asked, "Is that the one?"

"Yes. In about two hours you will see an engine pull up and hook up to those cars. Then you and your mother can get on it. I will sell you the tickets there and we will be on our way."

Mother looked at me expectantly, and I explained to her what the man had just said. Since we had to wait and we were hungry, we decided to eat our sandwiches. Mother was extremely weary and slumped down on the rock where we sat. It was as though she had expended all of her energy in the process of escaping that horrid Russian holding camp. The stress of not being able to communicate in German added to her nervousness. She clutched her stomach. She was faint, I could tell, but we had to stay put, or risk missing our train. Mother noticed my worried look and gave me a weak smile. "We've done well to get to Stuttgart," she said. "We're nearer to Göppingen and Hanusia!"

The first train arrived late in the morning, but it was headed in the wrong direction. An engine arrived later that afternoon and attached itself to the parked train cars. The same man whom I had talked to earlier fastened a sign to the front wagon, then motioned for us to come. "It is time to board," he said as he helped us with our belongings. Mother draped her arm over my shoulders and leaned hard on me as she stepped up. We found seats, and shortly after we started, the conductor took a small fee for the ride.

The train seemed to be running well. It made several stops, and we arrived at our destination in about an hour. Of course, this time there was no one to greet us and we were on our own to find our way to Frau Euler's and a reunion with my sister.

In contrast to Stuttgart, Göppingen appeared remarkably intact. It had been spared from the ravages of enemy bombs—at least this part of the town.

"Can you make it, Mamo?" I asked as we stood on the platform and the train left the station.

Mother nodded. She seemed encouraged that we were so near our destination. "Do you remember the address?" she asked.

"It's Hauptstrasse 36," I said. "I think I can find my way there if I ask someone here at the station for directions. Would you like to sit here and wait while I go get help?"

"No, I'm feeling better. I can't wait to see Hanusia!"

I asked directions from a lady who seemed to work at the station and learned that Hauptstrasse was only a couple of blocks away. We walked slowly in the given direction. Mother lagged behind me, but refused to stop and rest, sustained by the belief that rest was just a short way off. Her courage inspired me, and I recalled our first reunion with my sister, now more than two years earlier. I thought of the warm bath, the clean sheets, and apples. Those thoughts made me want to run up the hill. But mother leaned on me again and I slowed my pace to support her.

Ten more minutes passed, and we were there. We carefully looked at every house number to make sure we didn't miss the most important one. Now there was another unstated fear. What if we couldn't stay? What if Hanusia was required, like us, to return to Russia? Suppose the Eulers didn't want us here? After all, they were defeated, and we looked like downtrodden beggars. What would happen to us if they turned us away? We didn't have any other options; we were at their mercy and could only hope that they would have the heart to help.

We stood in front of the photography shop. The store was closed. A few people walked by or rode bicycles. A jeep with some soldiers sped by. No one seemed to take notice of us. Next to the photography shop was a door leading upstairs to the residences. It was locked.

"Ring the doorbell!" mother said.

"What doorbell?"

She pointed to the button next to the door. "Press it with your finger."

I pushed the button and heard a faint ringing inside the house. Nothing happened for a moment, and I looked at mother to see what we should do. Then a buzz sounded. I pushed the door and it opened. There, at the top of the stairway, was my sister, with her curly black hair falling over her eyes as she leaned over the railing to see who was there.

For an instant we were stunned. Then Hanusia screamed, "Mamo!" in delight and flew down the steps. Mother, sister, and I embraced and cried at the joy of being back together.

When we finally let go of each other, Hanusia grabbed our things and started up the stairs ahead of us. "I have a surprise for you!" she said. Mother grabbed the railing and with my support slowly made her way up the stairs. At the top, we turned into the Eulers' apartment and stopped in shock. For a second, I thought I was seeing a ghost.

"Tarasik!" I shouted and ran into my brother's arms. He picked me off the floor and gave me a big hug, then set me down and gently embraced mother. The three of us stood and hung on to each other and wept.

We were overwhelmed. The joy of seeing Hanusia, and then, as if he had stepped out of heaven, Tarasik! He had the biggest smile I had ever seen.

"How in the world did you get here?" asked mother, wiping the tears streaming down her cheeks. She didn't wait for an answer but hugged him again, then hugged my sister again.

"*Slava Bogu!* Praise God, we are a family again." This was said from the deepest part of her soul.

I just stood there and grinned until it hurt to smile. There was my brother, alive and well. What a happy moment!

Hanusia then guided us into the living room, where mother collapsed into a chair. "Wait here for just a moment," she said. "I'll run downstairs to the store and tell Frau Euler you are here."

As my sister ran off, mother said to Tarasik, "Now Senok, come here and tell me all about how you are and how you found your way here."

"I'm fine, Mamo. I just made it here myself two days ago."

Mother looked at him as though he had been brought back from the dead. His presence obviously gave her renewed strength.

"Please tell me what happened to you!" she said with eager curiosity.

Tarasik started with the time he said goodbye to us in Reichenau. "All those Hitler boys and I were trucked to a holding camp nearby. There, we were issued rifles and given a quick training in the basics of war. We marched, trained, took orders. No one knew where we were going, but there were rumors we were to be sent to Berlin. That was where the hardest and final battle was. And then there were rumors that the war was almost over. No one knew what was going on. I felt I had to escape, somehow. I was afraid to lose you and Emma. And if the war was over, I knew it would not be good for me to be found in a German uniform, especially since I didn't want to be in one to begin with. So one day we were marching and I saw some bushes and a farm beyond that. During a break, I went into the woods, supposedly to relieve myself. I started to run and kept running until I was in deep woods and could hide myself among the trees.

"The first thing I wanted to do was get rid of my uniform. But I had no other clothes. As I was wandering, I accidentally came upon another group of German soldiers. I told them that I had lost contact with my unit, so they gave me a ride on their truck. They were heading north, and that gave me the idea that maybe I should try and head for Göppingen. I knew Hanusia was there. But I wasn't sure because I also thought maybe I should go back and try and find you. I was torn on the inside.

"The soldiers dropped me off at a train station. When they were gone, I started walking and for the next few days, I hid in ditches and slept in the woods and tried to stay out of sight. I prayed for divine guidance to show me which way to go. I found some old work clothes at an abandoned farmhouse, so I quickly ditched my uniform. I felt a little more safe in the farming clothes. But still, I stayed out of sight as much as possible. I knew the war was over now, but I wasn't sure what to do. Should I try to get back to Reichenau? Should I join one of the convoys driving back to Russia? Or would I be better off finding Hanusia?

"I was hiding in a ditch along a highway and spotted a convoy of trucks loaded with our people—the trucks were marked with Russian flags. I didn't want to be seen, but I peeked out just in case maybe you and Emma were among the people in those trucks. Then I began to wonder if you had already passed, or if you were still in a truck to come. I was torn about which direction to go. I finally decided the best thing to do was to make my way to Göppingen and look for Hanusia."

My sister had returned and she picked up the story. "I was watering the flower boxes," she said, pointing to the windows. "I looked down, and there he was, my brother, just standing there looking up at me . . ."

Frau Euler came in and greeted us with a smile and a handshake. She listened as my sister translated to her what my brother had told us. Then Frau Euler announced, "I will see if we can make some arrangements for you to stay with Herr and Frau Lang for a few days."

"They are our neighbors," my sister explained. "They own the men's hat store next door."

"When do you have to go back?" asked Frau Euler.

Mother closed her eyes and quietly said, "We can't go back."

"What do you mean you can't go back?" Frau Euler inquired.

"We can't go back to the camp because then we have to go back to Russia, and we can't go back there.

"The Soviet authorities want us to go back home, to Ukraine. But I know that it is not safe," said mother. "They have lied to us. They have made promises, but I don't trust them. We can't go home. Not now!" That reply seemed to exhaust her and she shut her eyes again. I was scared, but said nothing.

Hanusia translated for her mistress, who nodded. My sister, with tears in her eyes, looked at me and then mother. "You're going to be OK now, Mamo."

"You don't have to go anywhere," said Frau Euler. "We will see what arrangements we can make."

Frau Euler's compassion had great meaning, for the war had taken its toll on the Euler family also. Young Wolfgang had died a year before from an appendicitis attack, unable to get medical attention in time. Uli was glad to see me, but was more subdued than I had seen him two years ago. There was a hole left by his brother's loss, and I sensed it immediately. The bear we had played with two years ago sat ignored in the corner.

A few days later, I found my sister talking with mother. Mother was holding her stomach in discomfort. Hanusia explained that a Russian official had come by the house. "They found my name in the local police register," she said. "I have been told that I have to go home to Drushkovka."

"What are we going to do now?" I asked.

"We can't even think of making a trip—not with mother's weakened condition. But the official said he would be back. I'm not sure what to do next."

We held a brief council to discuss the situation with Frau Euler. "For how long is your permit to stay here?" she asked mother.

My sister had to translate. Mother handed Frau Euler the paper. She looked at it with concern in her eyes. "We must act quickly and secretly. It is best if you and your family stay indoors for now, so no one will know you are here. For the moment the officials are only concerned about Hanusia."

"But you can be sure that soon they will be looking for the rest of my family, too," said my sister.

"Here's what we can do," said Frau Euler. "The Langs have three children and could use some domestic help. Now that the war is over, everything will slowly rebuild. In return for household help from your mother, they will provide what food they can, and you can hide in a small space in their attic, which is next door to our attic."

"What about my little sister?" Hanusia asked.

"Her German is fluent. She is blond and blends in well with the children. I don't think anyone will be suspicious. But it would be better if your mother stays inside all the time."

"And what about Tarasik? What can he do?" mother asked.

"He can work for me in the photo lab downstairs. I need to train someone who can specialize in this work. He will be a real help to us."

"The photo lab is connected to here through a passageway on the ground floor," Hanusia explained. "That passageway connects to the Hinterhouse (the house in the back). Frau Euler also owns that building, and she has made some workrooms on the second floor. There is also a little unfinished apartment above those rooms."

"Tarasik can sleep there," said Frau Euler. Then, turning to mother as Hanusia interpreted, she added, "I have talked with Frau Lang. We will also have to rename you for your protection. You are now Frau Fischer."

My mother looked surprised.

"Children talk," my sister explained. "You must remain hidden until this issue with the Soviet authorities is settled. We feel that a German name will help camouflage us until we know for sure what to do."

"Remember, you will be Frau Fischer," Frau Euler repeated. "Your daughters are Emmi Fischer and Ann Fischer. Your son is Thomas Fischer. Everyone in both of our households will be instructed to call you by those names." And so we assumed German identities.

A short while later, we climbed up two flights of stairs and emerged on top of the flat roof. As we walked on a platform that was connected to the building next door, which was owned by the Lang family, we passed through a badly weathered door and descended into the Langs' attic. Against one wall was a bed, and the rest of the area was crammed with boxes—various old family possessions. The room had no running water, toilet, or heat. Through a small door were stairs that went down into the residence. The family bathroom was on that floor, but we could only use it for urgent needs and to wash our face and hands. "Like most other households, bath time is once a week—usually on Saturday," Hanusia explained.

The attic was a bleak room made of rough wood, hot and stuffy in the summer heat, and bitterly cold in the winter. In one corner, it was impossible to stand because of the sharply slanting roof. But this was an ideal place to hide. As long as mother stayed inside, there was little chance that anyone in the neighborhood would detect her. But right now, all she could do was collapse on the bed. The weakness she had been fighting off for weeks finally consumed her. She gently clutched the area below her rib cage—something I had seen her do more frequently in recent weeks. Her stomach ached from nervousness, and all she wanted to do was rest.

I was playing near my sister upstairs the next time a Soviet official came. Frau Euler called to her to come down. I followed close behind, hiding in the shadows on the stairs as Hanusia talked with the man.

"How come your mother is still here?" demanded the official.

"What are you talking about?" Hanusia said.

"She had a five-day permit. She never came back. We know she is here somewhere."

"You don't know where she is."

"She's staying here. We know that."

"She's very sick and unable to travel," my sister answered.

"Tomorrow we are taking you and your mother back home," the man said.

"How can you?" my sister shouted. "My mother is in no condition to travel!" Tears came to her eyes, but she fought to control her emotions.

The man put on a sweet, artificial smile, as though to assure my sister he had considered it. But his charm was unpracticed and made me shiver in fear. "We have good doctors. We will take care of your mother. We have medication. There is a hospital for her. We have everything she needs. You just be ready tomorrow morning." Then he turned and left.

The four of us and Frau Euler talked that evening. We were all upset and frightened, and we agreed that we could not possibly go back with the Russian official. Besides, at this point, my brother still hadn't been discovered.

The Russian officer appeared again the next day, as promised. "You must come with me now!" he said gruffly, his charming smile gone.

"You don't understand," my sister protested. "How many times must I tell you? You must allow time for my mother to get well."

"We will make sure your mother has the best medical care possible!" he said sternly, as though issuing a command.

"I know you promised that. But we must wait until she is better."

"Two days!" said the man. "I will give your mother two more days to get ready. You will then come with us!"

That afternoon, Frau Euler brought Dr. Buddhe, the family doctor who lived across the street, to see my mother. After examining mother, the gentle woman doctor wrote out a certificate stating that she was too ill to travel.

The Soviet official returned and shook in anger at the notice from the doctor. "How long?" he demanded.

"I don't know," said Hanusia, fighting the tears.

"One more week!" he said, stalking off.

*　*　*

In the more than two years since we had spent those nights with the Eulers on the way to Reichenau, conditions in Germany had deteriorated markedly. Those wonderful apples my brother had devoured were no longer available. Fortunately, Frau Euler had special connections with a farmer in the nearby village of Ottenbach, and she was able to obtain vegetables that were not available in town. "Many people have nothing," my sister said. "Only business people who have the right contacts can get some food now and then."

Everyone had their hands full trying to survive. The addition of more mouths to feed could not have been welcomed by the Langs, but they graciously added us to their table. Everyone was issued food stamps—ration cards that provided a family with certain limited essentials such as bread or half a pound of butter for a month. Potatoes and cabbages were available maybe once a month in certain stores. Otherwise, there was nothing on the store shelves. Stores opened only when a truckload of food arrived, then closed again as soon as the produce was sold. People, clutching their ration cards, lined up outside a store where a delivery was scheduled and hoped there was enough left when their turn came.

Obtaining food was an important part of our day. Everyone kept eyes and ears open for news of a delivery to a store. Someone would hear that a truckload of potatoes was arriving the next day at a certain location. The line usually started to form before daybreak, with people holding bags to collect the produce that would be distributed. Sometimes I would be asked to go and stand in line for a couple of hours to hold a place for Frau Lang. People in line would comment on how the store shelves used to be full of all kinds of candy and other nice items. I could not envision such a picture. Then I would be relieved by Frau Lang, who would then purchase as much as she was allowed for her family—that is, if the produce arrived, and if there was any left when her turn came.

A couple of days later, we would learn that a load of cabbages was arriving, and we would repeat the process. We had to take advantage of every opportunity that came along because having the ration cards didn't guarantee the food would be available. Often we obtained far less than the rations permitted. The only way many people survived was through the black market, which was evident everywhere. But to work the black market, you needed money, American cigarettes, or coffee. We had none of these.

American soldiers provided much of the illegal trade, for they had the most access to food. Cameras, clothes, paintings—anything of value could be traded. Sometimes the trade was for goods that could be used as currency, such as coffee, cigarettes, chocolate—Americans had plenty of these items. Of course, the black market was against the law, so only a few civilian people were significantly involved in this illegal activity. Most of the trades were done secretly, always with American soldiers who alone had access to the desired supplies. Frau Euler did deal with cameras. I never saw the transactions, but the evidence was visible—American coffee, chocolate, and sometimes cheese and tea.

The Langs refused to use the black market. Instead, they had a limited supply of men's felt house slippers, gloves, socks, wool scarves, and occasionally a velour hat, which they could trade with their longtime friends in the country who farmed. By supplying these friends with house shoes or a warm scarf, in return they could bring home a jar of molasses, sauerkraut, or other items.

The Langs were kind people, and didn't demand that mother begin work immediately. She needed rest to regain her energy. Two of the Lang children became my friends. The boy Armin was my age, and his sister Gerda was a year younger. With them, I explored the neighborhood. My German was now fluent, and I could converse with people without revealing any accent that might raise questions.

One day we were playing in the street when two American soldiers passed by. All of us stopped and stared, for the two men were black! Immediately, I thought of the Dutch men in Reichenau who had mentioned black soldiers. Here, for the first time, I was viewing black men in real life, and I didn't know what to think. They were dressed like all of the other soldiers I had seen. As the men were about to turn the corner and disappear down the next street, they saw us, changed direction, and headed our way. They came right up to us and reached into their pant pockets. With a huge smile, one of the soldiers opened his hand and offered me a colorful little package.

"For you!" he said. "Lifesavers!"

I didn't know what he meant, but the object in his hand was obviously something I could put in my mouth. I took the package and picked at the end to open it. It smelled sweet, and the colorful wrapping paper was so pretty. All the other children gathered around to watch. Inside were pretty round candies. He indicated I should pry one out. The top one was red. I pulled it out and underneath was an orange one. I put the red one in my mouth. My smile must have told him thanks. He then handed each of the other children a roll, and then as fast as they had appeared, the men were gone around the corner.

Thus I met my first black man and realized that he was just like other men. In fact, I thought he was even nicer. That summer, several other army men gave us candy or gum when they happened upon us. We began to look on the American soldiers as friends. We also heard through rumors that there was more food here in the American zone than in the other three areas of occupied Germany. This was confirmation that we were in the right place, and we were thankful for that.

* * *

Mother was still terrified about having to return to Russia. She began having nightmares. I was scared the first night she screamed in her sleep. Her first yell woke me, and her noise continued—gruesome and frightening.

I shook her and tried to wake her. "Mamo, Mamo!"

Finally, she awoke with a jolt and looked at me as though in a daze. Then she seemed to recognize where she was. "I'm sorry, Dotshitshka. I'm so sorry. I was having a terrible dream."

"You were screaming," I said.

"I didn't know I was screaming. This man was stalking me in a dark street . . . I was being chased by a crazy man. He was trying to kill me. He had a knife in his hand and an evil look in his eye. I was running as hard as I could and shouting for someone to help me. But there was no one who would help, and he was getting closer and closer. . . ."

The nightmares became almost nightly occurrences. Sometimes she dreamed of dark streets and the NKVD knocking on the door and taking her away. Other times she dreamed that there were snakes everywhere, that someone was trying to shoot her, that people were fighting and she got in their way, or that people were chasing her and trying to kill her. And always, she would see someone coming for her. She knew they would find her, yet she still had to defend herself and run away. These nightmares exhausted mother and caused her nerves to remain on edge. They also left me unsettled every time I had to shake mother awake and bring her back to reality.

* * *

Across the street from the Lang family was a church. It was an unusual building; it had a tall steeple on top and the clock chimes that rang every fifteen minutes could be heard clearly in our attic room. At first it startled us; it sounded like a big gong clanging right over our heads. But after a while it became a part of the routine sounds of the day.

I found myself drawn to this unusual building. I admired the strange architecture, trying to figure out what it might be used for. But I found no clues. Finally, I asked the Lang children.

"That's where we worship God," said Armin.

"Grandma Lang goes there every Sunday morning," added Gerda.

"What do people do in there?" I asked.

"Oh, they sing hymns," said Gerda.

"Hymns?"

"You know . . . songs about God. And they pray. And a man in a robe talks about God."

"Why don't you come with us and see for yourself?" said Armin.

"Yeah!" chimed in his sister. "Sunday morning put on a nice dress and come."

The next Sunday, while mother slept, I got up early and walked to the church with Armin and Gerda. As we walked across the street, the bells rang continuously—it was different from the simple melody they played the rest of the week. It was as though they were inviting me and everyone else in town to come and discover the secrets inside the building. I followed Armin and Gerda into the church and climbed the stairs to the balcony. I immediately noticed the simple but elegant interior and knew that this was a building that demanded my reverence.

Though there were people inside, it was very solemn and quiet. Downstairs, the benches were filled with adults and a few children. I looked around and wondered about the pipes against the wall directly behind where I sat. Downstairs and in front, there was a table with a cross above it and a man on the cross. *Why was that man on the cross?* I wondered.

Then I heard music. A man sat on a bench with his feet moving on what looked like a row of boards, and his fingers were moving over a keyboard. Armin told me that was the organ. From his fingers and feet a thunderous sound filled the church building with beautiful music unlike any I had ever heard before. There was energy in this sound, and the power of the music which came from the pipes behind me was overwhelming. The congregation stood to sing, and I stood with them. Armin and Gerda showed me a book with the words of the hymn. I did not join in their singing, for I had never heard these songs before. There were too many new impressions on my senses; it was too much for my mind to comprehend.

The service got under way and I watched a man dressed in a black robe, with an unusual white collar around his neck, ascend some stairs and stand in a balcony above the congregation below. He read from a book, then talked about someone named God. I had never heard of God. I had no idea who He was or what He was like. But as I listened, I began to understand that God was someone special.

The following Saturday afternoon, I played hide-and-seek with Armin and Gerda in the attic right next to where mother and I slept. One of the dressers held old items from World War I. Apparently they belonged to Grandfather Lang before he died. There was a steel helmet with a long, sharp point sticking out of the top—it looked like someone could get hurt by it. In one corner hung a musty old uniform that looked completely differ-ent from the ones we had seen in the recent war. Against the wall hung a huge knife—actually, a saber in its sheath. We were told not to touch anything, but I was certainly fascinated by the mysterious objects.

When it was my turn to hide, I squeezed into a narrow space between the uniform and an old box. I sat still, hardly breathing, while my eyes searched the area around me. Then I saw a strange object. At first it looked like a watch. I picked it up and found that it had a needle in the center that jiggled nervously. At the four corners were the letters N, E, S, and W. I was intrigued, and the object was small enough to hide in my hand. No one knew that I had taken it. That night, I played with it in my room.

The next day, I attended church again, and learned that God knew everything and everyone. He knew who I was. He knew all about me—even what I was thinking and feeling. He knew the past, the present, and the future. And He loved people; He cared about them. Yes, He knew *me*, and He loved *me!* My eyes must have been wide open—I sat quietly, soaking in every word. This was absolutely astounding. If it was true, this was the greatest revelation imaginable. No wonder these people came to this building! Who wouldn't want to know more about a person as wonderful as God?

Then I thought about that strange object I had kept yesterday. Frau Lang had strictly warned us not to touch anything. All of a sudden I realized that God knew what I had done. Deep in my heart, I was convicted. What should I do? I couldn't wait for the service to end. I ran up the stairs to our room, found the compass, and quickly returned it to the place where I had found it. Immediately I felt better.

The following week my mind meditated on what I had seen and heard in church, and I had a rather interesting experience that made an unforgettable impression on me. At the end of the block opposite the Lang house was a bakery. During the war, it was closed. Since the occupation of Germany by the Allies, however, once a week, on Wednesdays, it had its wooden storefront roller shade slightly raised. We discovered that the U.S. Army used the facility. One morning, we were playing on the sidewalk just in front of the four steps that led to the bakery door. A wonderful aroma wafted through the space below the rolled-up shutters. There was no sign that the place was open for business. But the smell was unmistakable—sweet, inviting, and foreign. It did not smell like German food. After enduring rations, our stomachs knew this smell meant something quite tasty. We were like bees drawn to honey.

All of a sudden, the roller shade lifted a few inches higher and a small tray appeared out of the darkness. It was filled with doughnuts—a treat none of us had ever seen before. All the children eagerly grabbed for one, and within seconds, the tray was empty and everyone was munching on this delicious-looking pastry—everyone except me. I had held back in my typical shy way and the doughnuts were all gone before I reached the tray. I was so used to the fact that I had no rights that I could not make myself push forward and demand any privilege. Inside, I was overcome with the feeling of being rejected and overlooked. Once again I was left out, just like always, and I ached with disappointment.

As I stood there watching everyone eat and lick their fingers and lips, I saw a man's hand come out from under the partially raised roller shade. In his hand was a single doughnut. "This is for you!" I heard a voice say. I could not see who it was until I stepped up and reached for the doughnut. Then I caught a glimpse of a man with black hair and eyes. He had seen me! He hadn't forgotten me. Never had any food tasted better than that plain cake doughnut!

And at that moment, deep in my heart, I learned something: Be comforted in the midst of rejection, for God sees, and He cares and will reward you. The link with what I had learned in church was unmistakable: God really does see our hurting hearts. I knew I would have to get to know more about God.

* * *

The Russian officials continued to harass us. One day after a particularly nasty exchange, my sister was in the photo shop scrubbing the floors as tears streamed down her face. "What are we going to do?" she sobbed to her mistress. "We can't go back. My mother can't travel. It would be suicide for all of us to attempt to go home at this time."

Ann (Hanusia) continued her cleaning as the bell above the door jingled and a sharply dressed man entered the shop. He went right to the counter.

"May I help you?" said Frau Euler.

"I am Herr Scheinbaum. I wonder if you could help me with developing some photographs. . . ."

My sister ignored the man as he conducted business with Frau Euler. But the man noticed her and asked, "Why is that girl crying?"

"Her situation is really bad," Frau Euler answered in a low voice. "She has worked for me for four years. Now her mother is here, and her brother and sister. They are Russian and some military officials want to ship them back home. But their mother is very ill at this time."

"Do they not want to go home?" he asked.

"It isn't a matter of not wanting to go back home; rather, they are all concerned about their mother's health. The Russian officials were here a few minutes ago threatening them and forcing them to go back now. We don't think that their mother can survive in her current condition."

The man looked at my sister again, then said, "I work for the American military government office that is just a few blocks from here. Maybe there is something I can do to help. Send this girl there tomorrow and have her tell the story to my superior. Maybe he will know what to do." Herr Scheinbaum then handed my sister a piece of paper with a name written on it.

Ann immediately sensed a glimmer of hope. She stopped sobbing, got up off her knees, and took the paper from the stranger. "*Danke Shoen*," she said. "Thank you very much. I will go tomorrow."

That night as we talked, all of us had a renewed sense of optimism. It wasn't much, but it was more than we had felt before. Mother was lying on her bed. She smiled as she said, "Tomorrow morning, you will go right away!"

"Yes, Mamo!" my sister said. "I will be there when they open the office."

My sister was back before noon the next day, and we all gathered around her for a full report. She had a beaming smile on her face, so we knew that the news was good. Mother sat up and listened intently. "I arrived at the office promptly at 8:00 A.M. A secretary invited me to come in. I gave her the paper, and she led me down the hallway to an office. The door was open and we went right in. Behind the desk was a gentleman in an American military uniform. He offered me his hand and said, 'Come on in. My name is Mr. Miller. What can I do for you?'

"The receptionist translated for me into German. So I proceeded to tell our whole predicament, and about your poor health, Mamo. Mr. Miller became quite agitated. 'Why do these Russian officials put demands on you? This is *our* territory, and *we* determine what is acceptable and what is not.'

"I explained to him that we were helpless and asked him for advice on what to do. Mr. Miller motioned for the secretary to sit down at the typewriter, and he dictated an official document stating that our family was not to be forcibly taken anywhere, and with the protection of the American military government, we were to be allowed to stay in Göppingen as long as we wanted to. Then he signed it and stamped it with a seal. He seemed quite pleased to have the upper hand over the Russians. As he handed me the paper, he said, 'This is our sector. We decide what is done around here!'"

My sister then brought out the document and held it up for all to see. "The pressure is off!" she announced.

But in the back of our minds, we knew that this crisis was not over. There were still those officials in Singen, waiting for us to return from Göppingen. We knew they fully intended for us to go back to Russia.

As promised, another Russian official appeared a few days later. Immediately my sister showed him the document. I could not hear what he said, but I could tell he was very angry. He shouted and screamed ugly names. My sister shouted back, no longer intimidated by his bluster. The document gave her a new sense of confidence. Finally, the man turned on his heel and walked out, slamming the door behind him.

Even though it seemed like things were temporarily settled, mother's nerves tensed up more after this last encounter. *Would they come back?* she wondered. If they did, and we got sent back to Russia, we knew we would surely die on account of all our confrontations with the officials.

13

A New Awareness

"Shine your shoes, Emmi!" Armin, Gerda, and their little sister Gisela were busy with rags and shoe polish, shining up all of their shoes. It was December 5, and because of the cold, everyone had stayed indoors.

"Why are you shining your shoes?" I asked.

"Don't you know?" asked Armin.

"Santa Claus is coming tomorrow!" said Gerda.

"Who's Santa Claus?"

The kids laughed. "You mean you don't know who Santa Claus is!" exclaimed Gisela.

"I'll tell her," said Gerda. "Santa Claus comes every year on December 6. We all polish our shoes and leave them outside our door before we go to bed. The next morning, there is candy or some other special treat in the shoes. By leaving a small gift in our shoes, Santa Claus lets us know he is coming back on December 24!"

"If you're good," corrected Armin. "If you're not good, he leaves a rod to spank you with."

This was all confusing for me. But I took off my high-top boy's shoes that Frau Euler's older son Uli had outgrown, and joined the party. That night, I put the shoes with those of the Lang children outside their bedroom door—I figured that Santa was not going to find me in the attic. Sure enough, the next morning, everyone's

185

shoes, including mine, had candy in them. I guess I was a good girl! I thought that was a rather strange but fun activity to do.

The children told me there was more to come. Something special was definitely going on at the Lang home! The door to the living room was locked, and we could hear something going on there. The children were all excited with anticipation. *"Weihnachten!"* they said. I had heard that word before—from the German officers at our house in Drushkovka. So now I was going to be introduced to Christmas! I shared their excitement without knowing the reason, and wondered if mother and I would be included.

On December 24, Herr Lang told us to be ready. Mother and I obeyed. Herr Lang could intimidate you with his black hair receding above his forehead, dark eyes, and stern expression. No one doubted he was the boss of the household. Mother told me that though he was strict, he was also fair and meant well.

I feared Herr Lang, but learned some important lessons from him. One day soon after we arrived, as we were eating with the family, Herr Lang looked up at me from under his bushy eyebrows.

"Young lady!" he said. "You must not chew with your mouth open. And do not smack your lips when you eat."

I was stunned and did not know what he was talking about. No one had criticized my eating before. I was totally unaware of how I, or anyone else, ate food. With a lump in my stomach, I tried my hardest to concentrate on keeping my lips together as I chewed my food. Thus Herr Lang introduced me to the etiquette of polite society; I quickly learned to eat quietly and properly.

On another day, Herr Lang sent me on a mission to purchase milk. Right after the war, the milk hut was open only twice a week, from 10:00 in the morning to noon. Every family had an aluminum container, with a fitted top and a handle, to carry milk. One container could hold up to three liters of liquid. Mr. Lang handed me some money and the milk can.

"Run up to the milk stand and have them fill this up for me."

I was glad to run the errand and when I returned, I handed Herr Lang both the container of milk and a few pfennigs (cents) change that the store owner had given me. Herr Lang counted the seven German pennies, then looked at me sternly and said, "They did not give you the correct amount of change!"

I had no idea how much I was supposed to bring back, if any. "Go back right now and tell them that they shortchanged you two pfennigs!" Inside my stomach was an unpleasant knot. I felt uncomfortable about having to go back, but I had no choice. That experience left a deep impression on me—some people take two pennies very seriously. My family, even though we had little or nothing, had more of a sense of freedom about such matters. Two cents did little to upset us! Still, from that moment on, I always took care with money in order to account for every penny.

While Herr Lang could be stern, he clearly cared about this family that had been foisted upon him by the war. He had no obligation to us, but when it came to this year's Christmas celebration, he insisted that mother and I be included. There were certain traditions the family observed, and the excitement of the Lang children caught me up in the festivities. On the evening of December 24 we waited in front of the living room doors, anticipating the moment when Herr Lang would open them and announce that Christmas had arrived. I could barely contain myself. The only ceremonies in the Soviet Union had revolved around the Communist party, and I had only heard about them; we had never participated in them. I was now realizing that the elements of wonder and celebration were important in life.

Finally, when we couldn't possibly wait another minute, Herr Lang opened the doors and the children rushed in. I hung back at the entrance, astonished by what I saw. In front of me was a tree decorated with glittery bulbs of all shapes and sizes and silver tinsel. On the ends of many of the branches were candles in bright little metal holders. Each candle was lit and seemed to shine a light into the darkness that had comprised so much of my life. I gazed in amazement; I was sure I had never seen anything more beautiful. And the smell! I breathed in deep and savored the aroma of the live pine tree.

Beneath the tree were packages wrapped in colorful paper. In one corner of the room, there was an electric train on the floor, its steam engine pulling little cars around in a circle. Against the opposite wall sat a big old-fashioned doll with porcelain head, hands and feet, dressed in a dark print dress and black high-laced shoes. Herr Lang saw me eye it and warned, "Be very careful with that doll, children. It once belonged to my mother. It is old and valuable, and some parts are breakable."

"Emmi, come see!" Gisela pulled on my arm and I turned to see a miniature toy house and store. They were built of solid wood and painted in bright colors. There were little dolls and inside the house were miniature tables and chairs for the dolls. In the play store there were little drawers, with dried split peas, rice, millet, and sugar. It had a tiny cash register, scoops to measure things, and play money so we could buy and sell the dried goods at this store. "This is special; we can play with it only at Christmas," Gisela explained.

I felt like I had entered a fantastic fairyland. I thought of the fairy tales my mother and sister had told me as a little girl. This seemed more amazing than any story! This was a miracle. I couldn't jump and shout like the other children. I had to look, to absorb it. I turned and looked at the tree. How incredible that anyone could make something so beautiful out of an ordinary object! I had always admired the beauty of nature. For the first time, I was seeing the beauty man could create. I already knew man was capable of great destruction and ugliness. I didn't know such beauty was possible.

I looked over at my mother. She was sitting down, watching me with a pleased look. I went over to her and hugged her. I knew what she was feeling. We had done nothing to make this beautiful moment. We had no money to contribute to the occasion. This was the Lang family's celebration, and we were only guests. Yet there was a feeling of deep gratitude that we were allowed to participate in such a beautiful event.

"It is time for the gifts!" said Herr Lang. Everyone gathered around the tree. Mother and I hung back as Herr Lang handed presents to each of the children and to his wife. The children tore into them and eagerly opened gifts of clothing—mostly pullover socks, scarves, or a knit cap. The youngest child received a toy—a wooden top.

"For our special guests, we also have a gift," said Herr Lang. My mother and I were shocked as he handed us our present. It was wrapped in white paper on which was printed small green Christmas trees and red bulbs. We looked for a long time before we slowly opened it. I carefully undid the paper and mother opened the box. Inside were two pairs of slippers—house shoes, the Langs called them. They were lined with what looked like fur to keep our feet warm during the winter. They were perfect for us, as the Langs always insisted on wearing slippers in their home. And they were brand-new! Mother and I beamed our gratitude to Herr and Frau Lang. Since mother still spoke very broken German, on behalf of both of us, I shyly said, "*Danke*

Schön.'' They smiled back, pleased that we appreciated their thoughtfulness.

After the gifts were passed out, we sat down for a simple meal, capped by a special dessert. It was homemade vanilla pudding, cooled in a metal mold, then tipped upside down. We ate it with a fruit sauce. It was absolutely delicious!

That evening opened my eyes to a whole new world of wonder. Each time I put on my slippers I was reminded of the evening, of Christmas, and the kindness of this family. The celebration ended with the family singing some songs. They were all new to me. One of them seemed to capture the beauty of this celebration. With no other lights but the candles on the tree, the family sang:

> *Stille Nacht, Heilige Nacht*
> Silent night! Holy night!
> All is calm, all is bright
> 'Round yon virgin mother and Child!
> Holy Infant, so tender and mild,
> Sleep in heavenly peace,
> Sleep in heavenly peace.

The melody had a haunting sensation that remained in my mind as I went to sleep that night. What was it that so captured my imagination? This was a special night. But there was something more, and I couldn't comprehend what it was. Why was there mention of a child? It didn't make sense. Yet the music captured the spirit and beauty of the evening. I would never forget my first Christmas celebration.

Christmas season lasted for one week. My friends and I played with the toy store and house until the end of December. Then the doors of the living room closed again, and I was told that all the special decorations would be put away in the attic until next year.

JANUARY 1946

I went again with the Lang children to church. Christmas made me want to know more about God. Here in church, I experienced more of the wonder that I had felt in the celebration of Christmas. The organ music, the hymns, the readings, the ceremony, and the talk by the minister—together they opened my mind to a world I never imagined before. I heard often the name of Jesus—the Son of God, they called Him. At certain times during the services, they stopped and prayed to God and Jesus. I understood that anyone could talk to God, even little me. I could pray. I could talk to God and Jesus, and they would listen to what was in my heart.

During one service, we sang a song:

> Fairest Lord Jesus! Ruler of all nature,
> O Thou of God and man the Son!
> Thee will I cherish, Thee will I honor,
> Thou, my soul's Glory, Joy, and Crown!

With the organ playing and the people singing, that hymn seemed to capture the wonder of my discoveries. The truths in the song lifted me above the worries of the world—above my mother's illness and the uncertainty of our future—where we would live, what country would be our home, how we would eat. Here was God, and this God loved me, and He cared about all my uncertainties. How wonderful it was to hope in Someone greater than humanity, Someone who is in control at all times.

That night, I introduced myself to God. Before falling asleep, I said my first prayer. "God, tonight I'm going to pray to You," I started. "Now Jesus, don't be mad. Tomorrow will be Your turn. Tomorrow night I'll pray to You. Now God, thank You for my mama, and for my sister, and for my brother. Thank You for the Eulers and the Langs. Please take care of my mama. She is sick. Please make her better. Amen."

The next night, I prayed again. I wanted to be sure I didn't hurt anyone's feelings, so this time I prayed to Jesus. "Jesus, it's Your turn. I told You I would pray to You tonight. God, it's Your turn again tomorrow." My prayers were very simple. Thanks for my family, and a simple request that my mother would get well. "Please also help me learn in school" I added this evening.

I wanted to know more about God and Jesus. That was motivation enough to get up early on Sunday morning, before my mother was awake, and dress and walk down to the church. Each time another piece of the puzzle was added to my picture. I learned that Jesus had once lived on earth, and had performed amazing miracles and told some wonderful stories. But He was killed—I began to realize that was the reason for the cross, and that Jesus was the Man on that cross. What a tragedy, that such a great Man should be killed! But the minister said He died for our sins. There was also mention that He had risen from the dead. My mind couldn't comprehend that. Did that mean He was alive now?

Each night, I prayed, alternating between God and Jesus. Something within flickered, as though it might spring to life. I didn't understand what it was, but it gave me hope and encouragement and peace. It was my deep secret in the midst of a difficult existence.

*   *   *

There was no fuel that winter, so the attic was bitterly cold. To try and stay warm, all of us wore wool stockings to bed. They were terribly rough and itched the daylights out of me. Further, on really cold days, my hands tingled, a reminder of the time in Russia when I had suffered frostbite. I began coughing. At first, it was mainly at night. Then it continued all day as I sat in the cold classroom at school. Soon I was coughing constantly with a whooping sound. It was impossible for me or my mother to sleep.

"You poor thing," my mother noted one day. "Your eyes are sunken into your head, and swollen." The Langs tried to help, but there was little food and no way to heat their home.

My mother worried about how I could possibly recover. There was no medication available, so when nighttime came, mother would boil water and pour it in a pail over dried chamomile. Then she would set me on a low stool, put a blanket over my head, and have me inhale the steam. Though sweat dripped from my eyebrows, the tip of my nose, and my chin, I had to remain in this position for at least fifteen minutes.

After that, an even more miserable cure was put before me in the form of hot milk with a tablespoon of unrefined lard floating on top. First I had to stare at those sickening "fat eyes." Then, despite my protests and tears, I had to drink that potion, gagging and choking all the way. Dr. Buddhe examined me and reported that I needed special hospitalization, "where the air is pure and the nourishment healthy." But that was an impossibility. We had absolutely no money—mother, Hanusia, and Tarasik worked only for room and board.

During this time a gentleman by the name of Klotchkoff entered our lives through Frau Euler's business. He was employed by the American forces at the edge of town, where they occupied former German barracks. He was a fine person who spoke seven languages fluently. He befriended my sister and then all of our family. On occasion he would stop by and bring us some leftover food from the American kitchen. We were so excited and grateful. In my heart, I thought of God, wondering if He sent this person our way to help us.

Hanusia talked to Mr. Klotchkoff about my health. He speculated I might have tuberculosis and somehow arranged to help us. One day an American jeep came by to pick me up and take me to a place where I could get well. "Mamo, do I have to go?" I said in tears. Fear gripped me. I had never been away from my mother's side. Her constant presence meant more to me than my health.

My sister tried to comfort me. "Emotshka, this is for your good. You will be gone only for a short time. This good man has arranged for you to go to a children's lung sanitorium so you can get well. And Mamo will be able to rest, too, and get better."

I calmed down when I heard that this might help our mother. My sister joined me for the trip, and we went out of town and up into the hills to a place called Waldhausen. "You need fresh air!" the driver explained. "We will take you to a higher altitude where you will get lots of fresh air among the pine trees. That will help you get well." Deep inside, I dreaded being away from my family for the first time. The thought of being alone for a month was terrifying—it seemed like forever!

The sanitorium was a place for children who had tuberculosis and other lung problems. The therapy was simple: They had me drink a new beverage—hot milk diluted with weak tea (in order to stretch the milk supply). And I had to spend as much time as possible resting outside with the other children in the fresh air. The nurses weren't friendly, especially to me, a little Russian girl. Each morning we, the children, were placed outside on cots. With our arms straight at our sides, the blankets were wrapped around us tight. We were not allowed to play or talk. We just lay there like sticks for several hours. The memories of the frigid winters in Ukraine, confined to my bed, returned. I felt imprisoned and terribly lonely.

During the weekend, everyone was required to write a letter home. Each child was given a piece of paper and a pencil. The nurse came back after a while and saw I hadn't written anything.

"What is the matter with you? You good-for-nothing Russian! Why have you not written a letter?" the woman yelled at me. "Speak!" she ordered.

Tears came to my eyes as I tried to explain: "I don't know how to write a letter."

"What do you mean, you lazy girl? A child your age should know how to write."

"I just started school," I said. "No one has shown me how to write a letter."

"You are just rebellious. You don't want to work."

The woman yelled at me for a few moments, then walked off, disgusted. When no one was looking, I cried harder than I had ever cried before. I felt hurt, forsaken, lonely, and helpless. I was sincere and honest with this lady. Why did she not like me? The feelings of rejection I had experienced in Reichenau returned, more intense than ever. After feeling the acceptance of the Langs and Frau Euler, this woman's anger toward me was mystifying. Why did she hate me? Why did she treat me so cruelly?

The only bright spot came during Easter when my mother, brother, and sister came up to visit. It was a crisp and brilliant sunny day among the pine trees, and it felt so good to be with my family. They brought me a surprise present—a pair of new shoes along with a pair of knee socks. With the warmer weather, I eagerly removed the hated, itchy wool stockings and put on the new socks and shiny brown shoes. About a week later, I was declared cured and released to return home. That was thrilling news, for being away from my family was the worst misery I could imagine.

SPRING 1946

As soon as I could, I started going to church again. My friends didn't go often, so on many Sundays, I crossed the street by myself and sat in the church alone. One Sunday I noticed a large banner above the altar, with these words:

> *Ich bin der Weg, die Wahrheit, und das Leben.*
> *Niemand kommt zum Vater den durch mich.*

> I am the way and the truth and the life.
> No one comes to the Father except through me
> (John 14:6).

What unusual words, I thought. *What do they mean?*

A beautiful old lady with white fluffy hair, big brown eyes, and a sweet smile took me aside one Sunday after the service. She was in charge of children's work at the church. She knelt by me in the pew, looked me in the eye, and said, "I've seen you here several times. Where do you live?"

"Across the street."

We talked for a while, and her gentle ways made me feel comfortable. So I told her, "My favorite song is 'Fairest Lord Jesus.'"

"That is one of my favorite hymns, too."

I pointed to the banner above the altar and asked, "What does that mean?"

"Those are the words of Jesus. They tell us how we can know God. Would you like to know more about Jesus?"

I nodded my head. I wanted to know a lot more!

She gently explained, "Jesus is God. He came to earth to save us. Have you ever done anything wrong?"

Instantly I thought of taking the compass in the attic. Other examples followed. "Yes," I whispered.

"Jesus died for everything you have ever done wrong or ever will do. He died on the cross, but He came back to life three days later. Do you understand?"

I nodded my head.

"Would you like for Him to live in your heart?"

My eyes opened wider. I couldn't believe what I was hearing—that Jesus could live inside of me.

"He will come into your heart if you ask Him. Would you like to do so?"

"Yes."

"Then here is a prayer you can pray: *'Ich bin klein mein Hertz ist rein soll niemand drin wohnen alls Jesus allein.* I am little. My heart is pure. No one shall live in it but Jesus alone.' Would you like to pray that prayer?"

I repeated the words of the prayer. Then the lady explained, "Now Jesus has come into your heart. He loves you very much. He has forgiven your sins."

A warm feeling came over me, the same feeling I'd had as a little girl sitting on the step in front of my house when the sun shone upon me, letting me know I was loved. I didn't ever want to lose that feeling again.

That evening I thought about it: Jesus living in my heart? It sounded strange. It sounded wonderful. It didn't make sense; I wanted it to make sense. "Dear Jesus," I prayed. "God, don't be upset. Tomorrow night I'll pray to You. Jesus, I thank You for that kind old lady. Thank You for making me well and bringing me home to my mother. Please make my mother well. Amen."

*   *   *

During this time my sister had several meetings at the American army offices near us. "They have listened to my story," Ann reported. "They tell me that many, many others are in a similar situation. Russian refugees throughout Germany are refusing to go back to their homeland. Some people, rather than go back, have killed themselves by jumping off high buildings."

These tragedies had apparently awakened the American leaders. Ann was told that there was a way to end the harassment from the Russian officials and stay in Germany. "They recommend we give up our Russian citizenship," my sister explained to us. "That means we would become stateless. That way, no one can claim us or order us to do anything we don't want to do."

We held a family council to discuss this possibility. A decision had to be made. In one sense, we had already made it by rejecting the demands of the Soviet officials and hiding in this attic in Göppingen. Ann had gathered all the facts, and presented them to us.

"It means we will no longer be citizens of the Soviet Union. Essentially, we will belong to no country. Though we are staying in Germany, we are not citizens of Germany, either."

We all agreed with this option because we longed for a time of peace—a time when we would no longer live under stress and pressure and fear.

It was hard for me to comprehend the implications. I couldn't imagine not going back to our home. I thought of sitting on the stoop soaking in the sunrises and the beauty of nature. I thought of climbing on the roof and surveying the fruits we set out to dry from our little orchard. Why couldn't we go back to that beautiful place?

"We are already considered traitors," my sister stated. "The Russian officers who have come to talk to me make that very clear. At first they are nice and try to tell me everything will be wonderful. But when I question them, they change and tell me we are traitors and that we will be punished."

"That is true," mother said. "They will not forget. The NKVD doesn't forget. Now if we go back it will be even worse. We housed German soldiers. We worked here for the Third Reich."

"We had no choice," Thomas interjected.

"We had no choice, but that's not how our government thinks. I know. It isn't logical. They will blame us for trying to survive and save ourselves. They will say we should have committed suicide for the good of the motherland. They wanted us to destroy our land when the Germans invaded. To die was better than to be captured by the Germans. They didn't realize that our death meant nothing to the enemy. And of course, it would mean nothing to the Soviets," said mother.

"Some people say we are selling out our country," Thomas (Tarasik) said.

"No! We aren't selling out our country. We're buying our lives!" mother said. "We really don't have a choice. We can't go back. If that means we give up our citizenship, then so be it. I have to think of all of us, and what may happen to our relatives back home. We can't endanger them."

"What about Uncle Alyosha, or Aunt Fedorka, and all our cousins?" asked Ann. She didn't want to overlook any aspect of the discussion. "They may be in danger if we *don't* come back. You know how they treat anyone related to 'traitors.'"

"I have to concern myself with how to survive and protect my children," mother said. "That is most important. We must do the best we can here. Here, at least for the time being, we can survive."

"What about dad?" Ann asked. "If he is still alive, he won't know where we are. Do you think that he will ever find us?"

Up to now, the thought of our father was rarely even whispered among us. The grim war and conditions in Siberia did not give us much hope for his survival.

"We don't know anything," mother said. "All we can do is wait . . . and hope. We don't even know if he is alive. He is probably dead."

Mother hesitated as she said that, then added, "No, I can't think that. We must not give up hope. He may be alive, and if so, if God is willing, maybe we will see him again someday."

"If we don't go home now, then we probably can never go home," said Thomas.

"We cannot look that far into the future," mother answered. "For now, we will live one day at a time. We make plans, but God changes them—that is what your grandmother used to say. Let us live in unity and be thankful that we are together."

Ann then explained what would happen next: "We will surrender our passports. The occupation army will issue us new passports. On the line that asks our country of origin, it will say '*Schtaatenlos.*'"

That word, *stateless*, had a harsh, final ring to it. It made me feel suspended in air. I shuddered. Whom do we belong to now? Perhaps God?

Deep inside, I wanted badly to blend in with my German friends. Now, I felt we were being set apart again. We were different from everyone around us. It was evident not only by our language, but also our background, our total poverty, and our total dependence on the mercy of Frau Euler, who on occasion treated us as though we were still under her dominion. The difference would be plain in our passports—we were not German, nor Russian, nor Ukrainian.

Would we ever have a place to live of our own choosing? Or something to wear that we could buy with our own earned money? How nice it would be to have our own little home and not feel like an intruder. Our years in slavery and in constant dependence on the mercy of others had molded our inner beings into submission. Our own likes and wishes were of no interest to anyone—in fact, they were now irrelevant even to us. If even the tiniest spark of a dream were to start in any one of our minds, it would immediately be quenched by reality.

What was mother thinking? I wondered. *Did she have the same feelings that I had?*

"We must do what is best for the family now!" she said. "We do not know what tomorrow may bring, but we will hope for the best."

There was silence for a moment as the implications of mother's words soaked in. Finally, Ann said, "Then let us agree to stay here, and we will respond as conditions show us what to do next."

The process took a few weeks; the Russians didn't give up their own easily. But by now the American officials were aware that many Russians refused to go home and would rather die than face the terror they knew would confront them if they went back. So Ann turned in our passports, and they were returned to us stamped "Stateless." Now we were permitted to remain in the American zone in Germany. The Soviet government no longer had any control over our lives—nor did any other nation. We lived under the same rules as any German, but we had no voting or citizenship rights.

Mother seemed visibly relieved by the news. Her health improved almost immediately. She seemed to relax knowing that she and her children were now somewhat safe. And we were no longer required to hide. Frau Euler suggested we move out of the Langs' attic into the quarters above the photo lab. "The Hinterhouse" it was called—the house behind the real house. It had one bedroom, a tiny living room, and a small nook which served as a kitchen. It contained a sink with running cold water, a small electric unit for mother to cook on, and a small wooden shelf behind a curtain hanging on brass rings.

Since the quarters were directly under the roof of the building, the ceilings in all the rooms were slanted. The living room had one small window looking out onto Schlosstrasse. The bedroom was separated from the living room by a small hallway. It also had a window that overlooked a small courtyard and Frau Euler's kitchen balcony.

To pay for these accommodations, mother worked for Frau Euler by cleaning and maintaining her camera store and the lab area. And fortunately, by now business was booming for Frau Euler. The shop was open every business day, and Americans particularly were frequenting it. There was enough work to keep Thomas and two other girls busy in the lab.

We were thrilled with these arrangements, for it meant that we were now able to settle down. For the first time since that cart ride out of our quiet village of Drushkovka, we had a place where, under one roof, we could be a family again.

14

The Voice of America

The suffering in Germany continued long after the war. Almost every day we saw refugees from other German cities passing through town, looking for work or a little food or a place of shelter. There were Germans who had lost their homes to enemy bombs or who had been forced out of eastern European countries. There were many eastern Europeans who had been prisoners of war or slaves who now faced the awful dilemma of either returning home to certain persecution or staying and attempting to survive among their former enemies. It was heart-wrenching to see people who had lost eyes, or arms, or legs. Some were so handicapped that they had to be pushed in carts made out of plain wood boards and small wheels. Beggars appeared on the street corners. One man who had lost both legs sat playing a harmonica a few blocks from my home. Next to him was an old hat to collect the few pennies people dropped into it.

Everyone around us found his or her own ways to survive. Many young women were widows. Others had husbands missing in action. I saw many men traveling home with arms or legs missing, trying to find their families, many of whom were also homeless. So people survived with whatever resources they could muster. One of the best sources of food and other supplies were American GIs who had settled in German barracks after the war. The soldiers craved female companionship, which German women would exchange for food—a trade that seemed fair to many.

We heard numerous stories, some with unusual endings. One example was Vasylina, a Ukrainian girl we knew. She was an attractive, dark-haired young woman in her twenties with a slightly pockmarked face—the remnants of a bout with smallpox when she was a child. When she was eighteen, she fell in love with a German soldier while the Germans occupied her land.

"It was love at first sight," she told us. "I did not speak German; he knew no Russian. But for two weeks, it was wonderful. Every opportunity, we stole a glance, or squeezed hands when no one was looking. Then the battle turned. The German army was in retreat. The Russians surrounded our village, trapping a group of Germans. . . ."

Tears came to her eyes as she recalled how she hid her newfound love and guided him through the hills and woods that she knew so well. "We ran and ran. He would certainly have been killed if we had not escaped. We crossed a river, and he was reunited with his squad on the other side of the line. That was the last time I saw him."

Vasylina wound up in Germany as a slave girl working on a farm outside Göppingen. After the war she eventually married another German man, but in her heart she never lost her love for this soldier. There was an interesting turn to this story, for the soldier she loved spent years searching for her and finally found her. His appearance caused her great agony. But with her husband's agreement, she divorced and married the soldier whose life she had saved. Thereafter, whenever I saw Vasylina with her new husband, they were always holding hands, as though nothing could ever separate them again. He treated her like a queen, buying her the best of everything. It turned out that he was heir to a fortune from an old German business family. I guess that is one story where perhaps they lived happily ever after. At least, it appeared that way.

DECEMBER 1947

Christmas was approaching, and I desperately wanted to take part in the celebration. I had begun to experience some independence for the first time in my life by reaching out to other people. I became more involved in church and was provided the best of schooling. The latter was an unbelievable miracle: Here was a little girl with absolutely no finances receiving an education paid for by the city of Göppingen. I went to school with the children of business and factory owners, doctors, and lawyers.

At that time, schools were strictly segregated. A school had either all boys or all girls. My teachers were firm but nice. I was so hungry to learn that I was extremely attentive, and often ended up being the teacher's pet. In one class, the teacher put me at her desk to keep watch over the class when she had to leave the room for a few minutes. That sense of responsibility helped me feel better about myself; I loved and thrived on any form of recognition.

The years of turmoil that I had suffered gave me an intense desire to belong. I wanted more than anything to be accepted. Maybe that is why I assimilated German culture so quickly while my mother learned no more than the most rudimentary German words and phrases. Though I loved my mother deeply, I was embarrassed whenever she spoke in public because her accent blew my cover—it became obvious she was not German, and thus people would know I wasn't, either. But for the most part, I fit right into the German ways—their traditions, language, culture—and my school friends accepted me as one of them.

So naturally as Christmas approached I wanted to celebrate it just like the German children did. In school we learned new Christmas songs and practiced for a nativity play we would perform for our parents. I was chosen to play the part of the Virgin Mary—I guess because of my long, silky hair that, when unbraided, fell in waves over my body. I was excited about being chosen for the leading role, and literally acting out a part of what was now becoming my very life—that is, a relationship with Jesus Christ. When the play ended and the applause rang from the audience, I suddenly felt the approval I had always craved. Imagine me, a little Russian urchin, being applauded by German people!

As I remembered the Christmas we had spent with the Lang family, I began thinking about how we could have a similar celebration in our little room. My family seemed rather indifferent about Christmas, perhaps because we really had no financial means to observe it. But that didn't dampen my enthusiasm.

"Mamo, could we get a tiny tree for our table in the living room and decorate it with candles?" I asked. "It would be so nice."

"Dotshitshka, we don't have the money for luxuries like that," she explained. I recognized the look on her face—the same one I had seen at the outdoor market when I longed for a pretty dress that I could never have. Mother would have loved to fulfill my wish, but she couldn't. Still, I continued to express my desire to do something for Christmas because in school there was so much talk and preparation for it.

"All the other children are celebrating Christmas, Mamo, and I would like for our family to experience it, too. It would be so nice to celebrate Jesus' birth."

I asked my school friends where they acquired their trees. They said they either went out and chopped them down in the woods, or they bought them outside a grocery store. I told mother this, and one afternoon she suggested, "Let's walk across the street to the grocery store." My heart skipped a beat. At the Konsum's grocery store, we saw a few straggly trees leaning against the wall. "I have one mark and fifty pfennigs," mother said as we started looking. We carefully examined each tree and looked at the numbers written on the tags. Mother shook her head in discouragement. The prices were far beyond our means. All of a sudden I looked down and there on the ground, behind the bigger trees, a tiny tree was lying on its side. I pulled it out and set it upright. It was the cutest tree I had ever seen, and no more than two feet tall. Trembling, I looked at the tag. One mark!

"Here it is, Mamo! This is the one!"

Mother smiled as she paid the clerk. She said nothing as we walked home, but I knew the sacrifice she was making. One mark was a lot of money to spend on my happiness.

Soon after that I saw a girl I had befriended shortly before the holidays. Her name was Inge, and she lived across the street. We talked about Christmas and I told her about my desire to find some decorations for my little tree. "Come with me," she said. "I'll show you—we have some extra ones."

I had never been in Inge's apartment. I followed her up to the third floor to a small flat similar to our own, though much nicer. She ran in and began rummaging through a box of decorations. My friend soon returned with a box containing five white Christmas bulbs. "Here, you can have these! Your tree will look pretty now!"

I couldn't have been happier. My first Christmas tree, though tiny, was the most beautiful tree in the world. With five shiny bulbs hanging on it, we now had a spot of beauty in the midst of our dreary existence. I was so proud of it, yet it was also a reminder of how little we possessed. Still, this eased the pain of our poverty. As I gazed at my little tree, I realized it represented a celebration of Christ, who came into this world with nothing yet was rich because He was love. My eyes would fill up with tears as I listened to our small radio play beautiful Christmas hymns. Despite the suffering around us, the season seemed to bring a new ray of hope.

SUMMER 1948

One night, I was awakened by moans from my mother. She walked downstairs to the bathroom, which was next to several sinks filled with chemicals for developing photographs. She was gone a long time, and I dozed off. A crash jolted me awake again. I listened hard, and heard my mother's muffled voice. In terror I rushed down the stairs and found my brother already beside mother, who was lying on the steps.

I sat and hugged mother while crying and shivering in fear. Thomas ran down the steps, through the narrow corridor in the basement, and back up the stairs to Frau Euler's house to call my sister for help. Together, they helped carry mother back upstairs to her bed. I cried as I watched, wondering if she was going to die.

"She's very hot," my sister whispered. We had no medicine, but Ann tried to comfort mother with some cold, wet cloths.

While my sister took care of mother, I crawled back into bed and secretly cried and prayed the most intense prayer of my life: "God, please save my mother!" I pleaded. "I'm too young for her to die now. I'm only twelve, and I don't think I can make it on my own. Please let her live until I am at least eighteen and old enough to take care of myself. Please God, don't let her die!"

Mother remained in bed for several days, but slowly she regained her health and was able to resume her work for Frau Euler. There were more hot flashes, though they were not as frightening as before. My sister assured me that mother was going to be all right. With a tremendous sigh, I thanked God for His answer to my prayer. Every day with my mother would be a special gift from Him.

One night a few weeks later, a noise woke me. I looked over at my mother's bed and didn't see her form. There was a muffled sound from the living room. I pulled back the covers and slipped my feet into the house shoes. I entered the room and saw mother huddled next to the radio. I glanced at the clock; it was after midnight. Mother saw me and whispered, "Voice of America."

I sat next to her and tried to listen to the Russian voice speaking. Apparently the Soviets were trying to jam the signal, for it was hard to hear clearly. We had to strain to understand what was being said.

That moment, there was an announcement that the United States was opening up emigration proceedings for displaced people in Germany. Numbers were given—we couldn't make out the actual figures—but the message was clear. This was a chance for people like us to get a new start.

At the conclusion of the newscast, mother turned off the radio. "We will try to go to America, Dotshitshka!" she said. "It might take time; it might be difficult. But somehow, in America, there is hope for us."

Around this time we began reading in the newspaper that there were plans to open up emigration proceedings to all refugees in Germany. One could apply for a visa to go to Australia, Canada, Brazil, or the United States. Since displaced people knew there was no future for them in Germany, they began to look into these opportunities. For example, one Russian family we befriended emigrated to Australia and encouraged us to follow. In Germany they had made very little money and lived in poverty. The mother lived in a perpetual state of despair, but her three grown children—two sons and a daughter—hoped for a better life and were willing to risk the unknown to make it happen. In Australia, they obtained good jobs and eventually built a house.

Australia was the easiest country to enter because it was largely unpopulated and they needed workers for construction, farming, and building roads. If you were willing to work, you could make a good life. That kind of progress was impossible in Germany. Yet Australia sounded so far away. It was another world, far removed from the world we knew. Brazil was another option, but Canada or the United States sounded much more practical. My sister and brother knew a man who had emigrated to Canada.

In our hearts, though, the United States seemed the right place. That was the land of real opportunity. We were drawn there by the gestures of kindness we had experienced from the

American soldiers in Germany. Maybe it was the friendly GIs who gave me candy. Maybe it was the way the Americans helped us when mother was ill and worked with us and gave us permission to stay and not return to the Soviet Union. Maybe it was the way one of them helped when I was sick and needed to go to the sanitorium for fresh air. Maybe it was the way they helped provide food for us, ensuring that we didn't starve like many people did in the other sectors. All of those were surely factors that drew us to America. But going would require patience, for the United States had a quota limiting the number of displaced people they would admit.

1949-55

We wrote for applications to the Emigration and Naturalization office in Munich. When we received the forms, we carefully filled them out and mailed them back. Two or three months later, we received additional forms to complete. There were many questions about our schooling, about where we lived, about our health history. Then we were summoned to emigration offices in Munich to answer questions about the information on the application forms.

Using me as an interpreter, the interviewer asked my mother, "Did you fill out the application yourself?"

"Yes," she answered. "With the help of my daughter."

The man looked over mother's application, then asked, "Are you married?"

"Yes."

"How long have you been married?"

"I was married in 1920. So it has been almost thirty years."

"Where is your husband now?"

"I don't know."

"Is he alive?"

"I don't know."

"When did you last see him?"

"In 1938. He was taken to a labor camp in Siberia."

"Have you heard from him since then?"

"Not since the war started. After the Germans invaded Russia, I received no more letters."

"So he may still be alive."

"I can only hope so."

Several months later we received notice to appear in Ludwigsburg, which was about an hour away from Göppingen by train.

There, foreigners from all over Germany came for examinations and health checks as the final step in the emigration process. Thomas, Ann, mother, and I traveled together by train. We were housed with other strangers in a large facility formerly used by German soldiers. Each morning, we had to report to a building several blocks away and check long lists that were posted on the outside wall of the emigration office. If our names appeared, we were to wait there, then go inside for a test or examination or interview. If our names did not appear, we were to come back the next day and check again. We stayed a total of three months in Ludwigsburg, enduring the agonizing inefficiency of bureaucracy.

During this time my brother met a young man who had been accepted for emigration and was going to Chicago. "I will sponsor you as soon as I get there," he told my brother. "That will make it easier for you to come. A sponsor is a must and is responsible for housing and providing work for the new emigrant." This was good news and a ray of hope for all of us.

During this waiting period, we also met a young man named Misha (Mike), a Slovak who was being sponsored by his uncle to go to America. Ann and Mike became fast friends and saw each other often during the following weeks. Eventually, we got the news: Ann was rejected. There were spots on her X rays, and a doctor explained that the rules stated he had to make sure they were not the result of active tuberculosis (TB). He said that maybe in a year we would be called back for another examination.

However, for Thomas the news was good. He was accepted for emigration. He had a clean bill of health, and his friend, true to his word, had sent papers of sponsorship immediately upon his arrival in Chicago. It was exciting, and at the same time scary. We had heard that Chicago had gangsters. We had heard of the big cities in the United States and how the American people were concerned about crime and hoodlums. Germany was not experiencing anything like that.

Mother was also approved, but she did not want to leave Ann in Germany by herself. So the decision was made for us to stay with Ann and for Thomas to go ahead to America.

Frau Euler had a going-away party at her apartment. She invited Thomas's co-workers and our family to celebrate his good fortune and convey best wishes for the long journey. As the evening wound down, I had a private moment with my brother.

"Aren't you afraid?" I asked. "It must take a lot of courage to go alone to this foreign land and big, scary city."

"I will be fine," he said. "I will go and learn about America. And soon, you will follow and join me. I know I don't have to tell you this, but please stay close to mother. You know how much we all love her." Tears welled up in my eyes as once again I was reminded of the love and adoration all three of us had for our mother.

Mike was accepted at the same time as my brother, but decided to stay and wait until Ann was cleared. They were married in Göppingen and for the next three years, Mike worked for the city. They gave birth to a son whom they named Tom, after my brother. Meanwhile, we all waited for another call to be reexamined. One day the notice came to go to Ludwigsburg for a physical examination. During the three years after my sister's rejection, her health had stabilized to the point that a local lung specialist assured us that the scars from her past TB were not active. So we went back to be reexamined in another attempt to emigrate—only to face another blow of disappointment: Ann and Mike were approved to go to America, but now there were scars on mother's lungs. So Mike, Ann, and the baby left for America, but mother and I were left behind.

We waited anxiously for news from Munich permitting us to be reexamined. Once a year, we received a notice telling us that they were reviewing our papers. It was a preprinted message, and the news was always the same—wait. The next time we were asked to go to Munich, the end result was once again disappointing. We were told to go to another town—Schwabisch Gmund. We went through more tests, and again mother was rejected. Seven long years we waited. The wait was all the more painful because Ann and Thomas were now in America. But there was a good reason for the delay, as we would soon discover.

During those seven years, I grew from a little girl into a young woman. The older I became, the more I realized that because we wanted to go to America, I could not completely thrust myself into the German way of life. I was an eligible young woman, and there were numerous young German men who wished to date me. But I always found excuses not to go out with them. I knew now that Germany was not my real home—mother had often stated that. It was a temporary situation. I knew we couldn't go back to Ukraine. But I also sensed we would not remain in Germany.

SUMMER 1955

Sunday afternoons were often reserved for visiting friends. We frequently spent time with an elderly couple that lived on a farm at the edge of Göppingen. Mr. Shechowzow was Russian, and he and his wife were employed by a farmer. Mrs. Shechowzow was German, and she could speak Russian. She was about sixty years old, but looked much older. Mother and I would sit with this couple on a bench outside a barn and talk for hours. Of course, there was plenty to talk about and no fear of retribution if our talk ventured into political territory. By now, here in Germany, people were free to vent their feelings about communism and Stalin.

Mr. Shechowzow told us he had come from a region near Kiev and still had many relatives in that area.

"Do you ever hear from them?" mother asked.

"I have written two or three letters, but so far only one was received by them. They wrote back answering that one. The border is tightly controlled, and the Soviet agents have a spy syndrome. Every letter is suspected of being a coded message. It's absurd! So when I write, I ask only about their health. They are afraid to write about anything else."

"I haven't attempted to write to my relatives," said mother. "My husband was arrested in 1937 and sentenced to ten years in Siberia." Mother sighed. "I do not know if he is alive or dead. But I never give up hope. I live with hope that someday I will see my Fyodor again."

A number of weeks later, during one of our Sunday afternoon visits, Mr. Shechowzow told us that he had received a message from his brother in Russia. "It's only the second letter I have received from my family since the war," he said.

"Where does your brother live?" mother asked.

"About thirty miles south of Kiev," said Mr. Shechowzow.

"Do you think the next time you write to him, you could ask him if he or any of his relatives ever travel to the region of Konstantinovka?"

"I do not know. Why do you ask?"

"That is the region we came from. I was wondering if you would mind asking your brother or relatives if they could inquire about my husband Fyodor. Should any of them happen to travel near Konstantinovka, I would really appreciate it if they checked to see if my husband is still alive."

"Sure, I would be glad to do that for you, Maria Denisowna. It doesn't hurt to try. I will write again in a few days."

Mr. Shechowzow tore a corner off a brown paper sack and wrote down my father's name. "Fyodor Philipovich Wasylenko," mother said. "If he is still alive, he is probably living in the village of Drushkovka. Maybe they can find out what happened to him."

I was surprised and thrilled by my mother's request. It was a wild shot in the dark.

But maybe, just maybe, my father was still alive.

15

Heart to Heart

The possibility that my father might be alive stirred up many questions inside me. It was as though a secret I had kept buried deep in my heart now insisted on entering the light. I could barely contain my curiosity. One night after dinner, I asked, "Mamo, would you tell me about our father?"

Mother had a faraway look in her eyes. For a moment, I wondered if she had heard my question. Then she answered. "Of course, Dotshitshka. It is time that you should know about him."

That night we began a discussion that lasted off and on for several weeks. I started by asking, "Mamo, how did you meet Tato [Father]?"

Mother smiled, and I saw that for a fleeting moment she was a young woman again. She didn't speak immediately, as though she were reliving the memory.

"We met in Drushkovka, in the village where you were born. I had seen him; you couldn't help but notice him. He wore white suits, and had a ruggedly handsome face. I knew he was a teacher. He was an expert on Ukrainian literature. But I had no reason to talk to him. Of course, our family knew of his family—that was usually the case in villages."

Mother laughed. "There was a boy, Vasyl, who was infatuated with me. But he was terribly shy. He didn't know how to tell

211

me of his love. He was good friends with your father, who was not at all shy about expressing himself. Vasyl kept telling your father about me, and asked for advice on how he should approach me: Should he write to me first? What should he say to me? He was constantly talking about me, and after a while, your father became curious about this girl."

"Were you in love with Vasyl?" I asked.

"Oh no!" she giggled. "He was a nice boy. I had known him for years. He was a friend who lived in the village next to Drushkovka. That's all. He started writing me these little notes of affection. Fyodor had coached him in what to say. The notes were nice, but I didn't take them seriously. Then one day there was a party at a friend's house. We were singing and having a great time. The door opened and there stood Fyodor and Vasyl, coming in to join the gathering. They looked around, saw me and my girlfriend, and headed toward us.

"Fyodor wore a white suit and walked with a barely noticeable drag of one leg. But he was attractive, and he knew how to make conversation. He dominated a room by his appearance, and while the other boys were awkward and unsure, he knew how to approach a girl. So he and Vasyl walked up to me, and dad said, 'So this is the girl you have been talking about!' He smiled and his intense blue eyes looked straight into my eyes. I blushed and was flustered. He held out his hand, and I shyly reached out and shook it."

"How old was he?" I asked mother.

"Twenty-one. And I was just sixteen. After the party, he asked if he could walk me home. He was extremely polite. He encouraged Vasyl to find another girl, and he kept coming around to visit. My parents didn't approve of our dating."

"They didn't!"

"Oh no! They were just plain, simple people, and they didn't care for your father because he was from a family that my mother—your grandmother—did not approve of. Mother also had strong opinions about the personal qualities a man should have, and she most definitely felt they were lacking in your father. So in the beginning, I had to sneak off so I could see him. One night I told mother that I was going to my friend's house, but instead I went and met Fedija. We had a fun time together— this was probably our third date. It was after dark and your father brought me back to the stone wall by our house, where we always said goodnight. But this evening he had a surprise for me. He pulled it out of his pocket—it was a little box, and he handed it to me.

"'What is it?' I asked him. 'Open it!' he said with great excitement. So I opened the lid, and to my astonishment, it was a watch!

"I loved the watch, but I was afraid of what my parents would think about receiving such a nice gift from him so soon into our relationship. So I had to think of a way to hide the watch from them. First I considered the stone wall—maybe I could hide it between the big rocks and then use it whenever I was away from home. But what if it rained? No, I had to hide it somewhere in the house. So after your father said goodnight and left, I sneaked into our living room. Everyone seemed to be asleep. I looked around. There was no light except that which came from a tiny oil lamp that burned beneath an icon in the corner of the room. There was no place to hide the watch! This gift was becoming a burden to me.

"And then I saw the perfect hiding place—the icon of Mary holding baby Jesus. No one would disturb such a holy display. So carefully I placed the watch on a narrow ledge behind the icon. I thought it was safely hidden. Relieved, I undressed and quietly went to bed.

"The next morning at breakfast, father casually asked, 'Which one of my girls owns a watch?' We all looked at each other in surprise. No one had such a luxurious possession in our house. My heart sank as father looked at me. 'Is it yours, Maria?' Shaking with fear, I admitted it was. He took me outside and gave me a good spanking for deceiving him and mother. Later, when things calmed down, he told me what had happened. He had awakened during the night and thought he heard a strange sound—tick, tick, tick—coming from somewhere. He listened more carefully. Yes, he was sure he heard a muffled tick, tick, tick. Not wanting to wake up mother, he got up quietly and stepped in the direction of the strange noise. It was coming from the icon! He was terrified. Was this an omen from God? He got closer and listened carefully. Then nervously he reached behind the icon and found the omen! Now he knew what had scared him out of his wits, and he was extremely angry. I paid dearly for that."

I giggled at the thought of my grandfather, whom I had never met, being scared by a ticking watch in the middle of the night. Mother also seemed to enjoy the memory.

On another occasion, I asked mother, "You were younger than I am now when you married."

"Barely sixteen. That wasn't unusual. My mother married at about the same age, and she had no say in picking her husband."

"You mean it was an arranged marriage?"

"That's right. She told me that she remembers some neighbors coming over one night while she was in bed. They were the parents of an eligible young man whom they wanted to marry off into a family of the same or better means. Mother had not fallen asleep yet, so she could hear the conversation behind the curtain that divided the room. They were talking about property: We have so much land and so many head of cattle; you have so much land, and so on. They were talking about marriage like it was a business transaction, which I guess it was. My mother said she got up out of bed and peeked around the curtain to see who her future husband would be if the deal worked out. In jest, she stuck out her tongue at him, and thought, *'I am not going to marry this guy.'* But the parents arranged it and agreed to a merger of their children and some property. So mother married this man, and they had five children. It turned out to be a good marriage."

Then Mamo looked at me and smiled. "It's not as bad as it sounds. Would you trust me to pick the right man for you?"

I laughed and hugged my mother. "You know I would!"

"Well, I don't intend to choose a husband for you. But it's not such a bad idea to consult with your parents. They have experience and maturity, and only want good for their children."

Though I had never said this to mother, I knew I loved her too much to ever marry a man whom she didn't approve of.

Another time I asked, "How did dad get a stiff leg?"

"It happened when he was a young boy. He was an orphan. His mother died when he was three years old; he barely remembers her. His father died when he was six—some bandits robbed him while he was riding on a train, killed him, and threw him into a field. The news of his father's death devastated Fyodor. He became unmanageable, roaming the streets with his friend Arkady. His grandmother took him in, but she had problems controlling him. She was nearly blind and was an unhappy woman. Fyodor was active and alert, and he got into a lot of trouble.

"He told me that he and Arkady would steal food from booths at the bazaar and try to escape from the owners that chased after them. They often climbed into people's basements and helped themselves to whatever food was stored there. They were troublemakers, a nuisance to all who knew them. There was a neighbor who had apple trees, and when he was gone, the boys often climbed into the trees and helped themselves. One day the owner came home while the boys were in one of his trees. Arkady jumped off the tree first and ran off. Fyodor jumped and landed on the ground in an awkward way, twisting his knee badly. He managed to limp away, but he had injured himself terribly. Over the next few days, his leg got worse and worse. He found that the only way he could relieve his pain was to bend his leg back as if he were in a kneeling position. Eventually the leg locked in that position, bent at the knee, so he had to hop around on one leg. Unfortunately, no one really cared. His grandmother did get crutches for him, but he had to figure out how to use them."

"Why didn't she help him?" I asked. I couldn't comprehend such lack of concern for a child.

"She was a troubled woman, Dotshitshka. Your father told me about how his grandmother would make him kneel with her before an icon and pray. She would say some words and make Fyodor repeat them. If he mispronounced a word, she would whack him on the back of his head, and he had to repeat the word. If he didn't repeat it exactly the way she wanted, she would pull hard on his curly hair until he screamed. But still, he had no idea what he was saying because the prayers were in an old Slavonic language. And the picture in the icon bothered him. The man in the picture had what looked like a club studded with spikes, and Fyodor said he felt like the man would hit him with that club if he didn't say his prayers right. Those prayer experiences left a bad taste in his mouth, and after that, he avoided anything having to do with religion or church. To him, religion represented mean, legalistic, cold idol worship, and he wanted no part of it."

I thought of my recent introduction to church and my prayers to God. I didn't have the same reaction as my father. To me, God was real, Someone who loved me, and I could talk to Him. Then I thought of my passionate prayer that God would keep my mother alive after her fall on the steps that night several years ago. I was grateful that He had answered that prayer. But I didn't express these thoughts to my mother. No one knew about my friendship with God and Jesus—at least, not yet.

Mother continued talking. "Your father loved theater. As he was growing up, he wrote plays for the kids in school—mostly satire, making fun of religious people. In fact, at one time the NKVD tried to recruit Fyodor to be a priest."

I was shocked. "Why would they do that if he didn't believe in religion?"

"That's what he said. The fact is, the government infiltrated the church to keep track of churchgoers. When your father objected that he didn't know how to be a priest, they told him not to worry. They said they would teach him everything he needed to know and how to do all the ceremonies. He didn't have to believe any of the rituals. But he refused; he wanted nothing to do with it. The idea of informing on his fellow villagers was totally contrary to his thinking. He loved the people he grew up with. They were his friends."

"Did dad stay with his grandma until he was grown?"

"Oh no, Dotshitshka. She had no control over him. He kept getting into all kinds of trouble. So after a while, she placed him in an orphanage. There, he had an opportunity to learn some manners. One wealthy couple who were the benefactors of the orphanage were impressed and charmed by this curly-haired blond boy who seemed especially bright and talented. This couple was childless, so one day they took Fyodor home with them for a visit. The lady became very attached to him, so the visits were repeated often, and sometimes he even got to stay overnight. They lived in a beautiful country home, complete with servants. They would take Fyodor for rides in a horse-drawn carriage. They provided him with private lessons in language, music, and culture. I think they had ties to France, which, for the elite, was the culture to be immersed in at that time.

"However, the most important event was a visit to a surgeon. They asked the doctor to examine Fyodor's leg to see if it could be straightened. The surgeon said it would take several operations, but eventually it could be set so he could walk again. So the couple scheduled the first operation. Fyodor was excited. He would walk again without crutches. The first surgery went well, and with each progessive operation, his leg got straighter. Finally there came a point when his leg was straight, but it was still bandaged. He was so happy! He knew they weren't finished, but that didn't matter to him as long as he could eventually walk and run again."

"When was that, Mamo?"

"He was about nineteen when that last operation occurred." Mother paused for a moment, thinking. "Yes, it was 1917, and he was born in 1898. He was still in the hospital recuperating when the revolution started. When that happened, the rich land-owners and people of means had to flee the country. Everyone knew the Communists would kill the wealthy. One night, some-one who had connections with the Communist party warned Fyodor's benefactors that they were targeted to die and had to escape immediately. They had no time to tell anyone—they had to pack up and leave as fast as they could. Everything happened so fast that the couple couldn't even come to the hospital and tell him goodbye. They simply left and ran for their lives. He never heard from them again. All the doctors packed up and left, too. It wasn't safe for anyone to be connected in any way to the wealthy. A neighbor eventually visited Fyodor and told him what had happened."

I was amazed, trying to picture my father as a young man, lying in the hospital at the time of the revolution, with all his friends gone. I suddenly felt sad for him. What was he feeling? What was he thinking?

"Your father went back to live with his grandmother. He held a job or two as a clerk, then worked in the village office as a secretary. He visited friends and relatives, and because of his outgoing, friendly manner, he always managed to get invited for a meal. Fyodor was not bashful—if someone did not invite him to eat, he would wrinkle his nose and say, 'Do I smell something wonderful in the kitchen?' Flattered by his comments, women always responded anxiously, wanting to demonstrate their tal-ent for cooking. During the meal, he would tell some wonderful stories. And he always praised the food and the hostess, which opened the door for another visit. That's how he survived, and retained many friends and admirers."

Before and during the war, mother had been very tight-lipped about the past. But now that we had received permission to stay in the American zone, my mother became more relaxed. It was as though she needed to make up for the silent years—the times when she didn't dare speak her thoughts. Now that there was no danger of arrest, mother seemed more open. In fact, it was as though she *had* to talk, and I was the beneficiary, eager to listen and start piecing together a picture of my family history.

Among the few things mother brought with her in the bundle from our home in Drushkovka were some family photos.

She showed me a picture of my father as a boy at his father's funeral. He sat next to his grandmother, looking beaten down and sad, with an expression older than his years. A heavy shirt was buttoned at the collar, and his curly blond hair was tousled and windblown. The two uncles sitting with Fyodor and his grandmother had vacant stares, but Fyodor had a determined look, as though he was challenging the world. *Where did that spirit come from? I wondered. Was it sadness? Fear? Anger? Was he looking for someone to love and accept him?*

I tried not to interrupt my mother. I just listened as her tale unfolded. "Your father and I were married in 1920, in an Orthodox church where I often sang solos as a teenager. We had dinner with all of our relatives. Then we moved into Pashka's home because she had an extra room. That was nice because her house was near everyone we knew. Your sister was born in that house in 1921, and Pashka let us live there until your uncles and I built the house across the stream, where you were born.

"Your father had trouble finding steady work. He tried to obtain a teaching position in a local school. He ended up traveling to Konstantinovka, where he found a job teaching in a little country school in a village called Kurtovka. So we moved there, but we stayed only that winter. The school didn't have enough money to pay him; the only payment he received at the end of the month was ground cornmeal. We boiled it or I made bread from it, and that was all we had to eat. It was pretty monotonous, but we made fun out of the situation. We laughed a lot, and humor helped us keep from noticing the flavorless taste of our meager rations.

"He found another job at a school in Osynova, where the teacher was getting old and preparing to retire. She gave us a large room in her home. She had once raised chickens in this room, so we were in what was once a henhouse. Fyodor eventually acquired a little house to rent nearby. Since we had no furniture, we slept on the floor. But that did not matter; I liked it there. Everyone was friendly and welcomed us warmly. Your father took on extra students for tutoring. In return, the students and parents tilled and prepared the soil by our house and planted a garden for us, and they shared their stored food with us."

Then mother laughed lightly, remembering an event from over thirty-five years ago. "One night a young boy knocked on our window. We had already gone to bed, but I got up and opened the window. The boy placed a loaf of freshly baked bread in my hands. What a surprise! It was his way of expressing appreciation for us being there. We happily got up and ate that bread right away, while it was still fresh.

"The house also had a stable, so Fyodor bought a cow and we started to prosper (among peasants, anyone who had a cow or a horse was considered prosperous). We shared the milk with a neighbor woman who had four kids and no husband. I worked in the garden and it seemed like everything grew well; we had huge cabbages and lots of beets! We always had enough to share with our neighbor. One time when I gave her all the ingredients for borscht, she hugged me and kissed me because she was so happy. We felt like we were doing well—we had shelter and food, and all of us were healthy. Looking back, that was probably our happiest time. We lived there for a year and a half.

"But your father felt he needed to get a better education. For a long time he had wanted to go to the university in Charkow to study law. He had heard that they accepted poor students and that they had classes for all professions. He sent in an application and was accepted. So we moved again. But we couldn't find a place in which to live right away. Some distant relatives said we could live with them, so we moved into a room with a window that looked out over a pigsty. The house itself had once been owned by a wealthy man before the revolution, but the Communists had come in and destroyed its contents. They had stored coal in the room we lived in, and it was still filthy and black with soot. Even after scrubbing it over and over, from floor to ceiling, I could not get that room clean.

"Eventually a spot opened up for Fyodor to live in the university dormitory. He applied for us to live in the family dorm, but there was a long waiting list for families with children. So we were separated for a time—until finally he found an apartment and Ann and I rejoined him. It was a tiny place, with a bed and a table. We were now able to get food in the cafeteria, which helped tremendously. I tried hard to find a job, but there were many people unemployed. Jobs were difficult to find."

That seemed odd because the Soviet government was always bragging about how everyone worked and that there was no unemployment in this workers' paradise. But my mother's story showed that there was a major difference between the propaganda and reality. I nearly cried as I thought about how hard my parents had struggled.

Mother then told me about an early experience in Charkow:

"One afternoon on the way to the city park, we passed a bakery that had all kinds of bagels. We couldn't afford anything. I was barefoot—we didn't have money even for shoes. Fyodor wore old sandals. We sat down on a bench in the park and your sister was running around and playing. A man walked up and sat at the edge of the same bench. He opened a newspaper and quietly sat there reading. Ann had seen the bagels, and she came up to us and begged, 'Tato, buy me a bagel.' Your father leaned over and gently said, 'Little daughter, I would love to, but I don't have a kopek [penny].' Resigned, she ran off, but after a while she came back and said, 'Tato, can you buy me a bagel?' And again your father answered, 'I'm sorry, I can't because I don't have a kopek.'

"The man sitting near us saw and heard this exchange. He folded his paper, got up, and left. A few minutes later he returned and handed Ann a huge brown bag full of bagels—it was so full she could hardly put her arms around it. The man then introduced himself to us. Tscharlinkankevich—that was his name. He asked us how long we had been in town, and told us he was fairly new there, too. After your father explained our situation, the man handed us his calling card. 'Have your wife come by this address tomorrow,' he said. 'I'll see what we can do for you. You did say that you had experience as a cashier at a bank and other businesses?' he asked me. I said yes, I had.

"We were excited and encouraged with this heavensent friend. Naturally, first thing the next morning, I went and looked the man up. The address was that of an official-looking office building. I handed the receptionist the card, and immediately I was told to go upstairs, where the man met me. The first thing he wanted to know was 'How is Ann?' I told him I had taken her to kindergarten and she was enjoying it. He reached into his pocket and pulled out five rubles. 'This is for Ann, for bagels,' he said. I was stunned. I thanked him many times for the generous gift."

Mother shook her head. "Five rubles was a lot of money at that time. Then he took me to his office and wrote a letter to a certain person in a major department store that he knew needed some help. It turned out that he was the director of this store—the largest one in Charkow. I went there, handed the letter to the secretary, and a few minutes later my name was called. I met a gentleman who asked me what I was qualified to do. I told him I

had worked as a cashier at one time and had high recommenda-
tions, but I was willing to do any kind of work. 'Great!' he said.
'Our head cashier is going on vacation for three weeks. You
sound like an ideal stand-in. Report on Monday for work.'

"I loved that job. We also had access to food—it was a
government store with a cafeteria. Later, I was given the job of
head cashier permanently. Things were really looking up for us.
The manager was pleased with my work. I stayed there for three
years and saved up a nice sum of money. Fyodor thought I
should buy myself a Persian lamb coat for the cold winters. But I
had a secret dream; I wanted to use the money to build a little
house of our own."

Mother paused for a while. I wondered at the way her needs
had been provided. Was this how life worked? We had known a
lot of difficult times, but always, just at the right moment,
someone appeared in our time of greatest need to help us—to
provide food, a job, or a piece of clothing. I had to wonder why
our family was spared from destruction so many times.

"When your father graduated from law school, it was hard to
find a job in his profession. So the head of the university hired
him to teach courses in Ukrainian language and literature. I had
supported him the whole time he was a student; now he was
receiving a good salary. I had been away from my family for too
long, so I decided to go back home and take a break for a few
months. Ann was in school, so your father insisted she stay with
him and finish, while I took Thomas with me.

"When I arrived at home, I got all of my brothers and relatives together and we discussed and drew up plans for a house
on the lot across the creek from Pashka's place. A couple of men
knew how to lay a foundation. Others were good carpenters.
Everyone pitched in, and we built the house in a month!"

I could tell mother still relished that accomplishment. Her
face glowed at the memory. "I'll never forget the look on your
father's face when he came to visit. He was able to get a short
vacation from school and he came home to see me. The day he
and Ann arrived, they went to your grandma's house where I
would normally have been. When he got there, Alyosha led him
to the site of our new house. I was there with all of my friends to
greet him. He was completely surprised!

"The men from my former church choir had practiced a
special dedication song, and they sang a blessing upon our new

home. Then we broke open some watermelons and had a celebration. Dad was overwhelmed. He wept as he examined the lovely little house. He liked the red tile roof and red brick walls. He only wished he could have helped. But he never was very handy; it was better that others did the work!"

Then a cloud came over mother's face for a moment. "You know, most of those men who sang with me in the church choir were eventually deported to Siberia." She shook her head, fighting tears. "How senseless!" she whispered.

"So you and Dad moved into the house and settled in Drushkovka?" I asked.

Mother shook her head. "No, your father had to go back to his job in Charkow. A relative occupied the new house and as payment finished off the interior for us. Before I went back to Charkow, your grandma suggested that we plant some fruit trees. We had some land around the house, and we knew the food would benefit us all. So we planted at least twenty cherry trees and plum trees. Later, dad planted quite a few apple trees." She paused, choked up at the memory. "Those fruit trees saved our lives many times, Dotshitshka. My mother was very loving, and very wise. She taught me that it was important to take care of yourself, to work hard, to do everything you can to provide for your needs. Then you aren't at the mercy of events beyond your control."

It was shocking to hear those words. Though it had been ten years since we had lived under Soviet rule, a deep fear still permeated our lives. It was hard to imagine that there weren't spies nearby, waiting to pounce on our words and arrest us for undermining the state. A pall settled over us.

"Your father was arrested for the first time in 1928. He had heard rumors of men being arrested and sent to prison for unknown reasons. One night the police came and searched our apartment, then arrested him. They ripped open our mattress to see if he was hiding anything, and fingered the seams of our clothing to see if anything had been sewn into the hems. Ann remembers that—it was a terrifying night. Thomas was too small to know what was happening. They took your father to a jail called *cholodna horah*—it literally means "cold mountain." I went there every day to try and visit him for a few minutes, but I wasn't allowed to see him. They never explained why he was arrested. No one would tell me anything.

"At the prison, I got to know a young Polish woman. She was a beautiful girl, newly married, with no children yet. Her husband's cell was next to Fyodor." Mother became quiet all of a sudden, speaking in a barely audible whisper. "One day when I was sitting in the waiting room, she went in to try and see her husband. A moment later, I heard some commotion, and then I saw some men carrying her out on a stretcher. They carried her outside the building and I ran over to find out what had happened. Someone whispered to me that she had just learned that they had executed her husband. No reason was given for it. The woman was crying hysterically, and the rest of us were in a state of panic. Later, I had a chance to talk briefly with the woman. She racked her mind trying to figure out why they had done it. Her only conclusion was that maybe it was because her husband had corresponded with some relatives in Poland. At that time, the government policy was that you couldn't correspond with anyone from another country—not even relatives. She couldn't think of any other reason why they would kill him. It was an awful tragedy, and all of us were wondering if this was going to happen to our husbands. . . ."

Mother was silent now, her body shivering slightly. I felt the fear she must have felt nearly thirty years ago. It was like she was afraid to even remember these things, but they were a burden on her heart. "It's OK," I tried to assure her, hugging her close. "Please, go ahead. You can tell me."

Mother nodded, but said nothing for a while. Finally, she admitted, "I have never told anyone that story. In the past, it was too dangerous to tell about an experience like that because it reflected badly on the government. They kept a good front, and people feared imprisonment or death if they told others the bad things they saw."

"Mamo, you can talk," I said. "It doesn't matter now. Things are not like they used to be." But I knew even as I spoke those words that they were not completely true. It was difficult to remove the fear that was pounded into all of us who grew up in the Soviet Union.

"You could never trust anyone," she explained. "It was too risky to talk. I've just kept this to myself all these years."

"They can't hurt us now. We're in Germany, not the Soviet Union. We're going to be all right."

Mother nodded like she understood, but the pain on her face showed me that she was not convinced. I knew then that she would never completely trust anyone except her own children. Too many years lived in constant fear had enslaved her.

A few more minutes passed before she spoke again. "Fyodor was in jail for eight months, and then was sentenced to three years in exile. They shipped him off to Shadrynsk, in the Ural region, without even letting him pick up his belongings. I did the best I could with work. Your brother wasn't even two years old then. Every day I had to take Ann to school and Thomas to day care. A while later, Fyodor wrote, begging me to sell whatever I had and use the money to come and live with him. He wrote, 'If you don't come and help me, I won't last much longer.' He couldn't get a job while in exile because of his label. Plus, at 11:00 every morning, he was required to report to a parole office. No one wanted an employee who was exiled and had to leave work every day to report to the authorities. He had to walk four miles to sign in at the parole office—in drenching rain or raging blizzard, even if he was ill with a temperature of 103. There were no excuses for not coming in, and the consequences for missing an appointment were grave.

"I hated to quit my good job, but your father kept writing and begging me to come. So finally I quit and moved to the Ural region to join Fyodor. It was a hard train ride; I had two small children and all the belongings I could carry. Two people, a man and a woman—I don't even know if they were married—helped me. They said they were students, and they kindly asked me where I was going. I told them I was joining my husband, who was in exile. We reached Shadrynsk, which is a small town at the end of the railroad. This couple unloaded all my luggage for me, carried it to a certain spot, set the children on top of it, then they just disappeared." She shook her head. "It was so unusual. I don't know why they took pity on me. I am so thankful for people like that. Where do they come from?" she said with amazement.

"Fyodor met us at the station with a horse-drawn basket. I had never seen one before, but that was the custom of this area. It was funny climbing into that big, square wicker basket with all of our baggage around us. We couldn't see out except when we stood up. Your father and I were so silly, peeking through the gaps in the woven basket, trying to see where we were going. We laughed so hard—we were almost giddy. For a few moments we were able to forget our troubles.

"We then hunted for an apartment. There is a beautiful river in Shadrynsk—Fyodor thought he might be able to fish there. We found a place for fifteen rubles per month.

"Your father wrote a resumé for me, and I got a job in a big department store called Gastronome. I walked in and handed a man my application, and he told me there was nothing available. Just then, another man walked up and asked, 'What are your qualifications?' I told him I was a cashier. 'That's exactly what I need!' he said. There was a girl leaving in a few days to get married, so I was hired on the spot. Amazing, isn't it? It was perfect timing that I should come in at that exact moment. It was like I was meant to be there.

"I worked there until they closed down that store and I was then transferred to another store in town. There, I was one of two cashiers. The other cashier had daily run-ins with customers who argued that she was shortchanging them. She was peculiar—the store wasn't that cold, but she would sit there bundled up in a fur coat and nice fur-lined boots and smoke cigarette after cigarette.

"The managers complimented me on my work. One of them said, 'You're my guarantee cashier. We could come in here blindfolded and take the money out of the register and know it would match the receipts perfectly.' That was a wonderful pat on the back, and it made me try to do even better.

"One evening, I was working late. A party official came in and purchased a bottle of wine and paid me with a crisp, new ten-ruble bill. He didn't realize there were two bills stuck together. I pulled them apart and gave one back along with his change. He couldn't believe I didn't keep that extra ten rubles for myself.

"That was a good job, but eventually that store closed, too. I was given a certificate of guarantee concerning my performance as a cashier, and that allowed me to get a job at the bank. I was to count the money and sign for it—in other words, I verified that the count was correct. They gave me two guns, one on either side of me, for protection, in case someone came in and tried to rob the bank. One day Fyodor came in to see me and they wouldn't let him come upstairs until I identified him as my husband! He thought that was funny; he said, 'I need permission to see my own wife! What an important position!'

"Really, it wasn't bad living in Shadrynsk for three years. At the end of that period, we were given the choice of three cities where we could live. We couldn't go back home for another three years, so we chose Kursk, because Fyodor knew they grew lots of apples there. He figured we should go where there was food. So we left Shadrynsk on a sled—there was still snow on the ground—and we settled in Kursk. We found a nice little apartment. There was enough to eat. I found a decent job at a vegetable distribution center which was for NKVD staff only. I was a cashier and bookkeeper. Your father worked in the central office managing the collective farms in the area. He was a good organizer, and that's what they needed. Ann was in fourth grade, and Thomas was just starting school."

Mother became quiet again, and I knew she was recalling another troublesome period in her life. I was learning now that she had suffered a great deal before I was ever born—more than enough to prepare her for the dark days of World War II.

"Fyodor was arrested again that year. I don't know why; they never told you why. This time they held him for three months. He was in a cell with two other men. They eliminated into a bucket, and there was a broom to sweep up the mess if the pail overflowed. Everyone was desperately hungry. In order to survive, Dad gnawed on the broom, and encouraged the other two men to do the same. When the warden came by and asked where the broom was, they told him that they ate it. So he gave them another one.

"He wrote to me from jail: 'Maria, I beg you, please, send something for me to eat.' That was a difficult request to fulfill because Ann, Thomas, and I were starving as well. This was during the famine of 1933. We could barely stand on our feet because we were so weak and skinny. But somehow I found two potatoes. I boiled them and chopped them into small cubes and put them into the oven to dry. They got very hard, like rocks. I wrapped them up in a small box and sent them to your father. But he never got them. A couple of months later the package was returned to me. The potato cubes were moldy and green. So we didn't get to eat them, and father didn't, either. I felt terrible about such precious nourishment going to waste. Two whole potatoes were a real sacrifice for us. Little Ann stood watching me cook them and asked for a bite. I had to say no; I told her that her father needed food to survive and that we would make it somehow."

There were tears in both of our eyes as mother remembered the pain of seeing her children go hungry. "Ann and Thomas found a patch of new, fresh-grown grass, and picked it and brought it home. I washed it, chopped it up, and put it in water to cook. It tasted just horrible—it was almost impossible to swallow, but we had to eat something, so we forced ourselves. I also traded a dress for a glass of flour. But then I couldn't do anything with the flour. I needed other ingredients to make bread. Later I traded a blouse to get some beans. The beans were counted ten at a time before the trade—that's how precious food was. May God protect us from having to live like that again! It was so bad, we constantly dreamed of food while we slept and thought only about how to obtain it during the day. Nothing else mattered.

"Your sister befriended a little girl whose family were party members. They had access to food. Ann was extra friendly to her, hoping maybe to get a tiny morsel of leftovers. One day, she met the girl while she was carrying a hot meal of meatballs and noodles. Somehow, in her carefree, friendly way, Ann talked the girl into sharing a meatball and some of the noodles. Of course, she didn't have any container, so she just lifted the front of her dress to make a pouch and the girl dropped the food right onto her dress. It didn't matter if the dress was stained—a bite to eat was all that was important."

"So some people did have food?" I said.

"Only very few. Mostly those who worked for the NKVD. They had storage areas of food that were locked up. No one had access except those with privileges. I worked at a place where they stockpiled food, and only certain NKVD staff had keys. They helped themselves to products while we starved."

Mother, who never expressed bitterness, sounded sad as she continued: "This was exclusively for important party members. Because I was the bookkeeper, I had to keep track of the transactions in this storage place. But I couldn't have any of the food for myself. Sometimes my manager would ask the officials if maybe something could be given to us employees. If we were lucky, we would occasionally get a few potatoes, or maybe a jar of pickles.

"After Fyodor was released from prison, he was assigned to work again in the same office he had worked in previously. This time, instead of money, they paid him with a loaf of bread and a sack of flour. From that, we would make dumplings. My mother heard of our hardship, and wrote to me and urged me to come home. She said there were one or two factories nearby where the workers got extra food rations. Fyodor said to go ahead and take Thomas; Ann needed to stay with him until she completed the school year. So I went home, and I'll never forget arriving in Drushkovka. My mother boiled some water and put some burned black bread into it to color it so it would look like tea. Then she removed the mush from the 'tea' and added sugar. That was a special treat!

"I had no problem finding a job in Konstantinovka. I worked in a factory office. They had a cafeteria there, so I didn't go hungry. It was a good job and I made some friends. Fyodor was homesick and begged the NKVD to let him come home and be with the family. When they refused, he wrote to me and pleaded for me to come back to Kursk. But I had a job that provided food, and I didn't feel I should let go of it. Then all of a sudden, he showed up at my mother's one day. They had released him and let him come back to our village. So Ann and Fyodor came home and we settled in our little brick home for the first time as a family."

"That was in 1933?"

"Yes. And even after your father came home, he insisted that I quit my job. He wanted to be the breadwinner. He thought that I liked my job too much and that maybe I could get along without him. At times he seemed jealous. We had some disagreements over this. But to keep the peace, I quit my job and stayed home. And he found a job in a new factory as a lawyer. Of course, they didn't pay him as much as they would someone who had not been in jail or exiled. So we had to get by on very little. He had to travel to other cities on assignments, and sometimes he brought home little presents for us. Also, every time he went to a different city, he brought home a different kind of apple tree. Eventually, we had a collection of twenty-five apple trees. We had big apples and little, sweet and sour, green and red and yellow."

I switched the subject and asked mother where I fit in. "Was I born yet, or on the way?"

"You were born in 1936. We had lived not quite three years in our new little house. During the last months of my pregnancy, it was colder than usual. Blizzard winds blowing snow and ice paralyzed almost everyone and everything. Your father was out of town on business. I tried to keep the house warm, but there was hardly any firewood. And water had to be carried into the house from a well. One day I bundled up and carried two pails with me. The ice in the well was thick, and I had to pound it in order to create a hole large enough for a pail to go through. It was exhausting and slippery work. Then I had to carry the two full buckets back through deep snow. The hard work caused me to go into premature labor.

"You weren't a pretty baby. You were small and scrawny when you were born. But we all loved you very much, and you gained weight quite fast and filled out all your wrinkles. Ann especially took to you. She would not let you go. Even when she was studying, she had you on her lap, sometimes rocking, sometimes singing to you. Your father also loved you, and as you grew and began to understand words, he would bring a little something home from work for you. He would hold up an apple, look at you closely, and say, 'Apple.' You would smile and say, 'La.' Then he held up a pear and tried to teach you to say, 'Pear.' All you would answer was, 'Lu.' That was all you were able to say when they came that night in October and took him away...."

A chill came over me even though it was warm. That fateful night had forever hung over me, depriving me of my father.

Mother went on: "The lawyer came out of your father continuously. He wanted what was right, but the government did not solicit his opinions, and they didn't like others listening to him. He could not keep his thoughts to himself."

I could see a war of emotions within my mother: On the one hand she loved him deeply, on the other she was frustrated that he had not been more diplomatic and that he often ignored her warnings. She had not lost hope that maybe one day they would be reunited. It had been sixteen years since he had been carried away in the middle of the night, but she waited. She remained faithful, committed to her marriage and her children. Yet there was also disappointment and deep hurt simmering beneath that love. She felt his arrests were unnecessary. He should have given in sometimes and played by the rules. Why did he have to stand up for what he thought was right? Why did he have to jeopardize the lives of his wife and children?

"Your brother was friends with a boy at school whose father was a party member. He sometimes stole food from his family and brought it to us. He once brought us a slab of bacon—he just hid it under his shirt and brought it to me. One day as they were walking home from school, he whispered to Thomas, 'I heard that some men are going to come and arrest your dad. I heard my father talking about it with my mom last night. They thought I was asleep, but I heard them talking.' This frightened Thomas and he immediately came home and told us. But Fyodor didn't take it seriously. I urged him to go away for a few days, but he refused. He thought he was safe. 'How many times can they drag a man back and forth?' he said. But sure enough, they came and arrested him about a week later."

With sadness in her voice, mother said, "It didn't have to happen that way. If he had believed the boy's warning, he could have gone away for a few days. But he was too naive. In fact, a friend of ours was supposed to be arrested that same night. The police came for him, but he conveniently managed to be out of town on a pretense of family illness. He returned two nights later, but they never came back for him. That kind of inconsistency happened all the time. If you knew they were about to arrest you, then you just conveniently took a trip or hid out somewhere for a while. Most of the time, the police never bothered to come back."

By now, mother had regained her composure and was simply stating matter-of-factly that her husband was a strong-willed man who said what he believed without counting the cost, who refused to run and hide from the party officials, who stubbornly took a stand for what he perceived to be the truth.

SUMMER 1956

Mother and I were eating dinner one evening when the doorbell rang. As was our custom, I looked out the window overlooking the street to see who was at the door three stories below. It was Mrs. Shechowzow. I hurried down the stairs to let her in.

"I have news for you," she said as she followed me back upstairs. Mother prepared some tea as our guest caught her breath.

"My husband received a letter from a relative in Kiev. He was recently down in the area near your village."

Mrs. Shechowzow didn't hold us in suspense for long. Speaking to mother, she said, "He inquired about your husband."

I felt my heart stop. I couldn't breathe. Deep within my heart I yearned to find him and to embrace him and to get acquainted with him. I felt like there was a missing piece in my heart that only he could fill.

And then Mrs. Shechowzow said, "He is alive and living in Drushkovka."

I tried to fight the tears, but failed. I looked over at mother and saw that she was crying, too.

This was incredible news indeed—father was alive!

16

Two Different Worlds

FALL 1956

Mother wrote immediately to my brother and sister in the United States, telling them about the good news. Then she wrote to father:

Fedija,

We just heard the good news that you are alive. Your whole family is alive and well. Emma and I are living in Göppingen, Germany. Hanusia and Tarasik are now living in America. We are eager to hear from you.

Yours,

Maria

A few days later, a letter arrived from my father. Apparently he had written as soon as he was contacted. Mr. Shechowzow's relative had given him our address. His letter was written in large, elegant Slavic script:

My dear, beloved wife,

My heart was warmed to hear that our family is still alive after so much suffering. My deepest desire is to see you all again.

Please write to me.

Your Fedija

This exchange took place at the height of the Cold War between the West and the Soviet Union, when all letters were censored. Thus our notes had to be brief. Neither of us could take any chances. If we said too much, our letter might never arrive to him. Nor did we want to inadvertently endanger his life.

While we were thrilled to communicate sporadically by letter, we knew there was no hope of ever seeing him. As a former prisoner, my father couldn't possibly leave the Soviet Union. And we couldn't go back. It was good to know he was alive, but there was nothing more we could do.

Mother continued to do cleaning work for Frau Euler, and we still shared the tiny apartment on the third floor above the photo processing lab. I was working in a china shop and enjoying an active social life. I spent a lot of time with the German Youth Association (GYA), which met in a vacant home just a block away. It was designed by Americans to foster better relations between the local townspeople and the occupying forces.

The GYA arranged, on Sunday evenings, for young girls and guys to attend chapel services with American soldiers at the post. There were English and German interpreters available to encourage joint attendance. An American-sponsored school bus would pick up young people who wanted to attend, and drive us to the post. After the services, we would go to a fellowship hall for snacks, music, games, and other programs. It was a lot of fun. Sometimes we would play charades, or a soldier who knew magic would demonstrate some tricks. I loved those two hours on the base; the American soldiers were generally nice.

Not much was said to me personally about associating with Americans, but it was clear that some older German people didn't like it. For example, Frau Euler turned up her nose at anything that wasn't German. Though she accepted help and business from the American victors, she resented their ways and behavior. "They are soldiers, and soldiers have only one thing on their minds!" she would say. Germans were often portrayed as reserved and disciplined, while Americans were viewed as uncaring, loose, and irresponsible.

Younger German people, however, didn't feel the same way, and we enjoyed meeting the soldiers and learning American ways. The men I met at the chapel were always polite and neither I nor my girlfriends ever experienced any misconduct from them. Though I had already studied English in school, my conversations with American GIs helped me become fluent in the language.

Those were fun years as I slowly emerged from the protective cocoon of my mother and sister and the horrors of the war faded into the past. But the bond with my mother never weakened. She not only remained my security, but also became my best friend. We talked about everything, even about the boys I met. Marriage never entered my mind; I was having too much fun going to dances and meeting new friends. So I was totally unprepared for Bob.

SPRING 1956

A neighborhood friend who worked at the army base selling *Stars and Stripes* and other papers and magazines told me about a job opening at the club for noncommissioned officers. "They are looking for a girl who can speak English," she said. "It's good pay—better than what you are getting here in town now."

The pay from my current job, combined with my mother's pitiful allowance, gave us barely enough money for food and other necessities. I had faithfully given mother all of my pay, and she would dole out some change whenever I asked her, which was not often. Sometimes I would ask for 75 pfennigs (cents) to go to a movie. The rest of our money was used as needed. If both of us needed new shoes, we would take turns. One of us would get a pair this month, and the other would wait until next month. So the higher-paying job at the club sounded attractive; I wanted for once in my life to be able to buy a new garment with my own money or to buy Christmas presents for my family and friends.

The next day, I met my friend at the post exchange and she pointed me in the right direction. I felt uneasy being on my own at the base without all my friends. I entered the club, which was a large room full of round tables with a long bar on one side and a small stage with a piano on the opposite side. Three men sat around a table next to the stage. Two were in uniform, the other was in civilian dress. My immediate reaction was to leave quickly, but I really wanted the job. Finally, boldness conquered my shyness. I went up to the table and spoke in my best English:

"Excuse me. May I speak to the manager? I have heard you need someone to work here."

The men stopped talking and looked at me. "I'm Sergeant Jones, the manager," said one of them. "What kind of job experience do you have?"

"I worked for a hat shop. And presently, I'm working as a salesgirl at a store that sells figurines and china."

"Have you ever waited on tables?"

"No." I didn't mention that at one time I had determined I would never wait on tables. But I swallowed my pride, and added, "I'm willing to learn whatever I need to do."

One of the other men grinned as I talked. "Go for it, sarge!" he said. "What are you waiting for?"

"OK. You've got the job," Sergeant Jones said. I stood there, shocked that it had been so easy. The sergeant laughed and said, "Why don't you stay right here? We can start you right away. Ellie, my senior waitress, will be here shortly. You can watch her tonight, then start tomorrow."

OCTOBER 1956

I was a waitress to sergeants and their wives, who would come in for hamburgers and drinks. I had worked there for a few months when a black sergeant came into the club and watched me the whole time I served him. As he stood to leave, he asked me my name.

"Amy," I said.

The next day, he returned late in the afternoon. With him was a tall, blond-haired soldier in civilian clothes.

"Amy, this is Bob," said the sergeant. "He's a buddy of mine."

Bob was smiling, and I smiled back and said, "Hi!"

When Bob finished his drink, he stepped onto the stage and played a few notes on the piano. I assumed he was a musician and was trying out this particular instrument. Then as he started to leave, he caught my attention.

"I leave on a three-week field trip tomorrow," he said. "Maybe when I get back, we can have a date."

"Oh, sure!" I said kiddingly, thinking that he would probably forget about me by the time three weeks were over.

Sure enough, three weeks later, he appeared at the club door in his field khakis and waved to me. I stepped outside for a moment. His faced beamed as he asked, "Can I take you out tomorrow for a coke? We'll go to the EM [enlisted men's] club."

"OK. That would be fun," I answered casually. Guys were always wanting dates with me. Once in a while I went out, but most of the time I laughed them off. That night, I told mother about meeting Bob. "His appearance reminds me of my cousin Paul back home. He has the same beautiful blue eyes."

The next day the weather was bitter cold. I walked the three-mile route to work bundled in a bright red wool coat with the wide collar up and wrapped around my face so that only my eyes were exposed. My fingers tingled from the cold, despite the heavy gloves I had on. The military policeman on duty waved me through the gate. There, just a few yards inside, was Bob, waiting to see me for a minute. He was wearing his fatigues and a warm cap. His hands were stuffed deep in his pockets, his nose and cheeks glowed a bright red, and he stomped his feet in an effort to stay warm.

I stifled a laugh as I told him, "You are the coldest soldier I have ever seen."

Bob's blue eyes sparkled and he smiled at my attention as he answered, "There is a good reason for that!"

"What's that?"

"I *am* the coldest soldier you have ever seen. I hate winter with a passion!"

"With what?"

Realizing that I didn't yet understand some of the nuances of English, he rephrased his statement: "I absolutely hate winter."

Remembering my confinement during the cold winter days in Drushkovka, I sympathized: "I don't like winter, either."

"I'll see you tonight?"

"Just take me to someplace warm," I laughed.

"Definitely."

He was waiting for me outside the club when I got off work. We walked down to the EM club and I ordered my favorite drink, an orange soda. There was a band playing at the other end of the room. Several couples were on the floor dancing, so we joined them. We danced for a few numbers, then sat down again.

"You remind me of a cousin," I said as we sipped our drinks. "His name is Paul, and he has blond hair and blue eyes, just like you."

"I would like to meet this Paul," Bob answered.

"Actually it would be rather difficult to meet him. He lives in the Soviet Union."

Bob was intrigued. "You're from Russia?" he asked.

"Actually, Ukraine."

Bob looked confused. "Where is Ukraine?"

"It is part of the Soviet Union. It borders Poland on one side. Have you heard of Kiev?"

"I'm not sure."

"You've heard of Moscow?"

"Of course!"

"Well, Moscow is the capital of Russia, the largest republic in the Soviet Union. Ukraine is the second-largest republic, and it's southwest of Russia."

"I thought it was all one country."

"It is, but the Soviet Union is made up of several republics."

"Like the United States?"

"Similar. But our republics were once separate countries. In fact, we have our own language in Ukraine."

"You mean you don't speak Russian?"

"Oh, yes, I speak Russian. I also speak Ukrainian."

"Is that like Russian?"

"It's similar but different. The Soviet government has made Russian the official language throughout the country, but we Ukrainians have kept our language alive. What we speak is actually a mix of two languages."

Bob's eyes sparkled as he was introduced to a whole new world. "So what is this Ukraine like?"

"Well, it's called Russia's breadbasket. We have wonderful farmland."

"How many people live there?"

"It's a big area, and I don't know how many live there. Maybe thirty million?"

Bob whistled. "I can't believe I have never heard of it. How long have you been away from home?"

"Thirteen years."

"Are you going to go back?"

"I can't go back. After the war, we gave up our citizenship. And now . . . well, it's a long story. Sometime I'll tell you. Right now, my mother and I are in the process of emigrating to the United States. My brother and sister are already over there."

"I hope you are admitted soon," Bob answered with a gleam in his eye.

Someone came up and tapped Bob on the shoulder. "It's time," he said.

Bob smiled at me and said, "I'm supposed to sing now."

"You're a singer?"

"I have been assigned to special services. My job is to entertain troops throughout Germany. I have just been given the job of putting together a traveling show with various musical acts. I'll be back in a few minutes."

Bob went on stage, talked with one of the musicians, then stood at the microphone and sang a couple of songs. His golden baritone voice was made for the romantic songs he sang! As I gazed at Bob, his music melted my heart. Then he announced, "For my final number tonight, I have a special song I want to dedicate to a new friend." He looked at me and smiled as he began to sing:

> Two different worlds,
> We live in two different worlds.
> And we've been told
> That a love like ours
> Could never be.
>
> So far apart,
> They say we're so far apart
> And that we haven't the right
> To change our destiny.
> When will they learn
> That a heart doesn't draw a line?
> Nothing matters
> If I am yours and you are mine.
>
> Two different worlds,
> We live in two different worlds.
> And we will show them
> As we walk together in the sun,
> That our two different worlds
> Are one.

As the crowd applauded, Bob made his way back to our table. "That was beautiful!" I said.

"I was thinking of you as I sang. Isn't it something that we should come from opposite sides of the world..."

"And meet in the middle, here in Germany! You have such a beautiful voice. You should make a record."

"It's funny you should say that. I have plans to contact Columbia Records when I get back home."

"So you are going to be a professional singer?"

"Those are my plans. But I also have a job with Armstrong Company waiting for me when I get back. They are a large flooring company in America. After I graduated from college, I went to work for them and took six months of intensive training with them. I did this so I could have something to fall back on in the event the music business doesn't work out."

I was impressed by Bob's thinking. He was a dreamer, but also a realist. "I hope you keep singing," I said. "My family has always enjoyed music. You should hear my sister sing. Everyone called her 'nightingale' because she has such a beautiful voice. We used to sing together a lot."

"I would love to hear all of you sing," said Bob.

During the rest of our date, we were both nervous and shy. But afterward, we couldn't wait to see each other again.

* * *

During subsequent dates, Bob spent many hours asking questions and listening to stories about the hardships of my life.

I also learned about Bob's home. On our second date, he told me, "I'm from Indiana, from a town called New Castle, with a population of about 18,000." He pulled out his wallet to show me some pictures.

Now I was the one to look befuddled. I knew little about the United States, and I had never heard of New Castle or Indiana.

Pointing to a family portrait, Bob continued, "This is my family. Dad, mom, my brother Dick, and my sister Eileen. My dad is a lawyer."

He looks like a lawyer, I thought, looking at his small mustache, smoothly combed hair, and nice business suit.

"My brother Dick lives with his family in Austin, Texas, and so does my sister. They are both married and have children." I looked again and noticed that everyone was dressed up, wearing hats, and the ladies wore white gloves.

Bob then showed me a picture of his home. It was beautiful—there was nothing in Göppingen that resembled it. The house was painted white and had arched doorways and windows. It looked like buildings I had seen in pictures from Spain or Italy.

"What a beautiful home and family," I said.

"It was a great place to grow up. Indiana is a hotbed for basketball—every boy who can do so plays the game. I played basketball in high school and college, and also sang with a band."

Bob's life sounded much more exciting than mine. "I wish I could have grown up in America."

"I wish you could have, too," he said tenderly.

I appreciated Bob's sensitivity. It was fun talking with him. Just as I told mother about everything else, I told her about Bob and our dates. I looked to her for approval and advice, and if there was even the slightest hint of disapproval, I knew I would not continue the relationship. Up to now, I had never dated anyone more than three times—that was the way I handled men. I did not know how to cope with their advances, so I always cut off relationships. The schools I had gone to were for girls only, and I had grown up without a father, so I was naive to the ways of men. I ended several friendships abruptly, hurting the young men's feelings. But my actions had nothing to do with them; I was simply insecure and my rejection allowed me to escape situations I didn't know how to handle.

I also never brought dates home. I was too embarrassed by our tiny place, and Frau Euler would have been most unhappy to see me host a GI. But I mentioned every relationship to my mother. She was my guide, and all she would have had to say was, "No, my daughter, he's not for you," and I would never see that man again. But with Bob, she just listened and smiled.

Bob was special. He tried to spend time with me whenever he or I had time off. One evening, he walked with me back to my home after picking me up from work. We entered the foyer and talked quietly. Mother heard the front door unlock and came down the steps to see who it was, so I introduced Bob to her. After he left, as I was preparing for bed, I asked, "What do you think?"

"He seems like a nice boy," she answered. That was an encouraging endorsement, and from that time on, Bob was the only man I dated.

One quality I loved about Bob was his surefootedness. I was deeply insecure and introverted. Bob was full of life and enthusiasm. Most of our time together was spent sharing our love for music. He had a ukulele that he would bring to our little apartment and we would sit and sing songs all evening long. We learned many new songs using sheet music that was available to the American soldiers.

Soon after we met, Bob invited me to ride with him on the train to Stuttgart, where he was doing a show. It was a relaxing trip, and it gave us a chance to talk more. As we chatted, Bob asked me to tell him more about my childhood.

"I grew up at the edge of a small village. My mother's family built the house. We had fruit trees and a garden. We were a close family."

"What about your father?"

I didn't answer immediately. I rarely talked about my father. *What should I tell Bob?* I wondered. *If this relationship is serious, he should know. But if not, why should I go into detail?*

"My father was taken away when I was a baby. I don't remember him," I said, hoping that would be enough.

"Taken away?"

"Arrested."

"Why?"

I shook my head. "We don't really know. My mother says he was charged with being an enemy of the people. But I'm sure he wasn't an enemy. That is how the government in Russia operates—many people are arrested for no reason at all."

"Is he still alive?"

"Yes. For over fifteen years we didn't know if he was dead or alive. But recently we learned that he is alive." I was silent for a moment, then added, "My father was a lawyer, too." That seemed like another link between Bob and me, though I had no idea if there were any differences between a Russian lawyer and an American lawyer. There probably were; almost everything Bob had told me about his life in the United States was dramatically different from what I had experienced. I was from the East; Bob was from the West. Hadn't I heard a saying somewhere that never the twain shall meet?

Bob reached over and touched my hand. My fingers slipped among his. His palm was sweaty . . . or was it mine? Whichever it was, I sensed a special affection deepening between us. We were from such different backgrounds, yet those differences seemed to draw us together. I especially appreciated his listening ear. He seemed to genuinely care about me, my family, and my father. It was easy to open up my heart to him.

On our next date, Bob jolted me with a new topic of discussion. "There is something I have often wondered about, and since you lived in Germany during the war, maybe you can help me understand. It's about the Jewish people. Were you aware of what was happening to them? Did you know about how they were murdered in the gas chambers?"

"What are you talking about?" I looked at him in disbelief. What he was saying sounded like fiction of the most gruesome kind.

"Surely you must have heard about it," Bob explained. "At least six million Jews were murdered by Hitler. In the United States, we have all seen the pictures. Our army rescued many

Jews from German camps at the end of the war. Didn't you see any of that?"

I shook my head, trying to comprehend the horror. "No. I saw none of that. And no one has ever spoken about it to me. The German people I know have never mentioned it."

"I suppose it's not something they want to talk about," Bob sadly noted.

"I've had some Jewish friends in school. But they never said anything to me. They are treated just like everyone else."

Bob's questions haunted me and I began to inquire about what happened to the Jews. Whenever I talked with my German friends, they acknowledged nothing, and changed the subject. I went to a library and read newspapers and watched newsreels, and gradually the truth emerged. I had no idea of the atrocities going on around me as a child. As slaves, we were not given any information or news. I began to realize that our family had miraculously slipped through the worst of the hellish system devised by Hitler. I shuddered to think of what had happened, and was unable to comprehend its scope. We had personally experienced the cruelty of the Nazis, but we had also met many Germans who were kind and who seemed incapable of such killing. I realized now that we had been totally unaware of the guillotine raised above our heads, and of the invisible hand of God that had moved it away.

FEBRUARY 1957

Mother and I didn't have a phone, so on the very rare occasions when we needed to use one, we used Frau Euler's. Frau got tired of calling me to her phone as Bob and I became more wrapped up with each other. Every free moment, we were together. Bob was now traveling all over Germany doing shows at military bases. Whenever possible, I went with him.

We spent a romantic evening in Salzburg, Austria. After a show, Bob took me to the Cafe Winkler. We reached it by riding an elevator to the top of a cliff and ate on a patio overlooking the birthplace of Mozart. A twenty-four-piece orchestra serenaded us, and we danced into the early morning hours. I believe that was when we began to realize that we were falling deeper in love and that maybe we wanted to spend the rest of our lives together.

When Bob wasn't traveling, he enjoyed being in our little apartment. Many times he wanted to ask questions about our past. He would ask mother questions and I would translate them into Russian, then translate her answers back into English. I honestly didn't think my life was that fascinating, but Bob was intensely curious about it. Through his questions, I learned more about my country and my father.

One evening, Bob got mother to talk about the years of famine, when my father was in and out of prison. "You say the government caused the famine," Bob said. "Why would they cause their own people such suffering?"

"In order to confiscate all the gold and silver," mother explained. "That is how the general population lost any power it might have. The government grabbed all valuables and hoarded them for themselves. There was a store in our town with food displayed in the window—rice, sugar, flour. And over the window was a sign that said, 'Available in exchange for gold only.' Once the people traded in their valuables, there was no option left but to starve."

Bob was astonished. "You actually saw people starve to death?"

"One neighbor across the street from us starved to death. Her daughter came home one day and there was the police, carrying away the body of her mother. I knew her well." Mother halted. She sighed, as if she was reliving the scene. "One day she came over for a visit and I shared some beets with her. They were leftovers from work, and they were tiny, bitter, and dry. I would chop them up and set them out to dry. They were so bitter that when you put them in your mouth and chewed them, eventually you had to spit them out. But they helped us survive."

Bob just shook his head, unable to comprehend such horror.

On another occasion, he asked mother to tell about my father's arrest. After she told the story, Bob gently said, "It must have been awful. How did you keep going?"

"There were many times I thought I couldn't take any more. That was part of the government's plan—they terrorized the family, too. You can't imagine how much it hurt. They wouldn't tell me anything about Fyodor. They made me go through all kinds of procedures in order to make contact with him, but then they wouldn't let me see him."

Mother was quiet for a while. I wondered if it hurt her too much, to recall these memories.

"When was the last time you saw your husband?" Bob asked.

"About a year after he was arrested—in 1937. He was on a train, about to leave for Siberia." Tears flooded my mother's eyes, and for a moment she was too choked up to talk. After so many years, the memory was as vivid as if it had happened yesterday. "He begged the guard to let him give me a hug. 'She won't be mine anymore after today,' I heard him say. So I yelled to him, so that all could hear: 'I'm going to be yours no matter what. I'm yours forever.' He signaled his love for me, and we looked at each other, communicating with our eyes that we loved each other. . . ."

Quietly, my mother cried. Bob and I cried with her. Finally she said, "I knew they were sending him to Siberia, but I had no idea where. After that evening, I didn't hear from him for nine months. Then one day a mailman came and handed me a note. The handwriting looked strange—like that of a school child. I thought maybe someone was playing a joke on me. I opened the envelope and inside was a note that said, 'Dear citizen, if you find this note, please mail it to the address on the back.' Our address was written on the other side. Fyodor had scribbled the note, folded it several times, and thrown it from the train window, hoping someone would find it. The note itself said, 'We have just passed Moscow and are heading toward Siberia.'"

"So they didn't even let you write to each other?" Bob asked.

"They let us write once a year. The next letter arrived with my husband's handwriting on the envelope. It was smuggled out by a man who had served his term and had just been released. It was a long letter, and Fyodor described in detail how he lived. Writing and delivering such a letter was dangerous; if Fyodor or the released man had been caught, it could have cost both of them their lives.

"Fyodor wrote that they were living like sardines in a barrel. 'I don't know how I got here or why I'm here,' he said. 'You hear only cussing, filthy language, and spitting. It's a raw way of life. It's an impossible situation.'

"That letter broke my heart. He also said I would receive a letter from him just once a year—that was all he was permitted to write—and that the next one would be short. I prayed after reading that letter, and begged God to protect him."

Bob respectfully asked, "Did you hear from him again?"

"The last time I heard from him was in the spring of 1941, right before the Germans invaded Russia. He begged me to come and see him. He said, 'If you don't come, we won't see each other until the next world.' But it was impossible for me to go."

Mother then nodded toward me. "I couldn't leave you and Thomas, and I didn't have any money for a trip. And besides, I didn't know if I would be allowed to see him once I got there."

"Now that you know he is alive, are you corresponding with him?"

"I have written one letter," mother answered. "And he has written one to me. But it is very difficult. I'm sure the authorities inspect our mail carefully."

Bob's eyes were moist. It moved me to see how much he cared about our situation. "Do you think there is any way you will ever get back together?" he asked.

Mother shook her head. "I suppose there is always hope. But the situation is not promising. The best we can expect is to receive an occasional letter."

It became quite evident that Bob was developing a love for my family. I could see he loved my mother, and she loved him. I thought it was special of him to care so much about the father I never knew. His care and concern made me want to be with him more and more. And I began to wonder if our two different worlds might really become one.

17

A Special Birthday

FEBRUARY 1957

O ne snowy evening, Bob and I came back from a romantic dinner at a little German restaurant. Mother fixed us tea. While we were talking, Bob asked, "Say, your birthday is coming up soon. What would you like me to get for you?"

"I don't know," I said, blushing. "Anything you want."

"Well, do you like jewelry?"

"Sure I like jewelry. But I have only two pieces that were given to me. Let me show you."

I ran to the back room and carefully picked up a little box on top of the dresser. I returned with the box and took out a watch and a plain, antique silver ring. "This ring was given to me when I was confirmed," I said. "So it's very special. That's why I keep it in this box."

"Why don't you wear it?" Bob asked.

"I save it for special occasions."

"Does it fit?" he said with a twinkle in his eye.

I slipped the ring on my finger. "See! It fits."

"It's a pretty ring!"

*   *   *

A couple weeks later, we celebrated my twentieth birthday. It had been three months since our first date. Bob arrived in the morning, but several of mother's friends and some neighbors had already arrived to wish me a happy birthday. He sat and squirmed nervously, looking flustered and impatient. I had never seen him this way, but there was no chance for us to talk with the constant flow of company.

Finally, after three hours, Bob could no longer wait for all the people to leave. Grabbing me by the hand, he guided me to the back room, saying, "Honey, we need to be alone for a moment."

As soon as the door was shut, he said, "Honey, do you remember the first time we met? I told my friend that night, 'That's the girl I'm going to marry.' It was love at first sight."

With that, he reached into his coat pocket and pulled out a small velvet box. His hands trembled as he opened it, revealing a ring that was a combination of white gold (American style) and yellow gold (German style). Carefully, he lifted the ring out and took my hand.

"Happy birthday, honey. Will you marry me?" He slipped the ring on my finger. "I love you."

For a moment, I was speechless. This was a total surprise! I stared at the ring. It fit perfectly, and it was so beautiful. Then I reached up and hugged Bob around his neck. "Of course I will!" I answered.

For a moment we hugged each other, then a knock on the door interrupted us. Mother stuck her head in and said, "Our company is leaving. You had better come and say goodbye to them."

So we emerged and announced our engagement, prolonging the celebration and congratulations!

Later that evening, I remarked to Bob that the ring fit perfectly. "How did you know my size?" I asked.

With a twinkle in his eye, he confessed, "It was easy. When you showed me your silver ring two weeks ago, I saw exactly where you kept it. You left the room for a moment, and I borrowed it. I took it to a jeweler in Stuttgart and had him measure the size so he could make the ring I gave you. The next time I came to see you, I was able to slip your ring back into its box without you knowing it!"

I giggled and said, "Well, how did you know I would say yes?"

"How could you resist?" he smiled.

*   *   *

Marriage was the first serious decision I had ever made. When I thought of leaving mother, I felt torn, even though Bob seemed like the perfect man for me. Bob still had another year of service in Germany, but then he would be going back to the United States. Of course I would go with him, but mother couldn't join us because she had not been approved for emigration. I couldn't bear the thought of leaving her in Germany by herself.

Bob understood my emotional struggle. "I've never seen a closer relationship than the one between you and your mother. You two are as close as a finger and a fingernail!"

"That's a good comparison," I said. "And what happens when you try to separate a finger from its nail?" Bob winced at the picture as I continued: "I know that when I marry you I have to let go of my mother. But it's going to be hard. We have been through so much together that I can't bear the thought of leaving her and going across the ocean to a new continent thousands of miles away."

"Why would you have to leave her? Why can't she go to America, too?"

"She has been denied several times. They say she has scars on her lung X rays. They want to keep checking to see if her condition changes. They want to be sure her scars are old so they won't erupt into tuberculosis."

"Your mother doesn't look sick to me."

"Well, she isn't. She has never had tuberculosis."

"Something seems wrong here. I'm going to check into it."

FALL 1957

Marriage between an American and a girl labeled a "DP" (Displaced Person) wasn't an easy process. The American government required an unbelievable amount of paperwork. Because I wasn't an American, I had to go through an intense investigation before the army would grant Bob permission to marry me. People at my job were questioned about my background and reputation. They were asked about my behavior: Did I smoke? Did I drink? and so on.

"Why are they asking all these questions?" I asked Bob.

"I guess they want to make sure you aren't a spy," he joked.

I laughed at that incredulous possibility. "Well, who would I be spying for? I don't even have a country!"

That statement struck Bob as very funny. He quipped, "I had never thought of that before. When you think about it, you were shot at by Russians, Germans, and Americans. There wasn't any country that liked you!"

"I wish we could get married the normal way, like everyone else, instead of having to go through this long investigation and all the paperwork."

"Me too, honey. Maybe it won't take too much longer."

Finally, after six long months, we were granted permission to marry. When an American soldier wanted to marry a foreign girl, the law stated that he first marry her according to American requirements, then to make it legal, marry her again in front of a German official.

The wedding was quite simple. Mother and I had no money, and Bob was a private first class in the army, so his pay wasn't much. Thus there was little to plan.

Bob had written to his parents about our engagement and his mother sent me a package with a lovely white dress. I used it for our wedding. The owner of the hat store where I'd had my first job made a veil for me. I bought a nice pair of white high-heel shoes. So I was all set for the big day! We had our American service in the military base chapel. Chaplain Blair officiated, and mother, Bob's supply sergeant Tom Brewer, and Tom's wife witnessed the event. Then we had a small reception in Frau Euler's living room where our friends dropped by throughout the evening to wish us well and have a piece of cake.

Newlyweds in Germany don't typically go on a honeymoon, but Bob wanted to do this the American way. However, it wasn't possible immediately. He had to apply for leave, and there was a waiting period. Several weeks later, we had our honeymoon—a whirlwind tour to Paris, then down to Rome and Venice, and finally back up to Austria.

Living space was scarce in Göppingen, so we set up house-keeping in the same small apartment mother and I had used for the last several years. She had the bedroom; Bob and I had the living room. Mother cooked for us on a hot plate in our tiny kitchen. The bathroom was one floor down, and in the cellar, down four flights of stairs, was our refrigerator. It was a cozy arrangement, and Bob seemed to relish it.

FEBRUARY 1958

The time was rapidly approaching when Bob's tour of duty would end and we would be packing to go to the United States.

While I was involved in all the paperwork for our marriage, Bob was working on getting approval for mother to emigrate. We went through the application process, and again the word came down: There are old TB scars on her lungs. Application rejected.

During Bob's first trip to Munich, he inquired at the American consulate why mother had been rejected year after year when she had never had tuberculosis. The official at the consulate insisted that her X rays showed scars that needed to be watched.

"But how can that be?" Bob protested. "The first time she applied, her lung X rays were clear. And she hasn't had tuberculosis since. She's in good health."

The man shrugged his shoulders and said there was nothing he could do.

Bob decided we should have mother checked by a local German doctor—a nationally renowned lung specialist. I went with them. Dr. Hradezki examined her and took fresh X rays.

"I find no scars on your lungs," he reported. "At least, none that look like they are active or have been active for years."

There was something wrong. How could the earlier set of X rays show scars, and this one show none?

"A switch?" the doctor asked.

"What do you mean?" I inquired.

"Suppose someone has diamonds or money. He wants to emigrate to America, but he has tuberculosis. He bribes a doctor or someone who has access to X rays to switch his X rays with those of someone whose lungs are clear. Poof! The X rays are replaced with those of someone who has no money. Problem solved. It happens all the time."

"Are you telling me that my mother's X rays could have been switched—that the X rays in her file are not hers?"

The doctor shrugged his shoulders. "I can't say for sure, but that is possible. I have heard that it happens."

Bob and I took the new X rays to the American consulate in Munich. Bob explained the situation and presented the evidence. "Let's place the two X rays side by side," Bob insisted. The official brought out mother's file. He took out the X ray and Bob put the new X ray next to it.

"Now look!" Bob said. "These are not the same lungs. It's obvious that the X ray in her file belongs to someone else."

The official seemed unmoved. "How do I know your X ray really belongs to your mother-in-law?"

Bob became angry. "There is one easy way to find out. Call her back in and take a new X ray yourself. Then you will see that she doesn't have tuberculosis and that she should be approved to emigrate."

But the official shrugged his shoulders, and said, "I can't do anything."

Now Bob was hot. His face was only inches away from the bureaucrat's. "Now you listen to me. It just so happens that my congressman is on the armed services committee, and he is a close family friend. How would you like for him to launch an investigation concerning this discrepancy, and possibly many others like it?"

The man turned a little pale, and told Bob, "I think our time is up."

"OK. I'll leave. But you will be hearing from my congressman."

Bob immediately wrote a letter to his family friend, Ralph Harvey, who was a United States congressman from his home district. All the facts were laid out. In a matter of days, a return letter was sent to the consulate. A few days after that, mother received notification that she was approved for emigration!

At long last, after a wait of seven years, we were now assured that mother could leave Germany. We would finally be all together again—this time, in a land of freedom.

FEBRUARY/MARCH 1958

America. To me, the name represented an earthly heaven. I was truly excited, for now I had a country I could call home. I was looking forward to a better life, to a chance to belong, to blending in and not being looked upon as different or foreign or poor. I imagined settling down with Bob in a little house with a white picket fence and living happily ever after—just as I had seen in movies and read in books.

At the same time, I was torn apart by many questions and anxieties. Mother would not be able to come for a few more months. Who would care for her after Bob and I left? She still spoke poor German. Would she be able to finalize her emigration arrangments by herself? Who would help her when it came time for her to travel?

Bob left Germany first, and I followed soon after on a space-available basis on a military ship. As I embraced mother at the train station, I was suddenly overwhelmed by the reality that I was leaving. I cried on the train all the way to Frankfurt, thinking about Bob's analogy of the finger and its nail. The hurt was much worse than I expected: Tearing a nail off a finger would hurt, but at least the pain is local. The pain I was experiencing now was deep inside, and nothing could relieve it.

At Frankfurt, I had instructions to board a special train for military dependents headed for the port of Bremerhaven. There, I boarded the ship *General Upshur*, and before we had even crossed the English channel and entered the Atlantic Ocean, I was horribly seasick! The ship doctor and Lou Ann, a young American lady I had met at the port, dragged me up to the deck each day in hopes that the cold air would help me recover. But my stomach didn't cooperate, and the mere thought of food was revolting. I lost all track of time until the news came that we were approaching the Statue of Liberty. Knowing the journey was about to end helped pull me to the deck to view this great symbol of freedom.

The sight of this great lady brought a chill to my spine. She reminded me of how much my life had changed. As the sea air revived me, I thought again of the early morning sights that I enjoyed while sitting on the step in front of my house in Drush-kovka. How simple my world was then! A few fruit trees, a stream, a garden, a three-room house, and a shed. If fate had allowed, I could easily have stayed and lived my life in that cozy environment. But events beyond my control had uprooted the family. I winced as I recalled the train trip to Germany—my brother, mother, and I crammed into a train car meant for farm animals. The horrors of the camp still gave me nightmares; I had never told anyone about the little boy beaten by his grandmother. The years in a camp for Hitler Youth, the year spent hiding from Russian authorities who wanted to take us back to the repression of communism, and the adjustments to living in a country that didn't want us but had to endure us . . . surely these had shaped my life. But now things were going to change. The great lady of hope seemed to say to me that my insecurity, fears, and night-mares would all fade away. A new life filled with unlimited possibilities was ahead of me. I would be free—free to be myself, free from criticism and persecution. And best of all, there was the happy prospect of married life!

As the boat docked, a large crowd drew near to greet us. I anxiously searched the faces, looking for Bob. Finally I saw him in the midst of the crowd, standing on his tiptoes, waving and grinning. I was so glad to see him that immediately I felt a surge of new energy, which was further intensified by the excitement of the crowd and the great city. Buildings soared higher than I ever imagined possible. People were everywhere, more than I had ever seen. But all I cared about right now was being with Bob again. We had a wonderful reunion in each other's arms. He then picked up my bags and we walked away from the dock.

After I told Bob about my trip, I asked him how his talks had gone with Columbia Records. He told me he had met with Arthur Willey, the vice president in charge of recording. "I called right after I arrived. He was very cordial, but he said to me, 'I'm sorry, Bob, but the music industry has changed. Sinatra isn't even making it any more, so it makes no sense to introduce a new talent with that style of music. The new star is Elvis Presley. That's what we're looking for now."

"You must be terribly disappointed," I said.

"No, not really. I thanked Mr. Willey for his kindness. I appreciated the opportunity. But now I'll move on. I have a job waiting for me with Armstrong. I don't know where I will be assigned, but I hope it's Texas."

"I'm sorry the music didn't work out for you. But we're together, and I'll be happy wherever you are."

We checked into a hotel and began a whirlwind of sightseeing. The top of the Empire State Building, a bus tour of the city, fabulous restaurants, a movie (*The Brothers Karamazov*), and the Rockettes at Radio City Music Hall. It was too much to take in. This was a totally new world filled with more possibilities than my mind could ever imagine.

On top of the Empire State Building, I looked out over the vast city and recalled myself as a little girl climbing on the roof of her little home in Drushkovka and thinking that Germany was just over the horizon. How big that world had looked, and how insignificant it seemed now. I felt like a little chipmunk who had emerged out of his hole to discover a world that was huge and terrifying and thrilling.

Then we packed the Volkswagen Bob had shipped over from Germany and began our trip to Indiana. The turnpike was jammed with cars as we left the city, and there were so many colors! In Germany, all the cars were dark—mostly black. Here, variety seemed to be the rule. Ladies' apparel bombarded women with infinite possibilities—in Germany, the options were varieties of brown, gray, or black.

After a long drive, we pulled into the driveway of Bob's boyhood home in New Castle, Indiana. His mother was waiting for us at the door, and instantly I noted how attractive she looked, far better than the pictures Bob had shown me. She was dressed stylishly in a beige-toned striped dress along with silk stockings and high heels. The home was like a fairy-tale castle; I had never seen such a beautiful home. All the floors were carpeted—it was the first time I had ever seen plush wall-to-wall carpeting. In Germany, I saw rugs in some houses, but the floors were largely wood or linoleum. Bob's home was filled with furniture, and it was all coordinated and of the finest quality. I gazed at a buffet that displayed a beautiful set of dishes and glasses, all coordinated in burgundy and pink. I didn't recognize the purpose of some of the pieces, so Bob's mother explained: There were dessert bowls, a shrimp dish (I had never seen shrimp, so that still didn't make sense), cocktail glasses (what were cocktails?), and rooster tails. *The American language has some funny names,* I thought.

Bob's father arrived home and greeted me warmly. Then we sat down for dinner. I noticed immediately that I was not eating my food the way they did—I held my knife and fork in the wrong hands. After dinner, Mr. George announced that it was dessert time. He asked me, "Have you tasted American ice cream?" I hadn't, so he suggested we go to the store for some. We drove to the grocery store, and just as I was about to push open the door, it flew open automatically and I stumbled in. My astonishment was just beginning! We went to the ice-cream section and Mr. George asked, "What flavor would you like?" I stared in amazement. There were so many varieties available, I simply couldn't choose among all the options. Bob's father laughed at my uncertainty and said, "No problem. We will just have to come back each night until you have tried every flavor."

Since the Georges were a prominent local family, I was soon introduced to a series of social events. The first one was at the home of a local businessman and his wife, close friends of the Georges. I arrived in a terra-cotta linen dress, hanging on the arm of my proud husband.

"Roger and Mary, I would like you to meet my wife, Amy."

"How do you do, Amy? It's so good to meet you. We have heard so much about you. . . ."

Bob would then move to another couple and say, "Mr. and Mrs. . . ."—there were so many names, I couldn't remember them all—"let me introduce you to my wife. . . ."

Then Bob spotted an old friend across the room and quickly made his way over there, leaving me alone in a sea of strangers. As I tried to follow him, a woman from a nearby group intercepted me: "We're so glad you are here. How do you like the United States so far?"

"Thank you. I like it very much," I said nervously.

"What a beautiful dress," said the woman. "Where did you get it?"

I mentioned the name of the store in Indianapolis, where Bob's mother had bought it for me.

"Oh, I absolutely love that place. You know, I got the most gorgeous blouse there recently. . . ."

I was trapped! The women in this group were talking about the latest fashions, a garden party, and their children. "Michael is doing great in college. He joined the Alpha Chi fraternity . . ." "My Michelle is performing in a play. She has the lead role . . ." "Ken made the football team. . . ." I stood mute, unable to understand their conversation, much less participate in it.

When I finally slipped away, I was offered a plate of stuffed celery. "Oh, no thank you," I answered. "The smell of celery makes me sick. I had some on the boat coming over. I still can't even look at it!" My blunt comment was greeted by a strange look from the hostess.

I listened in on some other groups. The men seemed to talk about business. "Just closed a deal with . . ." or sports, "The Hoosiers are going to have a great team this year. . . ." Who were the Hoosiers? What I was hearing was so different from the talk around kitchen tables in Germany. It seemed most of the people here had been to college and that everyone had something in common. There was talk about sports, money, business, social clubs, and cars. I got bored hearing about money and business. How different this seemed from the serious and often impassioned discussion of politics and world events that we'd had among the refugees in Germany.

My reaction was to keep my mouth shut as much as possible. Anything I said seemed to be misunderstood anyway. In Europe, people were open with each other; here, it appeared that a person had to hide his or her real feelings—or was this a matter of diplomacy? How was I ever going to fit in? When I did speak, people seemed to laugh or be shocked or embarrassed.

During dinner, I sat next to a teenage girl named Cookie, the sweet daughter of the Hammers. She only picked at her plate, eating a few bites of meat, and not even touching her vegetables. She looked pale to me, so later as we were saying our goodbyes and leaving, I shook Cookie's hand and said, "Cookie, you look pale. You need to eat better food, like vegetables and fruit. You really don't look well." She just blushed and there was sudden silence all around me. Bob's mother looked like she wanted to disappear into the ground, but his father was trying to suppress a grin.

Fortunately, Bob thought I was charming and humorous. Some people seemed to be amused at my bluntness. But I didn't mean to be funny or shocking; I simply didn't know how to be anything but honest. And I certainly didn't know the mannerisms and niceties of a small, conservative midwestern community. Thankfully, my life as a socialite didn't last long.

Bob, as he wished, was assigned to Dallas with the Armstrong corporation. Three months later mother arrived in America to live with my sister in New Castle, Pennsylvania, and we all settled down to a new life. Little did I know that though the long journey beginning in the village of Drushkovka had finally come to an end, I was now about to embark on a new journey of a different kind.

18

A New Master

I had not thought much about what life would be like when I was married. I'd had no example at home, so I didn't know what to expect. However, on the way to the United States, I did briefly dare to imagine living in a nice home with a picket fence and a man who was loving and romantic. However, it didn't take long before I was met with the stark reality of life. Within three years of our marriage we had two children, and I had my hands full.

I was totally involved with the raising of Debbie and Bobby. They were a blessing and served, in most instances, to keep my mind off the frustration I continued to experience. I was determined to work hard and be a model wife, mother, and house-keeper. The German work ethic was ingrained in me. There is a German expression, "*Sie hat den putzteufel*," which means, "She has the cleaning demon." I had him! Every day I scrubbed, polished, and washed. Everything was spotless. I also supported my ambitious husband in all that he did. I was behind him all the way.

Bob's work required him to travel every other week. He was drawn away from the family in order to invest more and more time in his career.

Before long, my old feelings of insecurity and loneliness began to surface. I was thankful for the security he provided with his work, but it seemed that his job was more important than his family—at least, that's how I felt. He would say to me, "Honey, I'm doing this for you. It's part of the job."

For some reason, however, I was never comfortable with that attitude. How about the children and me? Even when Bob was not on the road, he still worked late. And after work, many times he was in a bar with his clients. I felt that family was far down Bob's list of priorities, and I didn't like it. In fact, I felt more like a servant. Dutifully I kept the house and pressed his clothes—even his underwear and his socks. But he didn't even seem to notice or care. One day he came home and told me how he had gotten complimented for one of his accomplishments. My answer was, "That's great, but what about us?" That made him angry.

Every time I tried to express my frustrations about our marriage, it was like talking to the stones in the fireplace. Soon it became easier to simply say nothing. I became bitter on the inside. I felt like a duffel bag crammed full of resentment and frustration. Outwardly I stopped complaining, though deep down I yearned for someone to listen to me and understand. Wasn't there anyone I could talk to? Perhaps my mother . . . but I didn't want to burden her with my problems. And I was too private of a person to discuss these things with my female friends.

Bob's ascent up the corporate ladder was rapid. But for some reason his ambition exceeded his progress—the company wasn't moving fast enough for him. He came home one night and announced that we were moving to California. There wasn't any discussion. Being a good wife, I felt I had to support him wherever he went to earn money. Bob's first job in Southern California was that of managing a twelve-story office building. Over time, he became the owner of his own flooring business.

While this new business brought increased financial security, my loneliness intensified. Bob's routine of coming home late after entertaining customers continued. Many nights I cried myself to sleep. When was this going to stop? I was tired of the turmoil it caused our family. It seemed like Bob had no idea and did not care to know how to love me or our children. In fact, on more than one occasion, he said to me, "Honey, I love you as much as I could love any human being. But that isn't very much." Those weren't encouraging words.

On rare occasions we would go to church, but most of the sermons seemed to revolve around politics and social causes. There was little that applied to my daily life. Yet we continued to go because we thought it would provide a foundation for the children.

I was reminded of the simple love I'd had for Jesus as a child. I had prayed so fervently then, and God had answered those prayers. He was real, and I knew it! So I went back to Him and prayed, "God, I'm so tired of worrying about my husband. I'm tired of him going to bars and coming home late and ignoring his family. I know You don't like divorce, but I'm about at the end of my rope!"

One night Bob was out entertaining some business colleagues in a bar. He called early in the evening to say he was staying for one more drink and then would be home. He didn't call again, and he didn't come home. I knew the pattern. It wouldn't be one drink, but several. My anger rose as the hour moved past midnight. I watched "The Tonight Show," and then a late movie. Bob still wasn't home. I finally went to bed, buried my head in my pillow, and prayed, "Lord, I can't take this any longer. Surely You can do something!"

What were the options? Well, I knew where Bob was. "Lord, I could call the police and tell them where he is so they will arrest him when he comes out with liquor on his breath." No, I didn't want that to happen. Then I said, "God, maybe You could see that he gets into an accident on the freeway on the way home. Not a bad one! Just knock him out real good. Maybe then he will come to his senses." But was that the answer I wanted? No . . . so I went back to my earlier prayer: "God, surely You have another man, a better man for me."

Bob eventually made it safely home that night, without any arrest or accident. And we had the biggest fight of our marriage.

One evening a few weeks later, the phone rang late at night. It was Bob's mother. She told him that his father had cancer. He was at the Mayo Clinic, and had just gone through surgery to have part of his throat removed. The news hit us hard—Bob's father was a wonderful man, thoroughly honest and moral. He was probably the only person on earth Bob could say he deeply loved. Bob immediately flew back home to Indiana to be with him. When he returned home, he told me of some poignant moments with his dad.

Bob told me that when he arrived and walked into their beautiful home, his dad was standing in the middle of the living room. He weighed only about 125 pounds and had the most pitiful expression Bob had ever seen. Choking back their tears, they greeted each other and discussed dad's condition. Later in the evening, in garbled speech, his dad said, "Bob, I worked all my life to make enough money to eat anything I wanted to eat. Now I've got the money, but I can't eat."

Bob told me, "My heart sank when I heard those words." He related that after mom and dad went to bed, for the first time in many years he cried uncontrollably over the frustration of life. His attitude was best expressed in the song lyric, "What's it all about, Alfie?"

As in our early days of dating, Bob was beginning to open his heart and express what was happening inside of him. He also shared how he felt when he was flying out of Los Angeles: "I was looking down from the airplane after we took off. I realized here I am, flying back to see my father, and he is dying of cancer. Down below, I can see all of Los Angeles. But everything is so small. Somewhere down there is my big warehouse that I am so proud of, and I can't even see it from the plane—it's so insignificant. It makes you think. . . ."

Before now, Bob had refused to discuss the subject of death. Now he started to think about life and what it was all about. Was success in business the answer? Was it money or possessions? What did man live for? These and other questions haunted him as he saw his father's health deteriorate.

A few nights later, Bob called to tell me that he was stopping for a drink with his friend Fred before coming home for dinner. "Remember, mom is here," I said. "Please be home by seven so we can eat together." Bob promised he would.

Before Bob got home, Fred called, asking for Bob. "I thought he was with you!" I answered.

"No, I haven't seen him all day," Fred answered.

After I hung up the phone, I didn't know what to think. But I was hurt. When Bob arrived home, I asked, "Who were you having a drink with tonight?"

"I told you—Fred," Bob answered.

My hands were shaking as I tried to open a package of spaghetti noodles. I couldn't believe Bob would look me in the eyes and lie to me. When I couldn't get the package open, in total frustration I whirled and flung it at him. It missed and splattered against the wall, spreading noodles all over the floor.

Bob stared at me in disbelief.

I exploded. "What is wrong with you? How can you think of going out for drinks and lying to me about it when your dad is dying?" Unsure of what to say next, I turned and stormed out of the kitchen.

My mother was in the living room. Gently, she said, "Don't be angry, dear. It's not all that bad..."

"Look at him!" I answered. "He's a liar."

"Yes, look at him," she soothed. "I feel sorry for him being trapped in a lie. It shows on his face. He knows he is guilty. Don't be so harsh with him."

"How can I forgive him?"

"You need to calm down first. Why don't you two take a walk? I'll stay with the kids. Take your time."

Her soothing words swayed me. We took that walk, and for a while, there was silence between us. Bob finally broke the ice. He placed his hand in mine, and I accepted it. Slowly he tried to express some thoughts from deep within: "Sometimes I... I get this feeling like... like there is no meaning and purpose in life. You get up in the morning, go work yourself to death in order to make some money, go home, go to bed, get up the next morning, go to work, and make some money so you can go to bed and get up the next morning.... I don't know when I have ever felt so low. Let me explain what happened tonight."

Bob then shared how earlier that evening, for the first time in his life, he went into a bar by himself. "I sat there, drinking alone. I had always said I would never do that. But there I was, feeling so low, drinking by myself. The whole time I was there, I was asking myself, 'Why am I feeling so empty inside?' I have everything in life that I always thought would make me happy. I have my own business. In a few more years, I could be a millionaire. I know and hobnob with the celebrities and high rollers of California. I have a big, black Lincoln Continental convertible. I have a home with a swimming pool nestled in the hills of Southern California. So why should I feel totally empty inside?"

He paused for a moment, then said, "Honey, I shouldn't have lied to you, but I was so ashamed and confused that it seemed like the most natural thing to do. I couldn't have asked for a better wife or two more beautiful children. From the world's standpoint, I have everything anyone could want. But to be honest with you, I really do not know what purpose there is in living."

My anger melted away and my heart went out to Bob. "When you're feeling this bad, why don't you talk to me about it?"

"You know, honey, the one I think I really need to talk to is God."

How could I argue with that? Yet I still didn't understand why Bob felt he had to lie.

That weekend, we were flipping through the channels on the television and came across a special program. We listened as a group of young people talked about having a personal relationship with Jesus Christ. We could tell they had a quality of life that we hadn't seen before. Bob seemed particularly impressed with the testimony of a young man who had just won an Olympic medal in weight lifting. He stated that all of his life he had searched for power, and he found it in the Person of Jesus Christ. These people weren't talking about religion; they were talking about a relationship. At the end of the program, there was an offer to write in for a free book. Something seemed to touch us; we had never written anywhere for anything. But the next day, I jotted off a quick note requesting this book.

A few weeks later, we received an invitation to an open house hosted by the sponsor of the program. I wasn't particularly interested, but Bob immediately announced that he wanted to go. I was encouraged that Bob was open to this new direction, but I didn't see how this would change our problems.

The open house was held in an outdoor amphitheater with several hundred other guests. While listening to the speaker, Bob seemed nervous and jittery, but he hung on to every word. It was basically the same message we had heard on television. At the end of the presentation, Bob eagerly hurried forward to talk to the speaker.

I was not close enough to overhear what they said, but after a few minutes, I saw Bob crying and bowing his head, apparently praying. Then they talked a little more. Bob then brought the man up and introduced him to me. "Amy, this is Dr. Bill Bright."

Bill smiled, shook my hand, and then told me, "Amy, your husband just accepted Christ into his life as his personal Lord and Savior. Have you ever prayed and asked Jesus into your heart?"

I shrugged my shoulders. "I think so, but I'm not sure."

"Would you like to make sure?"

"Yes, I would." With that, we prayed together for the assurance of my relationship with Christ.

When we were done, Bill gave us a little more information, encouraging Bob and me to read the Bible together, pray daily, and share what we had learned with others.

On the way home, Bob exclaimed, "I feel like I have been washed clean with a scrub brush!"

Over the next two years, Bob and I buried ourselves in the Bible, and Christ became the central point of our lives and marriage. Everything started to change. And one day it suddenly dawned on me that God had answered that prayer I had spoken when Bob was out late in the bar.

That night, I asked to have him arrested. God answered, "No."

I then asked God to get him into an accident and knock some sense into him. Again, God answered, "No."

Then I said, "God, You must have another man for me." To that, God answered, "Yes!" What I didn't expect was that it would be the same man!

Bob started talking about Christ with everyone he met. But the main burden of his heart was his dad. While Bob's father was in Austin, Texas, visiting his daughter, he became very sick. Bob immediately flew to his bedside. Bob had already sent his dad material about Christ and had talked to him over the phone many times. Although there was an openness, he did not know where his dad stood in his relationship with Christ. Dad called Bob and his brother, Dick, to his bedside and told his sons, "All the things that you think are so important in life become absolutely meaningless when you're lying in a bed dying of cancer. What really matters to man is his relationship with God." Dad then looked at Bob, and said, "Bob, I have read the materials you sent . . . and everything is A-OK."

Bob left his father's side that night without shedding a tear, yet with the knowledge he wouldn't see him again on this earth. By the time Bob got home, the phone was ringing. It was his sister, informing him that his father had gone to be with the Lord. The first words out of Bob's mouth were, "In all things give thanks, for this is the will of God concerning you in Christ Jesus."

The dynamic of that experience is what solidified in our hearts the desire to spend the rest of our lives communicating the good news about Jesus Christ to anyone who would listen.

19

An Unexpected Call

SUMMER 1970

O ne day I was sitting quietly, praying. I began to pour out my deepest feelings to God, and felt again the warmth of talking to Him with the simplicity of a little girl who alternated speaking to the Father one night and Jesus the other so as not to "offend" either. I said, "God, I know it's impossible for me to ever see my father here on earth. But if You could, would You please allow me to be able to see him in heaven? Please send someone to him to tell him about the love of Jesus Christ."

Bob and I prayed many times for my father's salvation. And with that, a deep desire began to blossom in my heart to write to my father. I had never written to him, but felt now it was time to get in touch with him.

For a long time, I sat at my desk with a blank sheet of paper. How do I introduce myself to my father? What do I say to a man I haven't seen since I was a baby? Other members of my family had communicated with him—for the most part, my mother and sister. We heard from him once or twice a year. Undoubtedly, more letters never arrived. And every letter, coming or going, was censored. It was dangerous to say too much. Innocent statements could easily be misconstrued by the censors and cause problems for my father.

I held in my hand the last correspondence from him—a letter to my sister.

March 6, 1970

Dearest Hanusia,

I'm getting well!

The Reaper bypassed me this time. I'm still coughing and have a hard time breathing. It's a good thing that I never drank or smoked. In my lifetime I haven't smoked as much as finishing one cigarette.

I have, dear Hanusenko, a small request of all of you: Maybe as a group (or between all of you, as a family) you could obtain a pair of shoes for me—without shoelaces—and with soft soles. I cannot bend down to tie laces, and if someone puts shoes on me, I have to wait until they can help me to take them off. You once sent me a pair of slippers, but they had laces and they wore out a long time ago. Consult with one another and please help me because such footwear is unavailable here (even the devil does not possess any).

Greetings to all,

Your Tato and Grandpa Fedir

I tried to imagine the man writing those words. What had he endured since he was torn away from his family more than thirty years ago? What pain had he suffered? Not just physical pain . . . what was the condition of his soul? What emotions did he have when he thought of his wife and children? Had he found someone to comfort him and give him companionship after all these years?

My eyes moistened as I thought about how historical forces had cruelly separated my mother and father. For years, he never knew what had happened to his family, probably assuming we were all dead. Then he learned we were alive. How had he reacted when he found out we were alive but knew that he could never see us?

Surely he missed his loved ones. The one recurring theme in his letters was his desire to see us. His first letter to us, after he had learned we were alive, conveyed his hope that we would be reunited someday, somehow. It became his reason for living, and he would not leave one stone unturned in his attempt to find a way to come to us. But the Soviet government would not give him permission to leave the country. It was out of the question to allow a man with dad's background and experiences to travel abroad. He knew too much. They were not taking a chance with the possibility that he might tell people in the West about life in Siberia, about his persecution. And we certainly could not go to the Soviet Union to see him. An impassable chasm separated us. We were divided by ten thousand miles, but it seemed like a million miles. It was fruitless to hope. My father might as well have lived on the moon— seeing him was such an impossibility.

So what was I to write? I tried to picture him, sitting in a chair in a small room, his shaved head reflecting a dim light, his hands holding my letter. What would he think as he read words from a daughter he had last seen when she was only eighteen months old? What would he want to read? Maybe how I admired him, how my mother had praised him, or how his love of life had infected me.

Picking up my pen, I breathed a prayer: "Lord, give me the words to communicate Your love to my father." Then I wrote in Ukrainian, "Dear Tato."

Tato. That was the Ukrainian word for *father*. I had never called anyone father, or dad, or tato. It felt awkward and strange. But I wrote:

> *Dear Tato,*
>
> *I do not remember you, but I have heard about you all my life. Mom has always spoken well of you. I am married to an American, and we have two children, a girl Debbie and a boy named Bobby (that is the American name for Robert). My writing in the Russian language is very poor since I was educated only in the German language.*
>
> *Although I have never really seen you, through your letters to the family, I've learned to love you. I have another friend like that—His name is Jesus. And just like you, I've never seen Him. But through His letters to me in the Bible, I've grown to love Him. I hope you can meet Him someday.*
>
> *With love,*
>
> *Your daughter Emma*

Letters to and from the Soviet Union took months to exchange. It was nearly six months later when I received a letter from my father. I trembled as I carefully opened it and read:

Dearest Emotshka!

I am an atheist. You lifted me from the hospital bed with your letter. I read it and continued to regain strength.

It is pleasant and joyful for my soul as I saw for the first time in my life your handwriting and read your warm and sincere words.

Yours, Dotshitshka, was not a bad father, but his fate was different than that of other people. It turned out that you only grew up to know your mom. I am happy that all of you honor and love your mother. She deserves to be adored and pampered. She also has gone through so much.

But let's not touch old sores and open cuts. Let's not remind ourselves of the past, as these things bring back the fever and pain in the heart. May the devil take the past!

I am happy that all of you are alive, that you are united, that you see each other sometimes, that you are happy together, and that you are helping one another.

But please don't forget about us. Write, be brotherly, keep in touch. Hope for the best. Hope for a reunion.

I am embracing Robert and children.

Your Tato and Grandpa,

Fedir

I read and reread those words, and my heart was warmed. We were separated by so great a distance and so many years, yet there was such deep affection. But the first line in his letter puzzled me: How strange the "I am an atheist." Did he really mean what he wrote, or did he write that to get the letter past the censors?

"Lord, what do I say now?" I prayed. How else was I to touch father but through my God? "Lord, You love the whole world, so I know You love my father. I know that he hasn't heard of Your love. I know it's impossible to ever see him. But I want him to know that You love him, and that he, too, can one day be in heaven."

So I wrote again:

Dear Tato,

I will never forget you! Even though we may never see each other here on earth, it is my deepest desire to see you someday in heaven, where we will never leave each other again. Jesus gives eternal life to all who believe. Please trust Him in His forgiveness and His risen life. My prayers and love are with you.

Emma

My father's response was short but sweet:

Dearest Emotshka!

Received your warm letters. I am saving them and reread them often.

Fortunate are the people who believe and live godly lives.

I believe a little, but am constantly trying to live a godly life, not to do harm to anyone, not to hurt anybody.

Pray and ask the Almighty for a blessing—for us to meet.

Tato

His letter indicated that he didn't understand what I was talking about; there was no mention of Jesus—no understanding that only through Christ could he have eternal life.

1970-77

Since arriving in the United States, my mother and I visited each other once a year and talked every week on the phone. Much of our conversation concerned the children, Debbie and Bobby, who were growing into wonderful young people. Both of them had also come to Christ and were growing spiritually. Naturally, I wanted my mother to know more about how she, too, could come to know Christ as her personal Savior and Lord.

My mother had provided everything I ever needed in both a mother and a father. She had met my every need, especially my emotional needs. I had never struggled with her acceptance—she loved me and accepted me, so with her I always felt secure. I believe it was because of her love that I so readily recognized the unconditional love of God in Christ Jesus and opened my heart to Him. Ultimately, of course, no human being can fill the deepest need inside a person's heart. But my mother was a great comfort until the time Jesus came into my life.

During one of her visits to our home in California, I asked mother if she wished to place her trust in Jesus Christ and ask Him to come into her heart as her Savior and Lord. She was ready to take that step of faith and gladly prayed with me for Christ to be in her life. Later, she told me how she had learned a little about Christ in the Russian Orthodox church in Russia before the revolution. She had even sung in the choir as a soloist, but had never understood that she could invite Christ to live in her. This common love for Jesus now bound us together even stronger than before.

During this period my sister and her husband, Mike, and their family had also come to Christ. So upon mother's return to Pennsylvania, where she lived with my sister, they were all able to grow together in His love.

But what about dad? There was no way for us to get together in this world. Our only opportunity was for us to see each other in heaven. Yet how was he going to hear about Christ? I couldn't go and tell him. And it was too dangerous to write more specifically— our communication might be cut off by the censors. So again I prayed, "Lord, I can't tell my father about Your love the way I want to. But surely You have people in Drushkovka or somewhere in Russia who know You. Would You please send someone to him and tell him how much You love him? Would You please tell him about Your Son so that when he dies and when I die, we can see each other in heaven?" That was my constant prayer for the next five years.

MAY 1977

It was a Sunday night. As was our custom, we attended the evening service at church, and by the time we came home, it was ten o'clock. We had hardly walked into the house when the phone rang. I picked it up and said, "Hello?"

"Emotshka, this is your mother."

"Mom, hi. What is happening? Are you all right?"

"Yes, Dotshitshka. I'm OK. But please sit down." There was no place to sit except on a stool, so I stood as she continued: "Your brother just called from Chicago. He said an airline employee called and asked him if his name was Thomas Wasylenko. He answered, 'Yes, why do you ask?' She answered, 'Because there is an old man sitting here in the airport crying. He says he is your father.' Emotshka, your father is in Chicago!"

I gasped and sat down on the stool. "My ... I mean, our father?"

"Yes, your father!"

"I can't believe it," I stammered. "This just cannot be!"

Mother took a deep breath and, in a calmer voice, began to fill in the details. "He landed in Chicago sometime this afternoon. All he had was his passport, plane ticket, and an address book. He was feeling very sick."

I felt numb, unsure of what to say next. "How long is he staying?"

"I don't know. I didn't talk to him. He is not well, and he is worn out from the trip. Your sister is taking the first flight to Chicago in the morning. Once she gets there, she'll determine his condition and let us know the situation."

"Should I go, too?"

"Not yet. Let's wait until Ann gets there and see what happens."

That night I couldn't sleep. All of my family was in chaotic turmoil as we rejoiced at this impossible event. My father was in America! What were we going to do next? He was seventy-nine years old. The trip must have been quite an undertaking; I was glad Ann would soon be there to help him. Her medical training in Russia had prepared her to be a wonderful nurse. And it felt strange to know that at the age of forty-two, I was finally going to see my father.

I called the next day. Thomas was nervous as he talked to me. "It was eerie," he said. "I recognized father immediately. He looks just the same as I remember him last, but he is forty years older. He was wearing a black suit that was worn and shiny—it must be twenty-five years old. He had a bundle under one arm and a cane in his hand."

"How is he feeling?"

"Not well at all. He was sick when he started the trip, and was feeling worse during it. . . ."

Suddenly Thomas paused, and I heard another voice in the background. Thomas then said, "Father is standing next to me. He wants to talk to you."

My heart stopped. Thomas handed the phone to my dad. A raspy but strong voice said, "Greetings, little daughter!"

"Greetings, Tato." My voice trembled. What was I supposed to say to express what I was feeling? Words were totally inadequate to communicate what was on my heart. "I can't believe that I am talking to you."

"Yes, little daughter, it is a miracle. I finally made it to America."

"Will you have time to come and see us here in Texas? I can't wait to see you, and our family can't wait to see you."

"I have longed to see you for many years, little daughter. In a few days, after I feel better, Ann and I will try and come to your house. I want very much to meet you and your family."

"I love you, Tato, and I can't wait to see you," I whispered, fighting back the tears.

"I have often wondered what happened to you and if I would ever see you again on this earth. We have a lot to talk about. And we will . . . in a few days."

My brother came back on the phone. "This is unbelievable. It's like someone coming back from the dead."

"Thomas, I cannot begin to thank God enough for this miracle! I believe the only explanation for this is God's direct intervention in all of our lives. When do you think I can see Tato?"

"In a few days, we will see how he is feeling. We'll talk to him then about coming to Texas. Then Ann wants all of us to be together, at her home, for a reunion."

As I hung up the phone, I thought about how, up to now, my father had just been a picture or a story told by mother. But not until I heard his voice had I ever thought of him as a living, breathing, human being. My thoughts scrambled all over the place, trying to comprehend what had happened. I had just talked to my father—a voice from history! In a way, I was glad to have a few days to prepare for his visit. I needed to calm my emotions and to pray and thank God for this unbelievable miracle!

20

Face to Face

B ob, the children, and I pressed our faces against the glass in one of the terminals at Dallas International Airport. We had casually welcomed many planes over the years, but this time I was shaking in anticipation. Bob held my hand as the 727 jet taxied up to the gate.

We had prayed for my father, but not in my wildest dreams had I imagined that we would see him! During the last few days, we had talked several times on the phone. My sister told me that dad was a little apprehensive about coming to Texas. He knew that I was married to an American and wasn't sure how this son-in-law would receive him. However, I had assured dad that he was loved by all and would be well received.

All week long we had been busy preparing food, cleaning the house, getting our son's room ready for my father, and talking to friends who came by to share the excitement. The outpouring of love from our friends was a great encouragement during the times when I could hardly think about what to do next. I also appreciated my husband's attempt to focus on the bigger picture: "Honey, can you believe this? We were praying that God would send someone to your father. But God has chosen, instead, to send him to us."

"I never thought it was possible," I muttered.

By now the plane had stopped, and Bob, the children, and I wove through the crowd to the entrance of the gate, right in front.

No way was I hanging back this time! I wanted to see my father the instant he stepped off that plane.

The airline attendant opened the door and I looked down the short hallway. I had to tell my body not to jump in anticipation—I wanted so badly to run down and greet dad. Fortunately, I didn't have to wait long. He was the first one to emerge from the plane, leaning on a cane with his right hand and on my sister's arm with his left. There he was, slightly dragging his stiff right leg and wearing a new straw hat and a light gray suit that my brother and sister had bought for him in Chicago—perfect for the searing summer heat in Texas.

I gazed at him walking steadily toward me, sporting a painful smile. Instantly, before we even embraced, I felt an overwhelming love. The emotion swelled up, like a wall of water bursting from a dam, and the love I felt for my father emerged and flooded my heart. And then we embraced, hugged, and kissed, and the tears came—tears of overwhelming joy. A chasm of forty years, ten thousand miles, and countless heartaches closed in that instant. The past now seemed like a dream.

The crowd of other passengers emerging from the plane finally forced us to back away from the door. "This must be Robert," my father grinned, opening his arms wide to my husband. They embraced as though they were long-lost friends. "And my grandchildren! You must be Bob, and you are Debbie. I love you both!" I had to translate from Russian into English and back again so that everyone understood what each other was saying.

How natural this moment was—how right, how perfect!

I think we could have floated to our home. Of course, we drove. "How do you feel?" I asked dad as we brought him into our house.

"I feel wonderful. I'm much better than I was a couple of days ago. This is the happiest moment of my life—seeing my Emotshka!"

Leaning on my arm, he slowly toured our home and I showed him the bedroom where he would sleep. Then I seated him at the kitchen table. "Are you hungry?" I asked.

"A little," he said.

"He didn't eat on the plane," my sister said. "And we had trouble finding things he could eat in Chicago."

"It's my teeth," he whispered. He reached up and wiggled his false teeth. "Look at this! They are terrible. They just rattle around in my mouth and hurt terribly when I eat. It's a perfect example of the workmanship one finds back home in Russia."

The teeth looked like they had been fitted for someone else. Thinking quickly, I said, "I have some Jell-O. I can make oatmeal. Or, there is soup. And bananas."

"Bananas? What are bananas?"

"What is he saying?" Bob interrupted. I had forgotten that Bob and the children couldn't understand a word we were saying in Russian. I quickly explained his difficulty with his teeth, and that we were trying to determine what food would be easiest for him to eat.

"He looks hot," Bob noted. "Maybe he would like to change into some shorts while you fix him something to eat."

"Texas weather is warm!" noticed my father. "It's so different from the weather in Chicago and back home. But I like it!"

Father looked much more comfortable in shorts, though we could tell his pale-white legs had not seen sunlight in ages. But his face radiated and his gleaming head seemed to shine with the excess of his happiness. He took a bite of banana and a look of rapture overcame his face. He slowly enjoyed every bite, which didn't require him to use his tender gums. When he was finished, he asked for another, and praised this wonderful new fruit as he disposed of the peelings.

The doorbell rang. Some friends were at the door with flowers. I introduced them to my father and they smiled at each other. "We are so glad you are here. We have prayed for you," one of the friends said.

"*Spaciba!* Thank you very much," he answered. "The flowers are beautiful!"

"Did you have a good trip?"

"Wonderful, thank you. It is great to be here in your country. And with such gracious friends." Father's eyes filled with tears and he was unable to speak for a moment.

After our friends left, my father soberly noted, "In our country, they throw rocks at you and curse you. Here, they give you flowers." He thought for a moment, then added, "I was given strict instructions before I left Moscow. I am only to visit my family. No visiting with other people. No sightseeing. Just spend time with my family." His lower jaw started to tremble slightly. "Those were the orders," he said nervously.

I translated for my family. "You're safe here," Bob said. "No one will bother you while you are with us."

"You don't understand," father said after I translated Bob's words. "I would dearly love to see your beautiful country. I would love to meet your friends. But this is not a sightseeing trip. The people back home will know where I have been and all that I have done. They have spies over here. Believe me, they have ways of finding out. They always do. So I must be careful. I must obey their orders."

It was a sad reminder that my father was not a free man. His manner reminded me of a frightened animal expecting to be shot at any moment. My spine tingled at the thought that despite all the repression, he was still sitting here with me. God had done this; there was no other explanation.

*   *   *

The next morning, father looked fresh and rested. "This is the best he has looked since he arrived in the United States," my sister said. After a breakfast of oatmeal, with another banana, we started talking. Where does one begin to fill in a gap of forty years? There were so many questions, but I didn't have to ask. My father started instead.

"I can remember it like yesterday," he said. "You were a little baby. One evening I brought home for you an apple and a pear. I held up the apple and asked you, 'What is this?' and you said, 'La.' Then I held up the pear and asked you what it was, and you answered, 'Lu.' La and Lu. Apple and pear. You were so bright and curious." His voice started to crack with emotion. "But those were the only two syllables I ever heard you say."

He looked at me longingly and I gazed back into his eyes. They were crystal-blue, and strong—deep within this man was a tough, resilient spirit. Whatever he had suffered these past forty years, he had not been broken.

In those eyes I also recognized the pain. He shook his head and said, "You're all grown up. You're a woman. The last time I saw you, you were nestled in your mother's arms. As the NKVD took me away, I kissed your little hand and said, 'I'll see you soon...'" My father's voice broke with emotion. He took a moment to regain his composure. "Forty years...I'll never forget, as they led me away, looking back at the house and seeing you in your mother's arms as she stood in the doorway, framed by the light of the house. I have never forgotten that.

"I can't believe that little baby I held and loved is now a full-grown, beautiful woman with children of her own." His eyes moistened. Pain and sorrow masked his face. His most precious memory of me was as a baby saying her first syllables. He had missed my first steps. My first words. The joy of seeing his youngest daughter discover the world. Watching me go fishing. Pick flowers. Make up a song. Review my school lessons. That was part of the pain—he had missed out on all those years of introducing the world to his girl. I had grown up without him.

The childhood photo of me with my mother, my eyes wide open, looking for the bird, was in my hand. I handed it to him. "Tato, when I was little, this picture was taken for you."

A smile came over his face. "Yes, I remember this." He shook his head, fighting back the tears. "Your mother's letter with that picture was the last news I had from the family for almost twenty years." He looked up at me, then back at the picture, then at me again. "You were beautiful then, and you are even more beautiful now!" he said with a loving nod of his head.

My sister and I wanted to know what had happened to him during the intervening years. I didn't know where to start, but my sister voiced the question both of us were thinking: "Mother told us about the night you were arrested. And how the last time she saw you was when you were on the train, heading for Siberia. . . ."

"What a scene that was!" said father. "For a few moments, time stopped. They didn't let us touch, but we were together, and it was as though no one else was there." Then a cloud came over his face. "She didn't know the pain I was in. I wouldn't let her see it. They had beaten me in prison. Every one of us experienced cruelty and torture continuously."

"Mother says she got a package with bloodstained clothes," said Ann.

"They tried everything to get me to confess. They put two bandits with me in my cell. The bandits were actually informants—for their contribution, they would get a lesser sentence. I had to watch everything I said, for I knew it would be used against me. I had to be tough. Right away I had to prove that I was strong. Otherwise I knew they would beat me to death, kick me to death. The first time one of them attacked me, I stood firm and jabbed him with all my might by slamming my elbow into his ribs. Immediately he had respect for me and left me alone for the rest of his stay. But another man in my cell—an older man— was kicked to death by three other informants."

He sighed, then continued. "They wanted me to sign a confession. If I did, they said everything would be all right. But they were liars! I didn't believe them. The paper they wanted me to sign said that I had violated article 58 of the criminal code of 1926—suspicion of espionage, subversion of industry, and propaganda and agitation undermining the Soviet power. I told them I couldn't sign and admit to something I didn't do. Absolutely not! So they beat me. And they beat me again. They called me a counterrevolutionary—that's what they labeled everyone who didn't do exactly what the Communist party wanted."

"How long did this go on?" I asked.

"Off and on for probably a year, until they sentenced me. It was almost a relief to go to Siberia. That's when the questioning and the beatings ended. But you still had to be tough. I had to become like a criminal myself in order to survive. You didn't trust anyone. You were always suspicious, always careful about what you said. You never got close to anyone.

"Of course, I had been through some of this before. Ann, do you remember when I was in exile?"

"Not really. But mother told me about it."

"Shadrynsk. 1926. That was the end of the line for the railroad. It was hard. They wouldn't let me work—I had to report to the GPU every day, which kept me from holding onto a job to earn money for the family . . ."

"What is the GPU?" I interrupted.

"The secret police. Later, during the thirties, they were called the NKVD. Now they are the KGB. It's all the same thing. I'll call them the KGB. They approached me in exile and asked me if I wanted to work for them. They felt I had a persuasive personality; they thought people would listen and follow me. They said all would be forgiven if I became a priest and informed on the members of the congregation. I told them I knew nothing about being a priest. 'Don't worry, we will teach you,' they said. 'We will teach you what to say and how to perform the ceremonies.' But I couldn't do it. I couldn't inform on my own people. If I had wanted to be selfish, I could have built myself a nice life. I would have had all the food I wanted, a nice home, and nice everything. You can always tell who the KGB informants are. They live the good life. But I couldn't do it. I did not have the heart to betray my people."

I was amazed at the moral stand father had taken. Bob had tears in his eyes as he listened to my translation. Dad had suffered, but for the right reasons. There was nothing wishy-washy about him. He was dynamic, intense, strong in character.

"I wonder how I would have survived under that pressure," Bob said. "It must have been hard, thinking about your family. I mean, knowing what might have been, and remembering your family and wondering how they were suffering. How did you survive over the years?"

Father's answer surprised us. "Many men broke down because they couldn't take the mental pressure. On the train, as we were transported to Siberia, many of the men worried about what would happen to their families. They would agonize: 'How will my wife survive? What about my children? Who will take care of them?' They were in fear about their families and depressed—some were even crying. It was obvious some were going to crack up—you couldn't survive under that kind of mental anguish. I told them, 'Forget about your families! As of right now, you don't have a wife. You don't have any children. If you want to survive, put that out of your mind. You are not married. You don't have a home. Forget everything!' That's what I had to do to keep my sanity—put everything out of my mind. Whenever I started thinking of my family, I told myself I don't have a wife, I don't have children. There was nothing I could do for them, so mentally I had to give them up. I had to do it to survive."

I was stunned. There was a hardness in his voice as he said that. It made sense that he had to forget his family in order to survive. But could anyone really do that? It would require incredible determination to banish all thoughts about your family. Deep down, one would *have* to think about them. Maybe he simply buried those thoughts. If he did, surely they were instruments of torture, invisible yet sharper than any knife.

Father shared the details of his life in little spurts, oftentimes without a context. We didn't ask many questions; we decided to let him tell us only what he wanted us to know. He was cautious, afraid that something he said might get back home and incriminate him. He had lived in constant fear for most of his life and he couldn't relax, even in the midst of a loving family in America. He knew he had to go back; we could stay safely in this country.

Still, his stories, even the tiny incidents, left us breathless. He told about the trip to Siberia: "It was a long trip on the train. One time, they unloaded us in a remote field. They lined us up and began shooting—just executing us. They were about halfway down the line, almost to me, when another train stopped behind ours and an official got out and ordered the shooting stopped. If he hadn't arrived, I would have been dead. I would say probably half the men in that line were shot. It was a gruesome and terrifying sight."

Dad paused and contemplated his story. "Why was I spared?" he asked aloud. The question hung in the air, as if it were waiting for an answer.

Then he continued, "Later, we went north. I don't know exactly where—we were never told where they were taking us—but I think it was to the Kara Sea. Then they put us on an old, rusty, cold metal boat. It was like a big freighter or tanker—just a huge ocean transport made out of iron. All the prisoners huddled together so they wouldn't have to touch the frozen metal of the ship; you stuck to the metal if you touched it. I've never been colder. There was not a single spot on the ship that was not covered with ice. Many died on the way, and their bodies were pitched into the icy water. Even as we tried to huddle together for warmth, the razor-sharp winds tore into us. And all we had on were the clothes we wore when we left home."

"Where were they taking you?" Ann asked.

"All we knew was that we were assigned to work in the coal mines; at least, that's where our group went."

"They never told you where you were?"

"I don't even know for sure myself. I just know that it was awfully cold, and we barely had a bite to eat. We all lost our teeth from gum disease. Many died of malnutrition. It was so bad, they finally brought in a truckload of potatoes from somewhere. Everyone got a raw potato. But it was too late. All we could do was gnaw at them; we had no teeth for chewing. They should have given us the potatoes when we still had some teeth left.

"Fortunately, I didn't have it as bad as most of the men. They had to go to work in the mines. You had to crawl on your hands and knees to get into the tunnel. I could go in a little way, but I couldn't get back out because of my stiff leg—it simply got in the way. So they pulled me out and put me to work at a desk job— checking off the men as they went to work, keeping track of the work quotas, recording each load as it came out . . . that kind of stuff. So I had it easier. When I got out in 1947, there was only one other man still alive from my original group. I would never have survived if I had worked in the mines.

"I tell you, we lived like dogs, and all we thought about was survival. You cared only about one day at a time—one hour at a time. Your whole focus of life was that one day, that one moment—finding a little warmth, an extra bite of food. You never looked back; you never thought ahead. You just existed for today. Every so often our jailers would get generous and give the men a few cigarettes. I didn't smoke, so I would save my cigarettes and trade them with someone who wanted a smoke more than a piece of bread. That additional piece of bread gave me more strength. Those who didn't eat extra food got weaker, became sick, and died. Many died of pneumonia or tuberculosis. There was no medication available. Men died like animals right where they were."

I shook my head in amazement as I said, "God sure protected you. I can see it now. Jesus not only had His hand on you, but on all of us as well."

Father gave me a strange look, as though he didn't comprehend what I was saying. But my statement triggered another memory, and he continued: "In prison, there was a man beaten to death in my cell. Three men pounced on him. They would hit him with their fists and ask him what his name was. 'Jesus,' he would answer. They kicked him and he tried to hide under his bed. The only word he said, over and over, was the name 'Jesus.' That made a vivid impression on my mind. How strange it was. It didn't make any sense. As they beat him to death, the name of Jesus was on his lips."

There was a deafening silence in the room. We were astonished at the life he had lived. He then reflected on another time when he faced death, saying that once he had awakened in a morgue and found himself lying on a stack of bodies. "It happened at a time when they executed many of the prisoners," he said. "I must have fainted in the process, and as a result, they thought I, too, was dead. Anyway, there I was in this huge barn-like room, a warehouse with shelves. There were caskets with bodies all around. They were stacked on shelves, lined up row upon row, like apples in an apple crate. I have no idea how I got onto one of those shelves. But I was most assuredly not dead. I woke up, raised myself off the pile, and tried to find someone." He started chuckling at the memory. "There was a single guard outside the building. The door was locked, so I climbed up to a window and yelled for help. That guard was scared out of his skull!"

This story brought some comic relief to the tragic drama dad was revealing about his life. I felt a sense of awe as I realized that he had lived in and returned from a world of pain and horror that I could barely comprehend.

Ann then asked, "Dad, what happened when you came back home?"

"I was released in 1947. Khrushchev closed all of the labor camps and let us go home. I came back to Drushkovka at night, in the same clothes I left with ten years before. I didn't want anyone to see me; I wanted to be careful and not call attention to myself. Anyway, I found our house, and there was a light on. As I approached I thought that perhaps all of you were there. I knocked on the door, but no one answered. I knocked again, and someone yelled, 'Who is it?' But no one would open the door. I told the occupants who I was. They asked what I wanted. Immediately I knew something was wrong. I told them I wanted to know where my family was.

"They finally did open the door, but they wouldn't let me in. They were distant relatives on your mother's side—I don't remember how they are related. Anyway, they were afraid, maybe because I was back from Siberia and wanted my house back. When I asked about all of you, they didn't know where you were. They didn't know if you were alive or dead. They knew nothing. They said they had lived in the house for four years and had no intention of giving it up. Then they told me to go away and slammed the door in my face."

He paused for a moment, then added, "They wouldn't let me into my own home! That was heartbreaking for me. What was I to do? Where was I to go? I was so tired from the long trip back home. I felt like a dog who had been kicked out of his home because he wasn't wanted anymore by anyone.

"I slept that night in someone's orchard, on a bench, and slipped away before sunrise so I wouldn't be seen. I was afraid that people would shun me because they were afraid to associate with a political prisoner. The next day I found some old friends. They cautiously fed me a meal, and then I went looking for anyone else I might know from the past. After a number of days of sleeping anyplace I could find, I accidentally met a woman about Ann's age who had once been married to a distant relative of mine. She had compassion on me and took me in. I have lived with her now for about twenty-five years. I was so desperate that I really had no other option."

That night as we went to bed, Bob said to me, "There is only one place for dad to go when he dies, and that is heaven. It's obvious that he has already lived in hell!"

* * *

The next day I had a number of errands to run, and I invited my father to ride with me. It gave me a chance to show him a little of Dallas without actually "sightseeing." As we drove on the freeway he looked around in amazement at the city skyline in the distance. He was used to plain, uninspiring office and apartment buildings and remarked at the attractive designs of these buildings. He also noted all of the cars. "I have never driven a car," he said. He looked at me for a moment. "You drive well."

"Thank you, Tato."

First I stopped at a bank. I used the drive-through so dad wouldn't need to get out. As we slowly approached, he stiffened in fear. I placed my checks and deposit slip in a drawer, and the teller pulled the drawer inside. "What is this?" he asked.

"Don't be afraid, Father, it's just a bank. I need to get some cash."

As I waited, my father's mouth tightened, and I noted the slight, quick back-and-forth movement of his lower jaw. Why was he so nervous about the bank? I received my cash and eased the car out into the parking lot and stopped for a moment to put the money in my purse. I looked over at him again and he was still tense.

"Dad, this is a simple daily transaction that American people take for granted. We think nothing of it."

"That was a bank?" he asked.

"That's right. I come here all the time. We keep our money in here."

"I thought it was some kind of police checkpoint. As we were approaching, I saw a man in uniform up by the window."

"Oh, he is a security guard. There is nothing to worry about."

"I'm sorry. I thought they were going to check my papers."

"This is America. They don't do that here."

He smiled with relief. That's when I realized that what was mere routine for me was traumatic to him. I had forgotten what it was like to live in a totalitarian country, always worrying about the police, carrying papers, and being prepared to stop anytime and be searched.

"Are all the banks like that?" he asked. "You don't have to get out of your car?"

"Not all of them. But yes, using the bank is easy. People can choose to walk in or just drive through."

"That's nice," he said with awe in his voice. I saw this as an opportunity to begin to try and explain about God and His great love.

"Dad, a bank is somewhat like God. God, in His love and grace, has given us *everything* we need for life and godliness. But this gift is in His Son Jesus. If we want to access this gift, we have to come to His Son, just as we have to come to the bank to have access to our money. It's there in the bank waiting for us to write a check and use it. We don't have to beg for our money or promise to earn it or try to be good enough to receive it. It is ours, and it is in the bank. Likewise, God has given us salvation in His Son. We also don't have to beg for it, or be good enough to receive it, or work hard enough to get it. It is a free gift . . . and it is available in His Son."

Dad didn't answer, but it was clear that he was thoughtfully contemplating what I had just said.

Next, we went across the street to the local Tom Thumb grocery store. I slowly led him by the arm, and he stopped just inside the entrance. His eyes scanned the building from one end to the other, as though this was the most amazing sight he had ever witnessed. "Let's go in, Father. I won't take long. I just need to pick up a few things."

"Wait. Is this a special store?"

"What do you mean?"

"Is this the store where all the tourists go?"

"Oh no, this is just a typical grocery store, open to everyone. They are everywhere. Actually, this is smaller than many. It's closest to our neighborhood, and I am accustomed to it and know where they keep the things that I need."

"All of these stores have this much food?"

"Oh yes! Some have even larger selections of merchandise."

"There is nothing even close to this back home. It will be a hundred years before we ever catch up!"

I got a shopping cart. Father took my arm and we walked slowly up and down the aisles. He watched my every move so as not to miss anything. He stopped and examined the many varieties of bread. In the produce section he was overcome by the abundant array of fruits and vegetables. Many of them he didn't recognize. "What is that?" he would ask, and I would name such vegetables as zucchini and broccoli, and fruits such as kiwi, mangoes, papayas, and seedless grapes. He looked at the watermelons and remarked, "They are twice the size of any melons I have ever seen." He was pleased when I picked up a bunch of bananas. "I could eat those every day for the rest of my life!"

On the way home, I pulled up to the drive-through window of a Dairy Queen and ordered a soft-serve ice-cream cone. I handed dad a tall swirl of soft vanilla. He took one lick and broke into a smile bigger than any child tasting candy for the first time. "What is this?" he asked.

"A special kind of soft ice cream. You buy it at Dairy Queen, and there are many little stops like this throughout the country."

"It's the best ice cream I have ever tasted." After each lick he made a complimentary remark about the taste, the texture, the flavor, how smooth it went down, or how refreshing it was. "If I could have one of these ice-cream cones and a piece of bread every day for the rest of my life—that would be heaven. I couldn't ask for anything else!" I made a mental note to make sure we visited Dairy Queen every day.

*　*　*

My father was intrigued by my frequent references to God and His goodness. The next morning I mentioned again that his visit was not an accident. "God has done this!" I said. "God brought you here. There is no chance of this happening by accident. It is a miracle from Him."

Father looked at me with wonder. "Dotshitshka, I have been thinking about what you said yesterday. And now again . . . tell me who taught you to talk like that?"

"What do you mean?"

"In Russia, I hear words of hate. Here, in your family, I hear words of love! Who taught you to say those words about Jesus? I have never heard such words. Where did you learn to talk like that?"

For a moment, I was surprised. Then it dawned on me that the mention of God and miracles was foreign to him. "I learned from the Bible," I answered. I had a Russian-language Bible and pulled it off the shelf to show it to him. "This book contains God's Word. It tells about Jesus and His gift of eternal life. I asked Him to come into my heart a few years ago, to be my Savior and

Lord. He changed my life. He now lives in me and teaches me what the Bible means. Every person can read what it says, but only the Spirit of God, who lives in each believer, can teach you what it means."

Bob suggested that maybe my father would like to read some of the Bible.

Dad nodded his head after I translated Bob's comment. "I have heard of it, but I have never read it," he said.

"Why don't you have him begin with the Gospel of John?" Bob prompted.

I opened the Bible to John, and father began reading aloud: "In the beginning was the Word, and the Word was with God, and the Word was God." Dad continued reading on through verse 14, saying, "The Word became flesh and made his dwelling among us."

He stopped and seemed like he was trying hard to understand the meaning of those words. He read them again, slowly absorbing them. I asked, "Do you know what that means, Tato?"

Dad's face suddenly brightened with excitement. "I believe this is saying that Jesus is God!"

"That's right, Tato! That is exactly what it says."

He continued reading, holding the Bible in one hand and gesturing with the other. His voice grew stronger and was filled with inflection and emotion. I recalled how my mother had said he was a good orator and an accomplished actor. By the way he read, I could see why the KGB tried to recruit him as a priest. He would have made a dramatic preacher.

Bob was at my side this whole time. The children were also listening to every word, eager to catch what their Russian grandpa was saying. Bob kept his eyes on our facial expressions and motions, not wanting to miss anything from this miraculous visitor. Already, the two had bonded; they loved each other. Now Bob wanted to guide his father-in-law as he was introduced to the truth of Scripture for the first time. Occasionally Bob would ask, "Do you understand, Dad?" My father would nod and say, "*Da!*" and continue reading.

The more my father read, the more amazed I became. He was not reading this book as literature, but as truth. I realized that for the first time I was seeing someone who had truly never heard of Jesus Christ. There was a wonder in his voice as he read, as though his eyes were opened and he was actually meeting Jesus, seeing His acts, and hearing Him speak.

He read through the scene in John chapter 3 where Nicodemus visited Jesus at night. As he read, I could almost see and hear their conversation: "Jesus declared, 'I tell you the truth, no one can enter the kingdom of God unless he is born again.' 'How can a man be born when he is old?' Nicodemus asked. 'Surely he cannot enter a second time into his mother's womb to be born!' Jesus answered, '. . . You should not be surprised at my saying, "You must be born again." The wind blows wherever it pleases. You hear its sound, but you cannot tell where it comes from or where it is going. So it is with everyone born of the Spirit. . . . Just as Moses lifted up the snake in the desert, so the Son of Man must be lifted up, that everyone who believes in him may have eternal life'" (vv. 3,4,7,8,14,15).

And then father came to that wonderful verse, one of the first that I had learned as a young girl: "For God so loved the world that he gave his one and only Son, that whoever believes in him shall not perish but have eternal life. For God did not send his Son into the world to condemn the world, but to save the world through him" (vv. 16,17).

"Have dad stop here!" said Bob. Speaking to him through me, he said, "Dad, read that verse again. This time, insert your name where it says 'the world.' In other words, 'For God so loved Fyodor. . . .'"

Dad nodded that he understood. Deliberately he read, "For God so loved Fyodor that he gave his one and only Son, that whoever believes in him shall not perish but have eternal life. For God did not send his Son into the world to condemn Fyodor, but to save Fyodor through him."

The light came on. Tears started rolling down father's face as he allowed the words that he had read to reach deep into his heart. The magnitude of God's love overwhelmed him. He looked at me, then Bob, and overcome with emotion, he was unable to read any further. Gently, Bob said, "Fyodor, God loves you so much that if you were the only person in this world, He would have died for you."

"Da!" My father understood. He lowered his head on the kitchen table and wept as we led him in prayer. "Lord Jesus, I need You!" he prayed. "I thank You for not only dying for all my sins, but for now offering me Your very life. I ask You to come into my heart to live, to be my Savior and Lord. Amen."

There was not a dry eye among us. The children were amazed at the miracle taking place before them. Dad raised his head and threw his hands up toward heaven in a statement of praise and surrender. "I'm a new man!" he shouted.

* * *

My father was indeed a new man in Christ. He was still weak and needed a lot of rest. But he would not let the Bible out of his sight. He was like a man who had discovered the world's greatest jewels and preferred to sleep with the precious gems rather than entrust them to someone else. I came to his room one evening to make sure he was comfortable, and found him reading. He was on the bottom bunk of the bed, holding the Bible close to his eyes. The only light in the room was from a weak night-light.

"Dad, how can you see?" I asked.

"I'm used to this kind of light," he said, continuing to read.

I stood and looked at him. It would be impossible for me to read in such light. But there he was, seventy-nine years old, without glasses, reading in almost no light. I wanted to say, "You'll ruin your eyes." But he had made it this long. . . .

One morning, as we finished eating breakfast, I opened the newspaper and saw the headline: "Podgorny Cut from Politburo."

I quickly read through the article:

> Soviet President Nikolai V. Podgorny was dropped today from membership in the Communist party's ruling Politburo, Moscow radio reported. The move appeared to presage Podgorny's retirement from the Soviet presidency, but this was not announced.
>
> Podgorny, 74, was one of the three men who replaced Nikita S. Khrushchev in 1964 as effective rulers of the Soviet Union. The others are Communist party-chief Leonid L. Brezhnev, 70, now the country's most powerful leader, and Premier Alexei N. Kosygin, 73.
>
> The decision to remove Podgorny from the Politburo was made at a meeting Tuesday. . . .
>
> [Moscow radio] did not indicate whether Podgorny's stepping down was voluntary. . . .

Podgorny, who recently toured Africa, proved himself one of the most durable Soviet leaders. He escaped Stalin's purges and the in-fighting that followed Stalin's death in 1953.

The news jarred me. Immediately I read the article to my
father. Dad sat and shook his head in amazement. "Podgorny
was the one who gave me permission to come to America," he
said. "I had tried to get permission from the Russian authorities
for over twenty years to see my family. For some reason, the
letters I had received from you gave me a new hope that just
maybe there could be a chance of getting approval. I wrote a
letter to President Nikolai Podgorny. I told him, 'I am seventy-
nine years old and have only a brief time left on this earth. I have
only one wish. I beg of you to give me permission to go to
America. I have no desire to sightsee or travel. I just want to kiss
my family goodbye before I die.'"

Tears streamed down my face as I listened to him speak. His
voice seemed to gain strength as he told me more of the story:
"That dear man gave me permission—may God grant him
health. As soon as I received his reply, I immediately left the
hospital and made my way back home. I picked up a few belongings and shared my good news with some of the people in our
village. I had saved up a sum of money through the years, but
when the people in the village heard that I had a chance to go see
my children, they all pitched in and helped me with the additional amount I needed to buy a ticket. What dear people! They
truly gave out of their poverty. Upon arriving in Moscow, I sat
three days and three nights at the airport to get clearance to fly to
America. I wanted to see all of you so bad that I would have
crawled on my knees and clawed my way just to see my children."

The miraculous timing of dad's trip to America was becoming more and more evident to all of us. If dad had written his
letter just a little later, Podgorny would not have been in power,
and dad would not have gotten permission to come to America.

Already, father was seeing life through the perspective of
God's sovereignty. "This is not by accident. Nothing in my life is
an accident. I used to curse the fact that my leg was stiff. If I'd had
one more operation, I would have had a normal knee. But the
revolution came, and my fate took a different turn. When I

couldn't crawl into that mine shaft because of my stiff leg, I didn't exactly consider it a blessing at the time. But now I see that it was what kept me alive. If it hadn't been for my stiff leg, I wouldn't be here today. Most of the men died from working hard every day in darkness and dust. And I wouldn't have met God. God must have been watching me all this time—long before this day."

Bob mentioned Romans 8:28, which says that God works all things together for good to those who love Him. That was all Fyodor needed to suggest we read the Bible. He constantly longed to read from this great book. It was more satisfying than food, he said. He couldn't read enough of it.

As I listened to my father read, I thought to myself that the Communist system had been terribly foolish to have wasted so wonderful a talent. This man was sharp, alert, intelligent, witty. He could have been an asset to the country, but instead they shipped him off and dumped him in a frozen wasteland. How many such people had this nation tossed into its slag heap? How many talents had been wasted? That was a monumental crime—how utterly foolish!

"Tato," I said. "For years, I prayed for you. So did the children, and Bob, and many people in our church. We prayed that someone would come and tell you about Jesus."

"That would have been impossible!" he answered emphatically. "I would never have listened to anyone talking about things like that back home. I would not have trusted them. I would have thought it was a trap. So what did God do? He brought me to you! You, I can trust. That is the only way I would have listened. What a wonderful God we have!"

"Tato, I think of my passionate prayers that someone would share the gospel with you. For years I prayed and asked others to pray. Now I realize that God has indeed answered our prayers, but in a way I could never have dreamed of or imagined. He worked through a complex political system, moving the heart of a now-ousted leader, and picked up a little old man—insignificant to the world, but precious in the sight of God—and brought that man to the one place where he would both hear and receive the truth."

Bob put it in perspective: "The Scriptures say that what is impossible with man is possible with God. When a situation comes to a dead end, when there is no other way, that's when I watch for God to act, because that's when He does the impossible."

The changes in my father were immediate. My sister noted that in Chicago, he had used rough language as she tried to make him comfortable. "His talk has completely changed here," she said. On one occasion father stepped outside in our tiny backyard, threw his hands in the air, and holding his cane with both hands, uttered a prayer of thanksgiving. He would ask me to read to him from the Bible, or invite us to sit and listen to him read.

On father's last day in Dallas, all of us wanted to show him the inside of the church we attended. He wanted to see it with all his heart. I could tell there was a terrible wrestling within him. But the threats and orders from the officials at Moscow airport were still loud and fresh on his mind: "When someone asks you if you want to go here or there, you are to say *no!*"

We drove downtown to Dallas and showed him where the building was. He looked through the car window. "I can't go in," he said. "I just can't. They would find out." So fear won, and we pulled away from the curb, slowly turned the corner, and drove home. How sad that the arm of fear can reach such a distance, from Russia to America, and grip the hearts of both slave and free! Of course, none of us wanted to do anything that might cause father any more harm.

During his stay, it was the little things dad appreciated so much—like soft towels. He loved the feel of the thick towels on his body after he showered. And American razor blades—they were so smooth. "At home, the blades are so poor that I'm a bloody mess when I'm done. Just send me home with razor blades, towels, and Dairy Queen, and I will die a happy man!"

*   *   *

Dad's week in Dallas flew by quickly. All of us were emotionally drained by the intensity of our brief encounter. While Ann and I would have another week with dad in Pennsylvania, this was the only time Bob and the children would see him on this earth. We went into the backyard, and much like one of the Old Testament patriarchs, father spoke to the family and gave us his blessing: "My dearest children, soon I will be departing for my country. It won't be easy, but no matter what happens, I will never forget you. I thank you for welcoming me as your very own father. It was hard for me to get here because of my sickness, but somehow I made it. I believe that the Lord God Himself is the

One who got me here. I saw an earthly paradise, but now I am looking forward to seeing my heavenly paradise. Once again, I thank you from the depths of my soul. May God give you grace to live a hundred years. May God bless you, my dear children."

Before Dad left, there was one more major surprise. As we looked at his plane ticket, we discovered that there was no return flight booked. "How did that happen?" I asked.

He shook his head in amazement. "You can't leave the country without a round-trip ticket. It was a mistake." For a moment, I wondered if this was a sign that my father should stay. But I pushed those thoughts out of my mind as he said, "The people I live with—the people who helped me come here—it would cause trouble for them. I can't do that. Maybe if I was younger. . . ." So through the kindness and generosity of our friends Andy and Joan Horner, a return ticket was purchased for him—a gift of love.

It was time for us to fly to Pittsburgh and drive from there to New Castle, Pennsylvania, to my sister's house, where the entire family would be reunited for the first time in forty years. My father had already spent time with his son and older daughter, and had met his younger daughter as well. And he had made the most important discovery of his life—he had met his Lord and Savior Jesus Christ.

One more reunion remained. This one concerned me. Mother was thirty-three and father thirty-eight when they were separated. Forty years had passed. What would it be like when they saw each other again for the first time?

21

Goodbye Is Not Forever!

MAY 1977

M other and father had not seen each other for forty years. She had waved goodbye to him as the door of dad's train car was closed that fateful day in June of 1938. Her heart went with him as she stood in the rain, watching the train round the curve and disappear into the night. For nearly twenty years, from the time the Germans invaded Russia until shortly before she emigrated to the United States, she had heard nothing about her husband. She had no knowledge of whether he was alive or dead, free or in prison. Except for a brief time of utter despair, she had lived with the hope that someday, somehow, she would see him again.

Then came the news that he was alive and living in Drushkovka. They had communicated by letter, but the Cold War conspired to keep them separated. She had lived another twenty years knowing that it was impossible for them to get back together. So they lived, each knowing the other was alive, but unable to bridge a political chasm far greater than the geographical distance between Moscow and Washington, D.C.

What should a couple do in such tragic circumstances? There are no manuals written to guide people through the practical realities of coping with massive political upheaval. They were just two of millions of pawns whose lives had been uprooted before and after World War II. What could they do? Father had found a woman who would take him in and give him shelter and companionship. And mother, resigned to the reality that the political powers-that-be would not permit them to be reunited, understood that father had made the best of an impossible situation. Recently, mother had been introduced to a widower, a Russian immigrant named Peter, who was lonely and in need of companionship. They comforted each other. So in 1974, after thirty-five years of waiting, mother married Peter. Though she didn't say much about it, I sensed this was more a marriage of convenience than of genuine love.

Now the impossible had happened. It was May of 1977, and father was in Pennsylvania, eager to see mother. All of us wondered what it would be like. Did mom still love dad? Did dad still love mom? If so, what would he think when he saw her with another man?

There was a knock on the front door. "Mom and Pete are here," Ann announced. I watched my father's face. He rose from his cot as everyone stood to greet mom and Pete. Father seemed calm and composed. The door opened and mom and Pete entered and stopped. Mom looked straight at dad, and he looked at her in silence.

Everyone fixed their eyes on them.

They just stood there, studying each other. Was there anything left from the past?

No one said a word. No one breathed.

I wondered what was going through their minds. What did they see as they gazed at each other? What memories did they recall? Did he still love her? Did she still care for him?

No one dared to break the spell.

It was the longest minute of my life.

Slowly they started toward one another. They extended their right hands. "*Zdrastvui*, Marusia," he said.

"*Zdrastvui*, Fedija," she answered. "Good day." They shook hands politely.

Mother then introduced Pete, who was standing a step behind her. "This is my husband, Peter Ivanovich."

"Fyodor Philipovich," said my father, introducing himself.

Father kept his eyes on mother as the family greeted mom and Pete. Then slowly he shook his head and said, "It is all gone." He turned and went to his cot.

What did those words mean? Did he mean the beauty of her youth was gone? Or that the years had robbed them of their love?

Was this reunion a heartbreak or joy? Or was it both at the same time?

No one dared to invade their privacy. All I could do was speculate that those words summarized everything. The life that they had enjoyed together had been torn from them, and it could never be recaptured. Circumstances had changed, and too much time had passed.

Ann had prepared a splendid meal: borscht with good meat, all kinds of breads, lunch meats, salads, and cake. "This country is truly blessed by God!" father said. "Look at this abundance of food! Wouldn't our people back home love to get ahold of some of this!"

Ann raised her glass and proposed, "Let us rejoice in the celebration of our father coming back from the dead. To your health, Dad!"

The rest of us raised our glasses and joined in the toast, then I offered a short prayer of thanks and we settled down to eat.

The huge spread of food reminded father of the famine in Ukraine in the early thirties. "Do you remember when we found that potato?" dad said to mom. "I think it had fallen off a truck. We thought it had fallen from heaven."

Mother smiled. For a moment she was a young woman again, recalling a tender moment. "Yes, I remember. We decided to eat it raw, and I insisted that you take the first bite."

"And I, being a gentleman, insisted you take the first bite."

"Kind of silly, isn't it? Two people, starving to death, arguing over who should have the first bite of a raw potato."

After supper, we all gathered in a circle around father's cot. For a while we fumbled around awkwardly, trying to decide what to talk about. After a few minutes of small talk, mom asked, "Fyodor, how is my brother, Alyosha?"

"He is just fine," dad answered. "I see him almost every day. He is a good friend. We talk about things I can't share with anyone else, as he is my only link to our past. He is a rare friend, someone you can trust and know that what you say will go no further." In Russia, a trusted friend was a man's greatest treasure. Father continued, "I also see all of Alyosha's daughters. All of them still live close by."

"What happened to my friend Pashka?"

"She died about ten years ago. But her daughter is still living in the same house."

Mother seemed saddened by the news. "Pashka was an important person for our family." Speaking to us children, she continued, "Your father and I were married in 1920 in the Russian Orthodox church. After the wedding, we all had dinner with our relatives. Then we moved into Pashka's home. She had an extra room, and we were glad to live there because it was near everyone we knew. Ann was born in Pashka's house in 1921. Pashka let us live there until my brothers and I built our house across the stream—where you were born, Emotshka."

I entered the conversation. "Mamo, wasn't Pashka the one who brought me the felt winter boots?"

"Yes. I traded some of our dried fruit for those boots. You wanted to play in the snow so badly, and Pashka's boots were a godsend to us."

I noticed a sadness come over my father's face as he thought of the poverty that his family had to endure while he was in prison. This was the first time he had heard the story about my boots. Mother then said, "It was Pashka who helped us when the Germans invaded our part of the country. We hid in her cellar."

"Indeed, Pashka was a dear friend to our family," said father.

Ann jumped in and suggested, "Maybe we shouldn't try to recall too many sad times. Old sufferings are best left alone. Why recall pain when we have such joy now? All five of us are still alive and now we're together after forty bitter years. What a miracle it is that not one of us was lost! And now, father has accepted Christ into his heart, as have all of us."

Dad responded, "How much more could God prove His love? How much richer can anyone be?"

Silently I wished that mom and dad could have an opportunity to be alone and talk. As I look back, I sometimes wonder what they would have said in private, without the rest of us around to hear. But that couldn't happen—not with Peter there.

The backyard behind my sister's home provided a beautiful setting for our reunion. It was a long, lush green embankment surrounded on three sides by trees. Mother and Pete joined us each day about noon, and would stay until evening. Every day, father would call the family together on the back porch and read from the Scriptures.

Staying within the New Testament, I opened the Bible for him and suggested various passages for him to read. The words of Christ took on new power as I listened to my father read aloud.

"I am the gate; whoever enters through me will be saved. . . . The thief comes only to steal and kill and destroy; I have come that they may have life, and have it to the full" (John 10:9,10).

"I am the good shepherd. The good shepherd lays down his life for the sheep" (John 10:11).

"I am the resurrection and the life. He who believes in me will live, even though he dies; and whoever lives and believes in me will never die" (John 11:25,26).

After that passage, dad stopped reading and looked at all of us as he said, "Do you realize that we are all going to spend eternity in heaven with Jesus? We will never again be separated by distance, or by war, or by terror."

We all nodded in agreement. I believe that was the evidence to my mother that father was a changed man. For as he read passionately from the Bible, she saw him in a new light. It had been only a week since he had asked the Lord Jesus Christ to come into his life, but God was already working in his life. Mother saw that, and it was powerful evidence to all of us that the gospel message was real and true.

My nephew, Ann's oldest son, came over with his wife, who played some hymns on Ann's player piano. We all joined in the songs. Though father couldn't sing along, he enjoyed the music, tapped his foot to the beat, and smiled sadly.

"Let's sing some Christmas carols for dad," Ann suggested. "He doesn't know what we sing when we celebrate Christ's birth."

"But it's May!" someone laughed. Still, everyone thought it was a great idea.

"Father, do you know what Christmas is?" I asked.

"Yes, I heard of it a long time ago, when I was a teacher. I had my students perform and sing songs about this holiday. But then it became forbidden to do that."

So we celebrated Christmas in May, singing "Silent Night," "Joy to the World," and many other carols. Afterward, father sang to us a sad Russian song in a minor key about a man near the end of his life desiring to live just a little longer. As I watched and listened, father seemed to me like a wounded man crying from deep within his soul. Every word had a facial expression. It was as if he were singing the words from a famous Negro spiritual: "Nobody knows the trouble I've seen; nobody knows but Jesus." Outwardly, he was joyful in our reunion. But his singing allowed us a glimpse within. Here was a man so talented, so eager to live life to the fullest, yet deprived of that chance.

Mother quietly hummed along as father sang, harmonizing to his melody. When the song was over, Ann noted, "We used to sing all the time when we were young. We would get together with a guitar and have a great time."

"Yes," father agreed. "People sat outdoors in the summer and sang. Evenings and weekends, we sat and sang folk songs, and made up new songs." He looked at Ann. "My daughter, you had a beautiful voice. Do you still sing?"

Ann then sang an old song about a beautiful nightingale that was heartbroken over its lost love. It dawned on me that this song—and dad's—expressed well the story of mom and dad's life.

I felt a yearning in my stomach, wishing we could freeze this moment so that I could go back and be with my father thirty years earlier. I wanted to be old enough to know him and young enough to still sit on his lap and experience his love for a daughter. I wanted to hear him recite a poem he had written, or sing a Ukrainian folk song, or tell me a Russian fairy tale. I wanted to sit next to him at family gatherings and participate with him in the singing. That is what I missed, though I never knew it until now. That is what I had been robbed of by Hitler and Stalin.

I'm sure the pain was intense for my brother as well. Thomas sat next to dad throughout our time at Ann's home. His eyes filled with tears as he listened to father tell about the hardships he had survived. What was my brother thinking? I couldn't tell for sure, but certainly he, too, had missed the joy of knowing his father.

Before the week ended, we assembled in the backyard for the first and only Wasylenko family portrait. Mom and dad stood next to each other. Gently, dad slipped his arm around mom's waist. It was a bittersweet moment. How eloquently that gesture expressed the tragedy of two people torn apart by the ravages of war and forced through uncontrollable circumstances to travel in opposite directions! Now they stood next to each other, and I could tell each one still had love and deep admiration for the other.

After the picture, dad spoke passionately to each of us. With a video camera we captured the poignant moments that followed. He proclaimed, "My dear children . . . " and then broke out in tears. A moment later, he was finally able to continue: ". . . Live in harmony. Get along with one another."

I placed my arm around my father and said, "I love you."

He gazed at me and responded, "I not only love you, I adore you! I almost worship you. You opened my eyes and now I'm as clean as an angel."

Then he held his cane up in the air and triumphantly shouted, *"Slava Bogu!* Praise God!"

* * *

Father had official permission to stay four weeks in the States, but he chose to leave after only three. His reason was typically Russian—to protect himself. "I would love to stay . . . I'd love to stay here forever! But if I stay all four weeks, the officials in Russia will accuse me. They will say, 'So you stayed the full term? You must have really liked it! What is wrong with our country?' I'm too old to go through that. I had better get back sooner and save myself such troubles."

As the time drew near for father to leave, our hearts became heavy. We wanted to prolong this joy, yet we had to be grateful that God had even given us this much time together. So the best we could do was to try to give him a few little gifts to take home—gifts that would offer him comfort for a little while.

"I wish to take only two things," he said. "I would like some of those wonderful razor blades!" He rubbed his bald head and grinned. "But I can't take them the way they are packaged. Let's open them and rewrap them in simple paper, and I'll put them in my top coat pocket. That way, no one will question me about the fancy packaging.

"And I would give anything to have some of the good fishing line they have here." Father was still an avid fisherman, and we had taken him to a sporting goods shop where he gazed lovingly at all the rods and reels. But in the end, all he would allow us to buy was some fishing line, and that, too, had to be removed from the package and wound onto a simple wooden spool. "I don't want it to look like I bought it. They would ask me questions." We would have loved to buy father a new fishing rod with all the trimmings and hooks, but he feared what awaited him at the Moscow airport—searches, questions, and having to explain everything they found on him.

There was one other item he desperately wanted to take. I had obtained for him a small, pocket-sized New Testament in Russian. He read it daily and treasured it. But when I invited him to take it home, his hands trembled and tears came to his eyes.

"This is something I desire more than anything else in the world," he said. "But I can't take it. I can't bring in any literature. And especially a Bible. That would immediately raise grave suspicion. That would mean certain arrest." Giving the Bible back to me must have been hard for him to do. He had fallen in love with the Scriptures and wanted nothing more than to immerse himself in them daily. But was it worth arrest and prison again at his age? Only he could make that choice.

Mike drove Ann and me and dad to Pittsburgh. Ann and I then flew with him to New York, where he would connect with his flight on Aeroflot to Moscow. The plane was scheduled to leave New York at 10:00 P.M. It was almost more than I could stand, waiting with him those final moments. There was an agonizing pain in my stomach; I knew I would surely not see my father again on this side of heaven.

But father was not sad. "Do not cry, Dotshitshka," he tenderly admonished. "Until I came here, I didn't know God. You have brought me incredible joy, and no one can take that away. Now I understand my life, and I see that God loves me and has watched over me all of my life. No, do not be sad, my little daughter. You gave me the greatest gift possible. I go back joyfully because I know I am going to see you again." There was a knowing look in his eye. "Yes!" he announced. "We are definitely going to see each other again! Remember—goodbye is not forever!"

With that, his flight was called. Father stood up and embraced us with hugs that said, "I never want to let go." Then, with a victorious look on his face, he walked to the gate and handed the flight attendant his ticket. Before stepping through the gate, he turned one more time and lifted his arms above his head with his cane pointed to the sky, as though he was a triumphant athlete. Yes, that was the joy and confidence he felt—much like that of a champion who has just claimed life's greatest prize. Then he turned and walked down the hall to the plane.

Ann and I were too tired and emotionally worn out to go look for a taxi and a hotel at night in New York. So we simply walked back to the terminal lobby, which was virtually empty by now, and waited for our flight back to Pittsburgh the next morning. We found a bench in a quiet corner and sat and tenderly held each other's hands. We were totally wrung out; never had we felt such a wide range of emotions, such intense joy and equally intense pain, in a mere three weeks. It would be impossible to live with such emotion for much longer than that.

During his time with us, father wrote several short notes expressing his feelings for us. I pulled one of the notes out of my purse; it was addressed to me and my sister:

> *After living through everything possible, horrendous, and frightening, how indescribably happy I am now that I have seen you, my precious children. Emotshka, wiping away tears from my eyes, you have removed the dark scales from them and opened them to light, and I have experienced God. Hanusia, you scrubbed and washed the dirt off my body, and embraced me warmly like a loving mother. I recovered, felt better, and was refreshed. I got well completely.*

"I am so grateful to God that we got to see dad," I said to my sister. "I will never forget this time with him."

I also felt intense appreciation to God for answering my feeble prayers. Silently I prayed; "Thank You, Lord, for letting me see my father. This is all Your doing. It is all by Your grace."

*   *   *

My father lived for eight more years after that trip. A few letters were exchanged—it still took months for mail to travel between the United States and the Soviet Union—and he always mentioned his desire to come and see us again. I'm sure many of our letters never made it to their destination. But even then, it was impossible to capture on paper the richness and depth of the relationship that we had experienced face to face. Father did receive a package from me with those thick, fluffy terry towels he so liked. I later learned that he considered those towels too precious to use.

Father's first letter came a few weeks after his visit.

> *My dearest little daughter, our dear Bob,*
> *little Debbie, and Bobby!*
>
> *I arrived safely at my destination. In Moscow, officials asked me where my suitcases were.*
>
> *I replied, "I don't have any."*

"And what do you have in your pockets?"

"Money and chewing gum," I answered as I showed it to them.

They all stared at me, a little surprised. "Whom did you visit?"

"My son," I answered. "And daughters."

"Do you mean to say that they didn't give you anything to bring back with you?"

"That's right," I said, "They wanted to, but I wouldn't take it because I was sick. I went to America not for stuff, but to say goodbye to my children before I die."

"You're a strange old man. Most people come back from America with suitcases full of stuff. You just bring back chewing gum in your pocket and want to say goodbye."

Truly, Emotshka, did I travel to you for things? I wanted to see you, for you grew up, matured, and had children without my presence. You didn't know me. I didn't know you.

You, my little daughter, loaded such joy into my inner being, my soul, that I feel like I have been born again in this world. My days have turned lighter and brighter, and the nights have turned warmer. You took the film off of my eyes. Now I can see.

May God give us friendship and unity, peace and quietness, pure love, truth, and goodwill among people.

Your Tato, F.

His final letter to me came a few months before his death in March 1986:

I have just reminisced about May 1977 . . . It is apparent that God Himself blessed the way and journey when He made the month of May warm, joyful, and bright.

Right now it is cold, almost as if at any moment snow may fall and cover our sinful earth with ice. My heart is so heavy, even white snow does not help to relieve it.

Ріджесенька дочечко,
дорогий Роберт Ф.
Дякую за поштовку.
Лягаючи і встаючи
думаю про вас і Колюсю
за вас. Сорочку і рушник
одвіз і ряді Нісоші,—
..е і Запракали.
поради

і пе...
ти...

Роберт Ф.
Може би там цирюри
з добрими людьми щось
придумаєтеі спасите
читаючу людину?..
Молюся за всіх вас,
Ваш тато і дідусь
Федір.

One of Fyodor's letters written to Amy after his return to Russia.

I am so sorry that I don't know your language, or I would write to our wonderful, gentlemanly Bob a big fatherly, friendly, brotherly, warm human letter. I have gotten to love him as a son, as a brother, as a friend, as one in Spirit.

I am glad that after forty years I got to see you, my dearest little daughter. To me you are the closest, the dearest, and most precious. Intuitively I feel your warm sincerity toward me.

Our mama, thanks to her, she writes, and keeps in touch. I have to say sincerely how sorry I am that things turned out so painful between us—that she is not mine anymore— not my partner and friend, but merely Maria Denisowna.

Your Tato, F.

There was no doubt about it, father still loved mother. In one of dad's last letters to mom, he asked her to come home to him. His dream was that they live out their years together and be buried side by side. Of course, that was impossible. But God had a better plan, for it is not where we are buried that is important, but where we will live eternally.

By summer's end in 1989, mom's health was failing, so I went back to Pennsylvania to spend a few weeks with her. On one warm summer evening, I took her outside, where we walked slowly in my sister's backyard and reminisced about our lives. I asked her, "Mamo, what kept you going through all those years of pain, suffering, and separation from dad?"

Mom thought for a moment, and then answered, "Hope. With hope in my heart, I lived for you children." Then she quoted her favorite saying: "Live one day at a time. We make plans, and God changes them."

After a moment of silence, I recalled the words of the apostle Paul and repeated them for mom: "Who shall separate us from the love of Christ? Shall trouble or hardship or persecution or famine or nakedness or danger or sword? . . . No, in all these things we are more than conquerors through him who loved us. For I am convinced that neither death nor life, neither angels nor demons, neither the present nor the future, nor any powers, neither height nor depth, nor anything else in all creation, will be able to separate us from the love of God that is in Christ Jesus our Lord" (Romans 8:35,37-39).

"What beautiful words, Dotshitshka, and so true."

"It's the story of our lives," I reflected. "Looking back, I can see that God was with us all along, and His hand was on all of our lives. When I think about dad, I think about this little orphan boy who, with his stiff leg, spent most of his life under persecution and imprisonment. Here was a man who, from the world's viewpoint, was totally insignificant, but in God's sight, was precious. He was *so* precious that God picked him up out of Russia and brought him over to us in order to draw him to Himself. Certainly we had times of great danger and suffering, but nothing could harm us until God fulfilled all He had for us."

"And now Tato is with the Lord," she whispered.

"Yes, Mom, that is true. As I think about all we have been through, I have come to a surprising conclusion. There isn't anything I would change about our life and past. It's all in God's hands. My heart overflows with gratitude for all His lovingkind-ness to us in the midst of our suffering."

I paused, but mom was quiet.

"The reason I wouldn't change anything is because God has worked everything for good. Even the bad circumstances have been covered with His goodness. I see His faithfulness, His love for each of us, and the love we have for each other—that could only come from sharing the hardships of life. And that is what makes life so meaningful—to know that God is in control."

The sun was setting as mom and I walked slowly back and forth, with her holding my arm for support. The afternoon warmth was rapidly leaving us, but the wonderful fresh air of all the foliage permeated the hill, and all around us nature was coming to rest. Some birds fluttered above, probably heading to their nests for the night. A squirrel scrambled up a tall tree.

There was still one question I needed to ask. Deep down, I had always wondered how mom really felt about dad. She had never really expressed how she felt, and the one occasion I had seen Mom and Dad together, time and pain had kept them from speaking openly. Reluctantly, I asked, "Mamo, did you really love dad?"

Without hesitation, she tenderly replied, "Of course I loved him—I loved him very, very much!"

Epilogue

As I write this, it has been sixteen years since the close of the events in this story. In the process of penning this book, many people asked why I took so long to put it into print. The primary reason was because of the potential repercussions against my relatives who remained in the Soviet Union. Until 1990, the Cold War still raged between the United States and Russia, and communism retained a firm grip on the lives of the Soviet people. It is very difficult for people in America to fully understand the tyranny of living under Communist rule. Sharing my story could have caused serious problems for my father, while he was living, and other relatives. So my concern for the innocent is what kept me silent until now.

Unfortunately, mom and dad never lived to see the miraculous fall of the Iron Curtain. When the political winds changed and communism was replaced by a new, hopeful leadership, I was encouraged to finally share my story—to encourage and give hope to those who have gone through and are hurting from life's trials and tribulations.

My last visit to my mom was in August of 1989. As I left her to go back to Dallas, she said to me, "I'm going away, Dotshitshka."

At first, I misunderstood her. "Where are you going?" I asked.

"I am going to see God."

I knew then that I would not see her again on earth. Two

months later, she joined dad in heaven, where they will live forever together in the presence of God.

During the early days after Bob and I gave our hearts to the Lord Jesus and received His life in us, we were awakened every morning by our clock radio that was tuned to a Christian station. Many mornings, the first sounds we heard were those of a man singing the hymn "Great Is Thy Faithfulness." Bob would gently take me in his arms and hold me as we basked in the truth of that song.

That hymn summarizes the course of my life. Looking back on the panorama of events, I now recognize that God was there all the time, even when I and my family were not aware of a living God. He saw us through all of our troubles. He protected us. He sent friends (even angels?) in the midst of our enemies to help us in our times of need.

He kept my family from starving during the years of famine in Russia.

He protected my father by allowing him to have a stiff leg, which prevented him from having to labor in the coal mines, which meant certain death.

He stopped the hand of death that persuaded my mother to take her own life during a time of utter hopelessness.

He kept us safe from bombs and artillery attacks when the Germans invaded our land.

He put in the heart of Major Euler to send my sister to his home to help his wife, thus setting in place the means by which we would escape from the labor camp.

He kept us alive as we worked and endured the harsh conditions in the labor camp in Nazi Germany.

He put into the heart of the kitchen manager at Reichenau the need to supplement my meager diet with a cup of milk everyday.

He put into the heart of the nurse at Reichenau to care for the sores on my hands—sores caused by malnutrition.

He put into the hearts of Frau Euler and the Langs to house and feed us after the war.

He made provision for me to receive special care when I had tuberculosis.

He brought into our lives the right people—including American military and government officials—to help us escape the persecution and death that would have faced us if we had returned to Russia.

During times when death was commonplace, He kept every member of our family alive. He then chose to reveal His Son to each of us, one by one. Yes . . . He guided our lives. Why? Because He had a plan—an eternal plan that none of us knew.

As I review the list of ways God intervened in my life, I realize that my story is really not my story. My life is really not my life. It is *His* story and *His* life, and I will spend the rest of my life declaring this truth to all who will listen.

There will come a time—none of us knows when—that each of us will be separated from our loved ones through death. The question is, Will that goodbye be forever? For those who have come to know Christ by faith, the answer is, No, it is not forever. I know beyond a shadow of a doubt that there will be a marvelous reunion someday in heaven when all of our family that is still here on earth will be reunited. I believe what the Bible says—that we will be absent from the body and present with the Lord (2 Corinthians 5:8). I believe that in that day, at that moment when death ends my life, I will immediately be taken into heaven, where I will see Jesus. I believe mom will be on one side and dad on the other, their arms outstretched as they say, "Welcome home, little daughter."

The apostle Paul said, "Listen, I tell you a mystery: We will not all sleep, but we will all be changed—in a flash, in the twinkling of an eye, at the last trumpet. For the trumpet will sound, the dead will be raised imperishable, and we will be changed. For the perishable must clothe itself with the imperishable, and the mortal with immortality. When the perishable has been clothed with the imperishable, and the mortal with immortality, then the saying that is written will come true: 'Death has been swallowed up in victory.' 'Where, O death, is your victory? Where, O death, is your sting?'" (1 Corinthians 15:51-55).

I would not be honest if I did not say that at times my heart aches and at times the pains of the past resurface. I would also not be human if I did not say that I miss my dad and especially my mom very much. But when I realize that they are in the presence of God and that someday I will join them there, the pain ceases and is replaced by an overwhelming joy. As the apostle Paul said, "For to me, to live is Christ and to die is gain" (Philippians 1:21).

So you see, the real reunion is still to come. Goodbye . . . is not forever.

A Personal Invitation
from Amy George

A Personal Word from Amy . . .

There's a God-shaped vacuum in the heart of every man. If after reading *Goodbye Is Not Forever* you sense an emptiness or that something is missing in your life, that you may never have accepted God's offer of salvation in Jesus Christ, Bob and I invite you to receive Him right now. John 1:12 says, "To all who received him, to those who believed in his name, he gave the right to become children of God." In Christ is total forgiveness of sins, total acceptance, and eternal life.

Salvation is a free gift that you can accept by faith. You are not saved by prayer, although prayer can be a way of concretely expressing your faith in Christ. For example, here is a suggested prayer:

> *Lord Jesus, I need You. Thank You for dying for the forgiveness of my sins, and for offering me Your righteousness and resurrected life. I now accept by faith Your gift of salvation. Through Your Holy Spirit, teach me about Your love and grace, and about the new life that You have given me. Begin the work of making me into the person You want me to be. Amen.*

Again, there is nothing magical about praying those exact words; God is looking at the heart that trusts fully in Him.

If you have received Jesus Christ through reading *Goodbye Is Not Forever*, or if your life has been changed in other ways through the ministry of this book, or if you would like more information about our ministry, we would very much appreciate hearing from you. Please write to us, Bob and Amy George, c/o People to People, 2300 Valley View Lane, Suite 200, Dallas, TX 75234-5737. May God bless you with a deep personal understanding and experience of His matchless love and grace!

Hear Amy George
Tell Her Story

*To receive a free audiocassette of Amy George telling
her story, please check the appropriate box below and
mail this form:*

☐ Yes, I would like to receive a free cassette copy of the **Amy George**
story.

☐ Please send details about how I can receive a limited-edition print
of Thomas Kinkade's painting on the front cover of *Goodbye Is Not
Forever.*

Name _____

Address _____

City _____ State _____ Zip _____

Mail your request to: **Amy George**
2300 Valley View Lane
Suite 200
Dallas, TX 75234-5737